"When I read **Creating WE** by Judith Glaser, I thought I had read one of the best business books. **The DNA of Leadership** picks up where **Creating WE** left off. Whether it's a strategic shift in the marketplace, loss of market share, or a merger or acquisition, leaders need to step up and lead. **The DNA of Leadership** pushes back against conventional wisdom to give the reader new and practical tools for creating an unstoppable organization in the face of change. This bright, innovative, and original approach shows how conversations are the 'carriers of a new genetic code' and the right conversations can trigger explosive business growth. This book is an indispensable resource for leaders and aspiring leaders. Direct, inspiring, and practical!"

—*Richard E. Stierwalt, CEO*
National Investment Managers, Inc.

"**The DNA of Leadership** is impressive in its scope and depth. It gives us an entirely new way of looking at how leaders lead, how they grow next generation leaders, how they impact the culture, and how they leap over other companies to create sustainable profitability. This is a must read for everyone who wants to be a leader."

—*Granville Toogood, author,*
The Articulate Executive in Action—
How the Best Leaders Get Things Done
(McGraw-Hill)

"The DNA referred to in this book could easily stand for *Do Not Assume!* Assumptions about accepted behavior and hierarchy that have been so ingrained in our corporate culture are not the most effective means to success. The groundbreaking ideas presented in this book are those that come from the very source of our human feelings and instincts. Communication through 'vital conversation' has already proven to be a cornerstone of corporate success that will continue to prove effective in the twenty-first century and beyond, and in **The DNA of Leadership** Judith Glaser masterfully presents a series of strategies designed to move leaders out of the 'Assumption' mode and into an 'Action' plan—an approach that is based in humanity and not humility. For those leaders seeking to develop a firm-wide cultural edge, and drive the organization to higher heights, **The DNA of Leadership** is an indispensable manual for success."

—*Michael Byl, President*
Palladium Global Partners, LLC

"In the midst of globalization and increased competition, the challenges today come down to one thing—exceptional leadership to survive in the twenty-first century. With more emphasis on succession planning, "We-Centric" leaders must be ready and willing to diagnose the toxic areas within their own organization as well as take the time, make the effort, and spend the money to ensure that future leaders are being nurtured within their organizations. In *The DNA of Leadership*, Judith goes deep-down to the molecular level of what it takes to develop and grow leaders that people will follow to greatness. While I thought *Creating WE* was the greatest leadership book I had ever read, this book is truly the ultimate recipe for leadership success. This is a must read for anyone aspiring for leadership greatness."

—Susan Peabody,
Professional Development Specialist

"True leaders must be secure enough to surround themselves with the smartest people they can find, as well as those who possess expertise that they do not have. They must set a vision and empower the team to create an environment that learns from the past, isn't afraid of admitting mistakes, searches for improvements, and looks toward the future. By doing these things, the 'collective DNA' will be able to adapt to change, face adversity, and come out on top. *The DNA of Leadership* is the most practical and inspiring manual for teaching this wisdom. If you buy one book this year—buy this one!"

—Robin L. Smith, M.D., M.B.A.

"Like Stephen Covey's *The 8th Habit: From Effectiveness to Greatness*, Judith has created a thoroughly original, modern day perspective into how great leaders are formed. Her engaging insights into generational influences, cultural connectivity, and conceptual genetic analogies give us a compelling—almost spiritual—view into the true code of leadership. It is invaluable at every level of management."

Angela Ahrendts, CEO Designate, Burberry

"The world is moving away from top down hierarchy and toward the horizontal spread of power. So, too, must leadership evolve from domination to stewardship. The 'genetic roadmap' in Glaser's book can guide your journey along that evolutionary path, and help you leave the organizational dinosaurs in the dust."

Edie Wiener
Futurist and author of the bestselling FutureThink

"*The DNA of Leadership* is a practical, understandable roadmap for managers and leaders who want to create a sense of commitment and innovation within their teams. Judith Glaser offers actionable insights that will undoubtedly energize, empower, and inspire your organization."

Linda Sawyer, CEO, Deutsch, Inc.

"*The DNA of Leadership* strikes at the heart of the matter; leadership is alive in everyone, just waiting to transform the business environment.

Glaser's book is the first to explain this in a simple, memorable way that pulls leadership principles off dusty academic shelves and puts them in the hands of the daily practicing leader."

Frank Palantoni, President & Chief Operating Officer,
Prestige Brands, Inc.

"Leadership is similar to elite running: It's not just one good race, it's the consistency of quality performance that counts most. In addition to hard work, one secret of performance is developing the unique gifts—the DNA—in each athlete (or organization) that keeps them winning again and again. *The DNA of Leadership* cracks the code on Leadership, Culture, and Brand in a way no other book has done in the past. It's a must read for anyone wanting to understand world class leadership."

Kathrine Switzer, 1974 New York City Marathon Champion, Author,
and TV Commentator

"*The DNA of Leadership* redefines leadership skills and commonalties— innate talent, skills, training, and experiences—and provides a leadership principle, step and process that connects the readers to the tools of real leadership and enables leaders to build thriving WE-centric success. Judith's insights, connections and the language she has created give an incredibly accessible path toward how innate leaders can create environments for all leadership to emerge and greatness to be realized. Judith's leadership insights are the touch points to thriving in the face of change, and a means to build leadership communities that will drive growth. It's a book that must be read and reread for everyone who wants to realize their leadership and inspire the same in their people and businesses."

Glen Ellen Brown, Vice President, Hearst Brand Development
Hearst Magazines, Hearst Communications, Inc.

"*The DNA of Leadership* has interesting parallels to the world of pharmaceutical drug discovery and research. The metaphor of enabling people to express their DNA reflects the human side of leadership, which is often minimized in theories about leadership effectiveness. Judith Glaser provides a practical and innovative approach to humanizing the workplace to enable higher levels of commitment, performance and productivity."

Donna Riechmann, Ph.D.
Director, Executive Education and Development
Pfizer, Inc.

"In her new book *The DNA of Leadership*, Judith Glaser again strikes at the root of culture change. Like a genie, she grants the reader's most profound wish—to tap into the gene power of authentic leadership to generate desired results."

Ken Shelton, Editor, Leadership Excellence

"Want to build healthy, vital and prospering organizations? This is the book for you! Going beyond an analogy, *The DNA of Leadership* offers a practical and human approach to leadership and business growth, outlining the necessary ingredients and steps to bind people, culture, leadership, strategy, and brand into a healthy system."

Robin Rodin,
Director, HROD Leadership, Strategy & Development
GlaxoSmithKline Pharmaceuticals

"With **Creating WE**, we built a new team with the same people. With *The DNA of Leadership*, we are now reinventing our organization and growing our brand based on our core culture. Merci, Judith."

Damien Dernoncourt, Vice Chairman, John Hardy

"Judith Glaser is one of those rare individuals who can translate the lessons she learned in life and in the classroom into lessons for the workplace. In her book, *The DNA of Leadership*, human behavior and development research become the basis for inspired guidelines for leadership in a corporation. Glaser writes with clarity, enthusiasm, and common sense, and her book is a must read for leaders everywhere."

Harriet Fulbright,
President of the Fulbright Center

"We transformed our business environment from the ME culture of the previous century to the WE culture of Judith Glaser's profound book, **Creating WE**. Now, thanks to the DNA of this gifted, visionary writer, we can inhale the literary fumes of *The DNA of Leadership* in all its metaphoric glory and create a new generation of prolific leaders."

Mikki Williams, CSP, Professional Speaker and Chairwoman of two
CEO Think Tanks, part of Vistage, International, the world's largest
CEO organization

"*The DNA of Leadership* teaches us exactly how to create a workplace environment where leadership greatness emerges not only in ourselves but in others. This book is loaded with practical, actionable, result-oriented leadership techniques that anyone can apply. Glaser's formula is mind-bogglingly simple and miraculous results have rippled throughout our organization. If you want to transform yourself and renovate your organization, *The DNA of Leadership* is a categorically imperative read."

Scudder Fowler, CEO, Liminal Group

"What struck me as I read *The DNA of Leadership* was Glaser's passion . . . a passion that comes from years of study and working with the top leadership teams in the country. Her perspective and lessons are diverse and provide insight for all businesses. Glaser has obviously incorporated these techniques into her own life, through her own journey of self-aware-ness and conversation to learn the truth."

Cindy Tortorici
President/Founder
The Link For Women, LLC

"As a physician, I was struck by the astuteness of Glaser's DNA analogy. Although written for larger corporate organizations, *The DNA of Leadership* also has incredible relevance to smaller and mid-size businesses. By using its principles, a staff becomes engaged, promoting an environment that is enormously more conducive to learning and healing."

Nikki Petti, M.D.

"*The DNA of Leadership* is about how we can shape and craft our cul-ture with precision and intention. Judith Glaser's book takes you on a wondrous journey into new thinking on leadership, culture and brand. She uncovers how DNA is laid down in companies through the conver-sations and rituals leaders establish. This book is a must-read for leaders who find themselves wanting to create a robust culture that attracts great talent. *The DNA of Leadership* is one of the most prescriptive and clear books I've read on this subject."

Carole Hyatt, CEO, Hyatt Associates, Inc.

"Judith Glaser has written another great work that shares its DNA with her excellent *Creating WE,* but includes enough original material and explanation to make *The DNA of Leadership* an invaluable resource for everyone who read *Creating WE* and for anyone who hasn't read it yet. She skillfully uses the metaphor of DNA to describe and explain varia-tion in leadership styles and organizations, how leadership is transmitted and organizations correspondingly evolve, and the differential success of organizations that either harness these principles and thrive or fail to engage them and disappear."

Ben Dattner, Ph.D., Adjunct Professor, New York University

"True leaders must be secure enough to surround themselves with the smartest people they can find, as well as those who possess expertise that they do not have. They must set a vision and empower the team to create an environment that learns from the past, isn't afraid of admitting mis-takes, searches for improvements, and looks toward the future. By doing these things, the 'collective DNA' will be able to adapt to change, face adversity, and come out on top. *The DNA of Leadership* is the most practical and inspiring manual for teaching this wisdom. If you buy one book this year, buy this one!"

Robin L. Smith, M.D., M.B.A.

"I always read books written by proven leaders. I like to hear their wisdom of how they have accomplished what they have accomplished. Judith a sharp, intelligent leader who has earned the right to comment on leadership. Her career shows that she understands *The DNA of Leadership* and we can all learn from that! Judith has a great deal of information to share and we are lucky that she is willing to do so."

Wendy Kaufman
President/CEO
Balancing Life's Issues, Inc.

"*The DNA of Leadership* reaches into the very core of the corporate soul, and, in doing so, teaches all of us how to maximize our inherent capabilities. Once again, by dissecting the components of successful management, Judith Glaser has given us the prescription we need to fully realize our goals and sustain them.

As a specialist in Occupational Medicine, I am confronted daily with the results of ailing corporations. This book can guide them, through the individual efforts of their leaders, back to health and, in the process, heal all of us."

Susanne Atkins, PA-C

"As an 'inside' consultant whose role it is to facilitate change within organizations, it is critical to have resources available that can be trusted, knowing that they are grounded in reality and based on the wisdom of experience. Judith Glaser's second book, **The DNA of Leadership**, is wise, informative, and effective. It is obvious that Ms. Glaser has explored deeply the true meaning of leadership and understands the critical role a leader plays in the ongoing health of a company.

Although every organization is unique, in my experience the people at the top—the leaders of the company—hold the key. Their behavior, beliefs, and style, as well as their ability to communicate and build communities, determine their company's ongoing good health or its continual struggles, sickness and disease. **The DNA of Leadership** shines clarity on what it takes to be a leader and why . . . it is a tremendous work that finally demystifies the myth of effective leadership.

I thoroughly recommend Ms. Glaser's book, **The DNA of Leadership**, to all leaders at all stages of their careers. We are all looking for answers; Ms. Glaser has cleverly woven her ideas and thoughts as well as her practical tools and solutions into an easy to read, engaging book, which I believe should take its place in all business school curriculums as well as on the desk and in the briefcase of leaders everywhere."

Christine Lewis Varley, CEO/President
Lewis-Varley and Company

the DNA of LEADERSHIP

LEVERAGE YOUR INSTINCTS TO:
COMMUNICATE
DIFFERENTIATE
INNOVATE

JUDITH E. GLASER
author of *Creating WE*

PLATINUM
PRESS

Avon, Massachusetts

Published by
Platinum Press, an imprint of Adams Media,
an F+W Publications Company
57 Littlefield Street, Avon, MA 02322. U.S.A.
www.adamsmedia.com

ISBN: 1-59337-518-2

Printed in the United States of America.

J   I   H   G   F   E   D   C   B   A

Library of Congress Cataloging-in-Publication Data
Glaser, Judith E.
The DNA of leadership : leverage your instincts to:
communicate—differentiate—innovate / Judith E. Glaser.
p.   cm.
Includes index.
ISBN 1-59337-518-2
1. Leadership—United States. 2. Success in business—United States.
3. Communication in organizations—United States. 4. Employee motivation—
United States. 5. Industrial management—United States. I. Title.
HD57.7.G652 2006
658.4'092—dc22
2005026049

This publication is designed to provide accurate and authoritative information
with regard to the subject matter covered. It is sold with the understanding that
the publisher is not engaged in rendering legal, accounting, or other professional
advice. If legal advice or other expert assistance is required, the services of a competent professional person should be sought.
—From a *Declaration of Principles* jointly adopted by a
Committee of the American Bar Association and
a Committee of Publishers and Associations

Many of the designations used by manufacturers and sellers to distinguish their
product are claimed as trademarks. Where those designations appear in this book
and Adams Media was aware of a trademark claim, the designations have been
printed with initial capital letters.

This book is available at quantity discounts for bulk purchases.
For information, please call 1-800-872-5627.

Contents

Dedication

Life is built on a tapestry of support, from one cell to another, from one relationship to another, from one generation to another. Without support we are unable to unfold our unique DNA. This book is dedicated to my husband, who gave me the spiritual and emotional support to find and express my voice, to my children Rebecca and Jacob, to my son-in-law Jeremy, and to my grandchildren Gideon and Eli, who are my wisdom teachers and who breathe wonder, joy, and life into me every day.

Acknowledgments

ONE COULD SAY that I have been a researcher on a mission since I was twelve, when I began writing this book—without the experience or wisdom to say what I wanted to write about—just the raw emotions of a young child trying to make sense of one's life, parenting, nurturing or the lack of it. At twelve, the title I picked for the book was *No Man Is an Island*, but when I found out that title was already taken, and with a dearth of things to say back then, I put the project away for another time.

In the 1990s, I made a visit to Nike for interviews on the same day that Phil Knight addressed his global organization about a precipitous stock drop. His leadership astounded me. He created a conversation with his whole organization, with everyone at the same time, to help address the issues openly and directly—the brutal facts—and at the same time created a sense that we are in this together; that we will make it through this crisis with integrity, and we will thrive. As Phil spoke of the steps that Nike would take and the changes that Nike would make, I knew in that moment I was witnessing leadership DNA unfolding. Then through interviews with Nelson Ferris, who was responsible for helping transfer the Nike culture through their Orientation Program, I realized how beliefs are transmitted and practices are established to reinforce the strength of the brand's DNA. The Nike culture, and how Phil and other leaders communicate to both preserve and evolve their leadership DNA, was a powerful metaphor that inspired this book.

In 1996, I dusted off my early writing projects, and began a decade-long endeavor that produced a 350-page bestselling business book called *Creating WE: Change I-Thinking to WE-Thinking & Build a Healthy, Thriving Organization*.

In 2005, when *Creating WE* came out, I thought I had said my piece, yet as the book was going through final editing, my publisher and editors at Adams Media knew that I had another book inside of me right behind that one, and we immediately forged ahead on *The DNA of Leadership* even before *Creating WE* was in bookstores.

The DNA of Leadership is my story of social evolution at work. This book could not have been written without the inspired conversations I had with my husband, Richard, as he was working on a parallel track with his cancer research project. Rich's interest was to find a healthy cure for cancer—one that did not use toxins to kill the cancer—one that used natural peptides to remind the cells how to be normal.

Through our discussions, I saw the metaphor of genes and DNA as a provocative vehicle for discussing the way we express our DNA at work. As the framework for this book emerged, I found I could draw upon the rich language of genetics to help provide new lenses through which it was possible to see culture and evolution from a totally new perspective.

The DNA of Leadership is rich with concepts and frameworks that enable leaders to see how conversations and the code of ethics, the code of conduct, and culture all connect. This book is about how our conversational environment creates culture—and how conversations trigger the expression of our DNA. So my first big thank-you goes to my husband Rich, who gave me the time and created the space for our very valuable conversations from which this framework emerged.

Writing this book has taught me that we evolve ourselves through the "coupling" and partnering that we do with others. Evolution is a "we-centric" phenomenon—culture is a "we-centric" phenomenon, and so who we partner with and the quality of our conversations is vital to our spiritual growth and to the unfolding of our potential.

My next big thanks go to the Adams Media Team: Gary Krebs, Scott Watrous, Karen Cooper, and Beth Gissinger who got excited and encouraged me to write book two. To my book editor Jill Alexander, for knowing when and how to push me to "finish my thoughts" on the subjects I am most passionate about—the nature of Human Nature. While we worked with a writing schedule that seemed almost impossible to meet, Jill helped me structure the process so that I could be successful in finishing the chapters, seemingly in spite of myself.

The next big thank-you goes to Bruce Scali. I don't know how he did it. Yet he was the best person to assist me with this book project, and because of his dedication to stay the course, encourage me through my resistance, and drive the process, the book evolved in lightning speed. Bruce's combination of gifted insight and anal compulsion about structure was the right alchemy to enable this book to be birthed in three months—and for his ability to keep me in the fast lane without crashing and burning, I am forever grateful. His mix of humor, thought-artistry, and creativity helped me see ways of saying big thoughts simply. A special thanks to Brian Penry, who for twenty years has worked with me to bring his exquisite "graphic eye" to play in every project I take on. He makes the invisible visible and brings color, texture, and presence to his illustrations. Thanks for seeing the luminous glow of DNA.

Many people have taught me lessons that support the underpinnings of this book. Special thanks to my sister Joan Heffler and my brother Jon Entine, whose conversations about family patterns and genes helped inspire me to keep the question—is it nature or nurture—always in front of me.

My clients and colleagues provided the essential laboratory for *The DNA of Leadership*, and many thanks are due to each one who provided a different insight worth sharing. In my conversations with Angela Ahrendts, then at Donna Karan International, then EVP at Liz Claiborne, now CEO designate of Burberry, I learned to see how the power of loving and nurturing parents can trigger confidence, personal courage, and leadership. Angela's incredible stories to me about the positive influence of her mother and father in her life gave me clarity on the essential importance of creating positive environments for growth.

Mary Wang, now President of DKNY, was another powerful example of leadership for me. When she was the President of Coach Wholesale, Mary, more than anyone, taught me how a leader's determination to change a culture starts with a commitment to change oneself—and how conversations with others crack the code on change. Mary's ability to create conversational shifts created dramatic positive ripples in the environment—nurturing profound growth in her employees, the organization, and the business.

Lindsay Farrell, CEO of Open Door Medical Center, a leader and teacher of wisdom, demonstrates every day the courage to make culture as important as breathing, and therefore sustains and nourishes those with whom she works. Leaders such as Lindsay are not afraid to speak up for what they believe in and hold the "culture container" with great respect—honoring the quality of conversations and relationships above all.

Lindsay, Angela, and Mary had big influences on my thinking, and gave me much to ponder as I worked on the shaping of this book. Together their stories convinced me that there is a **leadership gene**—our inherited and learned characteristics, that, if we learn to harness them properly, can transform us all into mutually supportive partners in our own and each other's development. By building environments with the essential ingredients for leadership, we actually enable leadership to emerge.

The DNA of Leadership contains stories and practices, rituals, and theory all woven together to create a new tapestry of thought.

Through this journey, I've come to realize that storytelling is the greatest carrier of DNA. Stories carry DNA from one culture to another, from one generation to another. The contributors to each chapter of this book are the water carriers, the storytellers, who enabled me to take you inside their lives and see how DNA gets created and replicated. Their stories elucidate the Leadership Gene and unfold its dimensions, chapter by chapter.

- Kittie W. Watson, COO; and Deb Jacobs, CEO of Innolect, Inc. along with Becky Ripley help tell the story of the C-gene—the story of how community is the essential foundation for expressing our DNA and we must honor that dimension since it is where the code of life is created.
- Dana Evan, CFO; Stratton Sclavos, CEO; George Haddad, EVP HR; and Ron Sacchi, VP HR of VeriSign, Inc. all help tell the story of the H-gene—the story of how our humanity emerges as we create environments that honor and respect the unique contributions we each have to offer.
- Michael Frieze, Chairman of Gordon Brother Group helps tell the story of the A-gene—the story of the importance of creating environments that enable our aspirations to emerge. Aspirations are the fuel for the expression of DNA.
- Alan Baral and Paul Apel, principals of New Wave Entertainment help tell the story of the N-gene—the story of the power of creating environments that enable us to collaborate, share, and engage and "fertilize" each other's thinking.
- Linda Milanowski, Director of Learning and Development; Andy Lock, EVP and Chief Administration Officer/EVP of Human Resources; Bruce Buursma, VP Communications; and Brian Walker, President and CEO from Herman Miller all help tell the story of the G-gene—the story about creating environments that sustain wonder, creativity, and generativity; these are the nutrients sourcing new DNA.
- Gary Rogers, CEO of Dreyer's and Edy's Grand Ice Cream, and William F. "Rick" Cronk help tell the story of the E-gene—the story about creating environments that nurture the expression of new DNA—giving voice to the next generation of leaders who are stronger and wiser than the generation before.

- Sam Palmisano, CEO; Tara Sexton, VP of Communications; and Bob Moffat, Senior VP/Integrated Supply Chain at IBM all help tell the story of the S-gene—the story about creating environments that foster and sustain reinvention which is the ongoing transformation of DNA to be more vital, life-giving, and life sustaining; this is a spirit running through us.

I am grateful to these clients and colleagues for sharing their stories and allowing us to learn from their wisdom.

And a special thanks to my associates who enabled this book to take shape with spirit and insight:

To Larry Butler, who helped me with *Creating WE* and whose expertise in harvesting new ways of thinking inspired the conceptual linkages between leader behavior and culture.

To Barbara Biziou, one of my Goddess friends, whose wealth of wisdom on rituals helped me shape the linkages from the past to the future trough the powerful anthropological stories you'll find in each chapter. Barbara is a ritual expert and author of *The Joys of Everyday Ritual* and *The Joy of Family Rituals*.

To Denise Lalonde, principal of Lalonde Consulting and Coaching, for her unwavering commitment and valuable contributions and support to adding strength-based dialogues and practices to this book that others could grow from.

To Bryan Mattimore and Gary Fraser, from the Growth Empire, who have been colleagues for two decades and whose work with Benchmark and our clients has always been inspiring and mutually successful. Their help with the IBM worldwide roll-out for the ISC created the engine behind the scenes.

To Geoff Grehert who helped me bring the wisdom of DNA to clients in a way that true transformation takes place. And to Natalie Shell who lives in the spirit of reinvention through every conversation she inspires.

To Jeremy Nash, CEO of Communication at Work, whose appreciation for breaking old patterns and creating space for new DNA helped me open the space for shaping the leader stories in each chapter. "DNA" is about the emergence of our "greater essence," and with this focus we support growth and vitality of the human spirit.

To Nancy Snell, Business and Personal Coach, who helped me realize that I needed to step inside of "fear" and see it in a new light—and that releasing fear triggers growth.

To the Liminal Group: Scudder Fowler and Granville Toogood whose belief in Transformative Leadership and my work has given me the inspiration to pursue this field with vigor. To Bryan Mattimore whose twenty year friendship has helped me keep innovation in the forefront of my mind. To Ken Shelton, publisher of Executive Leadership and a member of the Liminal Group, who encouraged me to discover my own unique thinking about the growing field of transformative leadership. To my other Liminal Group colleagues, Elizabeth Debold, Gary Fraser, Jim Mapes, John Ripley, Ed Bastian, and Matthew Cossolotto, who inspire me through every conversation. And to Gerard Senehi, whose "experimentalism" keeps me wondering and seeing the world in fresh ways every day.

To Dawne Era and Kathleen Ranahan, founders of ExecuGrowth Inc., whose vision for building the twenty-first century leader has brought us together to create new platforms for leaders to step up to their next level of growth. Special thanks to Drew Dougherty, CEO of Leadership DNA, for enabling me to share in this great metaphor.

Last, but in no way least, a very big thank-you to Al Zuckerman, my agent, who believed in me and my work, even when I was unsure, and to Judy Katz, my friend and PR maven, who continually helps me translate my big ideas into readable words.

So, to all of my friends new and old, to my colleagues, and to my family—I am grateful you are all in my life. Together we create defining moments, which become the triggers for our mutual greatness to emerge.

Introduction

Expressing the DNA for Greatness

WHEN YOU SHOW UP at work every day, you're there to handle issues, events, and circumstances specific to your own company. But what you are really doing is what every other top-level executive does: creating growth, value, and profitability in the face of change.

Whether it's a strategic shift in the marketplace, a merger or acquisition, unexpected customer demands, loss or gain of key employees or accounts, product obsolescence, additional competitors, unstable suppliers, industry contraction, or added government regulation, change is reflected in the crises and opportunities that show up in your in-box. How you react to these shifts determines whether your company will contract into a defensive posture, or move deftly and deliver knockout punches. You, and your organization, have a choice: will you stagnate or will you grow?

The DNA of Leadership is your user manual for capitalizing on change by creating environments where people can thrive and express their DNA for greatness. In the Chinese culture, the word for change is "opportunity." This book shows you step-by-step how to discard outmoded leadership thinking, conversations, and practices that exacerbate fear and cause everyone to run for cover. Fearful conversations "suppress our DNA" while vital conversations enable us to "express our DNA." Instead of resorting to the old top-down management approach, and trying to control the circumstances, the conversations, and the employees, *The DNA of Leadership*

1

demonstrates how to create environments—*defined by vital conversations*—that enable our individual and collective greatness to emerge. Through these empowering conversations, everyone connects in the spirit of co-creation to create environments designed to express our instincts for greatness. Vital conversations *crack the code* on culture change—and when we communicate with a powerful awareness of how our conversations trigger instincts, we collectively harness the power of our organizational DNA.

Wielding the dictatorial power that comes with a leadership position is seductive because it gets some immediate results. Someone is in charge; there is the appearance of stability. And sometimes you do have to apply a tourniquet to stop a hemorrhage. However, if you don't release the pressure at some point, harmful consequences, though delayed, will result.

The relationship between power and leadership is a given. *The DNA of Leadership* redefines it, by providing case studies of real leaders whose companies thrive in the face of daunting challenges. Rather than being threatened by change, these extraordinary leaders understand what kind of psychological environments (conversations and relationships) are necessary to trigger instincts—and they intentionally shape their conversations for leadership DNA to emerge.

They know that it's their job to create stability in the midst of flux. They know a deeper wisdom—which is the key to their success. *They know that everything happens through conversation.* Through conversations we trigger life. Conversations can be life affirming—or life negating. Those leaders, who know this wisdom—in the face of any crisis or opportunity—have the power to shape the future. Cultures and companies that operate this way evolve dynamically rather than struggle for survival. Their leaders recognize their dual role of growing the business and growing their people. Successful leaders in the twenty-first century invest in both, and in doing so grow stronger, grow smarter, and grow profitably as a result.

You could not reach a high position of leadership, or stay there very long, without innate talent and skill. That's the DNA you were born with and it is hardwired in you. *The DNA of Leadership* is not about the skills, training, and experience necessary for successful leadership. It's about discovering how to create conversational environments that enable the growth and expression of each person's unique DNA. It addresses the most important responsibility of leadership—creating environments that allow leadership greatness to emerge.

Which is more powerful: nature or nurture? The age-old debate for explaining evolution has been settled by recent science: it's both. It turns out that nature is nurtured; evolution is dependent upon inbred characteristics and outside influences. Psychological environments shape who we are and how we work, and leaders shape environments through conversations.

Nature and Nurture work hand in hand as allies to express DNA. This book adopts the rich metaphors embedded in the world of genetics. Yet, as you read, it goes beyond metaphors. Geneticists are discovering, just like the fact that there is a gene for "a belief in God" (see Dean H. Hamer's book, *The God Gene: How Faith Is Hardwired into Our Genes*) and that there is a gene for "Laziness" (as seen in a twelve-year study by Professor Bouchard's team at the Pennington Biomedical Research Centre in Louisiana), I believe we will discover that there are genes for greatness and genes for leadership. How you lead—most importantly, the conversations you have with others—creates the result you see. You can be a dominant, autocratic leader who imposes your will on others, or you can be conscious of creating an environment where the collective power of your organizational DNA emerges. For example, to achieve a goal, you could tell someone how to do it, or you could ask that same person how it could be done. The goal could be reached either way, but the long-term ramifications for the individual, and your organization, will be dramatically different depending on which approach you take.

Let's unfold this metaphor further. DNA carries the genetic information of cells, and is capable of replication. It consists of two strands of coded instructions and determines individual hereditary characteristics. Each strand is made up of genes linked together, and two strands combine when a gene in one strand bonds to its companion in the other strand, forming a double helix.

The premise of this book is that organizations, too, have their own "DNA." Organizational DNA is built on two strands that define its characteristics. One strand contains seven distinct leadership conversational practices. The other strand represents seven corresponding organizational practices embedded into the corporate culture. Corporate culture is the result of these two intertwined strands: your leadership conversations and the organizational practices.

Now let's develop this concept further by discussing the choices you can make as a leader. Each leadership gene can be expressed in one of two ways: to release or express growth, or to suppress it. The critical issue that spans this book is that how you lead—the quality of your leadership conversations and leadership practices—makes all the difference in the type of culture you create. Are you communicating through a commanding point of view from an ensconced bunker behind the lines, or do you get in the trenches with your troops and connect? Do you harp on deficiencies and failures, or do you acknowledge and get the most out of the strengths of others? Do you threaten, or do you instill hope? Do you protect turf, or cross-pollinate? Do you stagnate, or innovate? Do you stifle, or stimulate? Do you shut down, or turn on? What you do as a leader, and how you communicate, will either release the energy of your organizational DNA or suppress it.

There are myriad leadership styles: this book isn't about that. It's about the wisdom that underlies leadership. It's about your leadership genes expressed through conversations and practices (rituals)—which translates into how you treat individuals, how you foster teamwork, how you inspire others, how you communicate, how you bring out creativity, how you steer the ship, and how you maintain morale. All of this happens through conversations. Your conversational practices contribute to, and in many cases determine your corporate culture. In today's business climate, *The DNA of Leadership* is essential because how you and others in your organization express your genes determines whether you thrive, or even survive.

With this book as your guide, you'll be better able to:

1. **Discover and shape your brand:** Your brand is an anchor when the seas of the marketplace are turbulent. You'll define and realize your vision more clearly and meaningfully by creating conversations that tap the dynamics of collective collaboration in your organization. Your vision and brand are defined and lived through conversations that shape them.

2. **Live your brand:** Brands are more than products and services; they're the energy, ingenuity, and wisdom of your company's people and values. Instead of just spewing empty platitudes about your mission and goals, you'll use your conversations to stamp a real identity on your company that employees, vendors, and customers—each an integral part of WE—will recognize and associate with.

3. **Foster a dynamic corporate culture:** You won't have to demand "buy-in" from employees, nor worry about who's "onboard." Everyone will come to work excited and motivated because your conversations will inspire them to reach for greatness.

4. **Reshape the culture as circumstances dictate:** Instead of paralysis caused by rigid policies and procedures, you'll inspire a dynamism that makes your organization a living, breathing entity.

5. **Capitalize on change:** Instead of being blindsided by change and forced to "take a hit," you'll anticipate it and—through healthy vital conversations—take proactive measures to gain a competitive edge.

Leadership is integrally connected to brand and culture. Brand is what others see—the outside view of the organization; culture is the inside view. Great leaders ensure that a brand is manifested through-out the culture—and the key to unlocking the brand is the quality of the conversations.

How This Book Came About

The DNA of Leadership came out of my undying need to understand human and organizational behavior. There was so much I didn't agree with as I went through my education and training, and finding a new way to piece it all together has been an ongoing journey.

I was introduced to the "nature versus nurture" debate when I was a research fellow in human behavior and development at Drexel University. My graduate research clearly demonstrated that nature has to be nurtured for it to unfold. We studied children who lived in orphanages without a family core. What we found was that the circumstance of being abandoned was not as important as the atmo-sphere created by the caregivers. When social workers gave orders to children, punished them, or, even worse, ignored them, they devel-oped poorly, both physically and psychologically. They withdrew, and focused solely on survival. On the other hand, when the envi-ronment nurtured the children and encouraged individual expres-sion, the children were excited about exploring and learning. Their social skills and IQs advanced beyond what educators thought was possible.

Later, when I entered the business world, I was startled to see parallels between my research and corporate organizations. When leaders led with a top-down style, demanded compliance with estab-lished policies and procedures, and used threats and chastisement to achieve the goals they alone defined, the internal culture was one where development and growth were impeded. A silo mentality existed whereby employees only looked up for direction and down for execution. Territoriality and "turf wars" existed, internecine competition was rife, CYA exercises were commonplace, and blame was liberally spread around. Employees' motivation was to survive or get out at the first opportunity.

I also came across organizations where the atmosphere was vibrant, and palpable from the moment I went through their front doors. Employees exhibited genuine enthusiasm, curiosity, and excitement about personal development within collective growth. The leaders in these organizations stressed broad connectivity, collaboration, and conversations about shared goals, shared strategy, shared responsibility, shared pride, and shared ownership of success.

It was no surprise to me that the former companies were struggling, seemingly weighted down, trying desperately to hold on in the face of challenges and dramatic changes, while the latter organizations always took forward leaps and landed on their feet.

It wasn't a question about different natures: both types of companies had talented leaders and sufficient personnel, materials, and administrative resources at their disposal. That strand of DNA was equal. Their environments—the other strand of DNA—were markedly dissimilar, and leadership conversations and organizational practices (rituals) were at the core of the disparity.

It comes down to how a leader bonds intention with impact. Supremely successful companies—which are presented in the chapters that follow—are led by enlightened executives, who, while different and working in varied industries, exhibit patterns of conversation that nurture their environments. They consistently place emphasis on company-wide communication—not top-down, and not just that related to numbers and progress reports, but cross-divisional conversations with all employees that include their honest feedback, and their future hopes and dreams for themselves and their organizations. These leaders engage people passionately, and provide ways for them to do meaningful work and contribute, to build quality relationships, to strive, to access resources, to influence, to innovate, and to lead in their own way.

I came to the conclusion that the lessons I had learned over several decades would be instructive to a wide corporate audience. With the business landscape ever more uncertain, with executives under increasing pressure from boards and shareholders to get more from less, *The DNA of Leadership* is needed now more than ever. When you understand the power of vital conversations to effectively express the genetic dimensions that are discussed in depth, you'll transform yourself into a twenty-first-century leader who creates an environment that triggers the best in everyone.

Leadership in the Twenty-First Century

No one attains a position of high-level leadership without agreeing to first take on extraordinary personal self-awareness. You no doubt had new and broader responsibilities—and pressures—as you climbed the organizational ladder. You probably had new offices and new staffs. You might have relocated once or twice along the way as well. Your developing career might have involved leaving one company for another, or even entering completely different industries. You probably acquired new skills and knowledge from advanced education and executive training courses, and from dozens of seminars and conferences. You more than likely picked the brains of others to find out how they handled a particular situation, and incorporated some of those ideas into your way of doing things.

Thriving in the face of change is what brought you to where you are today. A natural tendency when people reach a certain level or certain point in life is to "kick back." Wanting a comfort level is perfectly understandable. But if you are still in a position where hundreds or thousands of employees and shareholders are dependent upon you for their future, then going out to pasture just won't do. Change won't let you; it will relentlessly refill your in-box.

If you are going to meet your responsibilities head-on, provide the necessary vision and direction, and continue your personal success, then you'll have to be "inside the change"—you'll have to embrace it, and be excited about the opportunity it presents. In short, you'll have to keep changing yourself, as transformational leaders—those who use change to grow and to catalyze leadership DNA.

The leaders presented in this book don't expect a "silver bullet" or quick solution to their challenges. They make a commitment to staying in the process of change, being a part of it, and thereby set the tone for others to do likewise. All of them lead with humility; none of them feel that they have "arrived." As a result, these leaders are part of a wonderful process of growth that positively impacts their employees, their bottom lines, and themselves.

The DNA of Leadership covers in-depth how their organizations thrive in any climate. Twenty-first-century leaders are masters of a new conversation. They live, breathe, and behave with a deep wisdom for what transformation is all about. To start with, they scrap the top-down (silo) structure for an interdependent (network) one that is more flexible and responsive to change. Through every conversation, they build inclusive communities where everyone is motivated, fulfilled, and partial owner of the decisions and achievements. Through conversation, such leaders empower others instead of dictate to them, and they establish a climate that produces the innovations that are essential to move forward. They foster reflection, dialogue, and rethinking of everything. They make sure that everyone stays focused on the big picture and on customers instead of on a personal agenda. And they view leadership as a journey, not as a station, constantly reinvesting in leadership development at all levels. As a result, every individual realizes his or her potential while the organization reaches its own.

The DNA of Leadership crystallizes the scope of successful helming by updating the challenges that leaders have faced from the beginning of time. And when I say the beginning of time, I mean just that. From prehistoric times until now, from the cave to the boardroom, those whom everyone relies on for survival and advancement of the collective have had to accomplish the same executive tasks—and these all take place through vital conversations:

- **Define the mission:** What, exactly, is the objective? You won't hit a target if you can't see it. Communicate openly and clearly so that all can see the target with you.
- **Communicate effectively:** How is the mission meaningful to everyone, what part does each person play, what does each person need to succeed, what problems exist, and what are the ideas that will fix them? Truth is not something to be feared; it's invaluable. Enable deep conversation so people can see where they fit and how they can contribute.
- **Reconcile individual and organizational goals:** The whole has to be greater than the sum of its parts. Individual reward and advancement must be framed in terms of both individual and group success—the "I" needs to thrive inside of the "WE." Conversations are not about "either your goals or mine"; they are about "your goals and mine," and how our goals serve our mutual success.
- **Create a thriving environment:** Instead of feeding others constantly, how can you ensure a self-sustaining organism? The brain cannot function without the lungs, heart, other organs, and interconnected networks. Conversations connect one to another. Be mindful of when you are pushing others away or bringing them close to you.
- **Foster innovation:** How can you tap the best and most exciting new thinking, and the wisdom inherent in each individual? Create conversational environments that nourish innovation.
- **Develop people:** Growth is a matter of people, not policy. Growth depends on the advancement of others into effective leadership. This will not happen by accident, and it's not a one-time workshop or a consequence of written policies and

manuals. It's an intention that breathes life into the organization. Healthy conversations are the lifeblood of healthy thriving organizations.

- **Replicate:** Companies wither and go out of business when they are unable to pass on and transform their DNA. To fulfill your ultimate responsibility for building an ongoing concern, you must constantly evolve products, services, policies, and procedures, and find and nurture the next generation of leaders who can steer the ship and weather the inevitable storms brought about by change.

Leaders who ignore people while pursuing financial goals place an organization's future at risk. While hierarchies must exist as a matter of necessity to avoid chaos, the important distinction in this book is that leadership is not the sole province of one person or a few top-level people. It is recast as everyone's responsibility. Employees are empowered to take part in the change process, and are chartered to lead their part of it. People feel honored and respected, and know they are contributing to something greater than they could envision on their own. This ensures two things: the tasks will represent the reality of what is, not that as seen from an ivory tower; and the entire organization will naturally get behind what has to be done.

The Book's Format

Chapter 1 explains the seven dimensions of twenty-first-century leadership—the genes—that comprise one strand of leadership DNA, and presents new terminology that describes executive practices. The next eight chapters cover each gene in detail and correlate leadership practices with resultant aspects of culture. Each chapter is introduced with a "'best-in-breed'" company that I have come across, or worked with, that clearly demonstrates what a particular dimension looks like when it is effectively expressed.

Each chapter has three parts that follow the introductory story:

1. A leadership principle, illustrated by a case study that shows what happens when a gene is not properly expressed.
2. A leadership step that shows how you can positively activate the leadership gene.
3. How you can nurture the gene in your culture and ensure its ongoing expression and replication for your organization's perpetual success.

Leaders have been faced with the same issues since the beginning of time. It also turns out that the knowledge our primitive ancestors gained about how to overcome threats to their existence is still available to us now. *The DNA of Leadership* was written to remind us of this great wisdom and to apply it to business to create growth-oriented environments. The "wisdom of the ages" so to speak, whether passed on verbally through honored tribal members, recorded in drawings on cave walls, practiced in rituals, or written in myriad forms and languages, has applicability to our lives—and businesses—today.

The third part of each gene chapter is introduced with an anthropological story that clearly shows how the responsibility of leadership has always been embedded in the best practices that have ensured survival of a culture and the realization of fantastic dreams. These stories confirm the concept that life—in or out of business—is all about "WE," and the lessons contained therein are invaluable to us all.

The last chapter pulls everything together and presents a series of practical exercises that you can use to "flex" your new leadership "muscles." Each exercise is designed so that you'll be able to express each leadership gene in the best way possible. When you see the immediate—and positive—effects that has on your organization, you'll be as excited about your personal evolution as you will about your company's.

How Will You Use Your DNA?

In the face of dramatic change, you can circle the wagons, batten down the hatches, withstand the blows . . . or energize your resources—your people—to get stronger in the face of challenges. You can use force in a futile attempt to impose your will . . . or harness the power inherent in those around you. You can use a stick . . . or a carrot. In effect, you can push . . . or pull, to motivate others to make forward progress.

The results you get are directly related to your methods . . . your conversational practices. Force produces resistance, requiring more force. The lessons from orphanages demonstrate that human beings want to belong and be appreciated so that they can grow. Nurturing does that, and when you nurture your employees so that they express their own leadership you build a generator that is never at a loss for power.

The choice about how you lead is yours. You can erect a silo, or construct a campus; you can install a court of law, or an institution of higher learning; you can instill a fear of change and of making mistakes, or the excitement about what is possible; you can build walls, or bridges; you can stifle, or you can resuscitate; you can dictate, or communicate; you can discourage, or you can inspire. It just depends on how you express the vital genes of your leadership DNA.

Chapter 1

Assessing Yourself and Your Organization

"To hear the unheard is necessary to be a good leader."
—from "The Sound of the Forest," an old Chinese parable

HUMAN BEINGS HAVE INSTINCTS that lead to patterns of behavior that enable the evolution of our species. These instincts are hardwired in our DNA and manifest themselves in how we relate to each other one-on-one and in expanded communities. In our workplace, instincts can drive us toward territorial and protective behaviors, motivating us to compete for resources, or they can trigger powerful and wonderfully collaborative behaviors that release energy and a collective greatness that is unstoppable. Leaders, through their own behavior, can reinforce the former, or inspire the latter.

This chapter introduces the leadership genes that are expressed in organizations that survive—and grow—in any business climate. It's a primer that covers the new words and practices that today's leaders use to constantly reinvent their organizations so that they remain among the fittest when the relentless forces of evolution effect change on personnel, products, and marketplaces.

▷ ASSESSING YOURSELF
What Leadership DNA Are You Carrying and Expressing?

In 1993, Dean H. Hamer, one of the best-known molecular geneticists at the National Cancer Institute, became a lively spokesperson for a new era of behavioral genetics. His then-controversial ideas have been bolstered by a number of studies that show connections between physiological states and specific human behaviors. In his book, *Living with Our Genes*, Hamer emphasizes that "Genes don't dictate a person's future; rather, they interact with each other, with the environment, and with an individual's response to these influences."

Understanding the links between your leadership genes and your workplace, and how you affect and respond to those around you, is critical wisdom for all who want to bring out the best in themselves for their people and for the success of the business. We can, indeed, use our DNA to achieve greatness!

All human beings have a need and desire for greatness. Everyone wants to be viewed as unique and special, and to be valued for who he or she is. When we join an organization, we believe we have been chosen among other candidates because we are "the best." We embody expectations, visions, and beliefs that we bring to work every day and through them we interact with our colleagues, customers, and bosses as we seek to fulfill our dreams and aspirations.

It is no wonder that the leadership challenge is so difficult and at times confusing to sort out. If each of us is seeking recognition and satisfaction, and if each of us wants to be promoted, internal competition can easily result. People might feel that, within the hierarchy of corporate life, there is only one ultimate level to which they should aspire, that there is one route to the top, and "may the best man win." In this model, some will make it and some will not, and those who don't must readjust their sights and accept less than what they planned. The successful twenty-first-century organization scraps this zero-sum model and builds in its place one where each individual at every level contributes his or her own greatness and reaches an appropriate level of success.

How can you as a leader in an organization realize each person's value, and at the same time guide and direct the whole organization toward its potential? How can you feed each person's appetite for greatness and at the same time keep the organization focused on its collective vision, mission, and purpose?

You can start by asking yourself what kind of leader you are. Are you one who is building a community of engagement, or a community of fear and defensive behaviors? Are you helping people to speak out and communicate even in the face of challenging times, or are you causing people to withdraw from you and others? Are you a "toxic" leader who poisons confidence and initiative, or one who fertilizes the corporate soil to grow the best in people?

The ability of organizations to reach their next level of greatness is determined by the atmosphere. The atmosphere is determined by the quality of the relationships. The quality of the relationships is determined by the quality of the conversations and behaviors. As a leader, you have in your grasp the ability to create and shape an environment that inspires greatness at every level.

Shorehaven Realty: The Buck Starts Here

Growing pains are normal. All executives who find themselves struggling with the challenges of growing a business face moments of desperation where they question their own capability to manage what is going on.

Even if you are the most confident businessperson, building a successful company is challenging. Rarely is your life filled with clear, risk-free decisions about how to shape your company's future. Rarely are your decisions black or white. There are always nuances and options and outcomes to weigh; you make your decisions and move in the direction of outcomes that you hope for.

Sales were not the problem facing the executives at Shorehaven Realty; disconnection was. "We saw strong-willed people going their own way," lamented Michael, one of the partners, "and as a result there was a lack of understanding between individuals and groups of people that ultimately led to a lot of fractionalization in the company."

As the consequence of people going off in different directions, management felt they needed to "take control and microman-age"—manage by force. Without seeing any other way to manage the attitudes and conflicts, the owners took the stance, "We own the company, so you do it our way."

In hindsight, power and control was inappropriate. Sandra, the other partner, echoed this realization, saying, "Back then we could have tried to build a culture that fostered respect for the talents of each person, but at the time, it was hard to see how to do anything else but use our positional power."

Michael and Sandra wanted to make their company great. They wanted to make Shorehaven an environment that would attract great talent. They wanted to have a company where people stayed for years. Yet neither of them was happy about the day-to-day reali-ties of managing and leading. It stopped being fun, and became a heavy weight they weren't sure they wanted to lift every day.

Like other leaders working in companies in a fast-growth mode, one morning you wake up and realize you've filled the space you own with more people than you can manage. You realize that the chal-lenges of cultivating new customers, and satisfying those you have, coupled with developing talent is a lot for a leader to focus on. And you realize that when you are treading water, you're not sure how to even think about the future, let alone create it.

The environment you come to every day is a mix of frenzied excitement and chaos—of elation and fear—of recognition-seek-ing and recognition-giving. Sometimes the world seems very unfair. Sometimes you can have the best intentions, but what you get are riots and rumbling. The organizational space you live in every day has become toxic. And when it's all said and done, executives feel a need to control the chaos, amplifying their role of authority, and the employees feel controlled, amplifying their need to undermine authority. The cycle can be fatal to a company's survival if it isn't turned around.

From Genes to Leaders to Organizations—
The Human Spirit Realized

Spreading greatness throughout an organization is not only possible, it's a necessary ingredient if companies want to succeed in the new millennium. The story of success is not just about money power, and it's not just about mind power. It's about heart, soul, and spirit power which can be released by creating healthy environments. Healthy environments are determined by the type of leadership genes expressed.

Everything happens through conversation. Language is the link that creates community, culture, and the future. Language is a large part of what makes us different from other living species. Language enables us to develop and handle complexity and ambiguity, to evolve and grow, and to teach others what we know. Colleagues who share common language, common definitions, and common meanings are a community.

Language is not neutral. Language triggers reactions, not only those we can see but those we can't see as well. Words communicate more than information. They are triggers that create ripple effects on those around us. When we communicate, the meanings of words reside in the listener as well as in the speaker. Sometimes we forget that and think that just because I told you, you get it. Communicating is a WE-centric process. For example, when a leader announces the new direction for the company in a large town hall meeting, a message is delivered by the speaker and received by the listener, and their meanings are often different. We listen from an I-centric—how it will impact me—rather than a WE-centric—how it will impact all of us—point of view.

While we listen, reactions are taking place in our bodies. Inside, chemicals are released, impacting how we think and act beyond what is obvious on the surface. Depending on the content of our conversations, chemicals can shut down our brain, blocking our ability to access an array of strategies we may have thought about the day before, or they can fire up the brain to integrate a storehouse of ideas. Some conversations cause us to label a person a foe, and others a friend. Some cause us to see our workplace as territorial and punishing; others cause us to see our workplace as friendly and supportive.

We all need to become sensitized to the way we use language and how language is a vehicle for creating the psychological environment that employees work in every day.

In a 2001 article on genes and behavior authored by Sophia Koliopoulos, she asks the question, "Could someone really be 'born bad'?" She goes on to explain: "It's not nearly that simple. Researchers on all sides of the behavioral genetics debate emphasize that the link between a gene and a behavior is not the same as cause and effect. Bottom line: a gene does not make people do things. It doesn't code for emotions or thoughts. It may not even turn on or off without an instruction from its surroundings. Instead, a gene may trigger a whole cascade of biochemical events in the body, interact with environmental and developmental influences, and—together with these—increase the likelihood that you'll behave in a particular way."

The psychological environment dramatically impacts our personal and organizational behaviors. How we talk about power and leadership, what behaviors we advocate and reward, and how we speak to each other all set into place a cascade of biochemical and physiological responses that determine the "feel" of our culture.

Understanding the link between the language you use and the reaction your conversations have on the behavior of others is essential and vital for leaders today. Without this wisdom you will have conversations that erode, rather than build, a strong community.

Without this wisdom you weaken your ability to create a strong, vital workplace. Through conversations you create the culture and set the tone for expressing your leadership DNA.

What Is Leadership DNA?

Leadership DNA is the practice you use to motivate or demotivate those you depend upon for development of your organization. Engagement drives evolution. As you engage with others through conversation and actions you either expand others' potential and catalyze growth, or limit others' contributions and perpetuate stagnation.

What motivates employees to give it their all and get engaged in building an identity and influencing the company's direction? What causes employees to create subgroups and fight with other divisions? What causes colleagues inside the same company to refuse to share important information with one another? What causes leaders to lose the faith of their teams, or lose faith in their teams? What causes leaders to lose faith in themselves? What causes a company to go out of business? What causes others to soar? These are all fundamental questions you must answer to be successful. How you answer these questions, and your leadership challenges, depends upon your understanding of what leadership DNA is.

Encoded Behaviors

Everyone has his or her own leadership style and personality, but effectiveness is determined by how you choose to lead: Do you dictate, or solicit original contributions? Do you assign blame, or appreciate experimentation? Do you "know," or do you ask? Do you engender fear, or encourage individual expression? Understanding how to create environments where employees bring out the best in one another is vital for the evolution of your business. Creating the kind of environments where employees are passionate about their work and contribute their gifts and talents to the good of their teams and, in turn, their company, is essential for twenty-first-century leaders.

Connections Throughout the Organization

In today's increasingly connected world, companies themselves must also be finely interwoven to connect effectively with their suppliers, partners, and customers. How you link your employees to one another, and to other teams and divisions, makes all the difference in how successfully you connect to your outside world. Do you withhold information, enforce boundaries, and defend territory, or do you cross boundaries to share knowledge, decision-making power, and ownership of ideas and success? Do you rely solely on your own knowledge and vast experience, or do you tap into the wealth of resources readily available in your team and across your company? Understanding how to foster connections lightens everyone's load and leads to greater success faster.

Corresponding Corporate Culture

How you express your leadership DNA determines the norms and patterns that govern how everyone works together, "the way it is around here." Culture represents how work gets done, from how you make decisions, to how you run meetings, to how you assign projects, to how you recognize and reward effort, to how you develop employees. These patterns stamp everything and ultimately define your brand. Do you hold people back, or challenge them to advance to the next level of skill and responsibility? Are you distant and secretive, or accessible and open? Is your vision created and implemented by a select few, or does everyone contribute to its definition and realization? Leaders who practice rituals that maintain stability while embracing change and encouraging personal growth will be the most successful in the new millennium.

How to Encode and Decode the Genes

Leaders influence the culture of an organization. We've identified a set of dimensions that, I believe, dramatically influence how leadership is expressed in organizations. When you focus your attention on these dimensions, you create environments where the human spirit can thrive in the face of internal and marketplace challenges. Leading with these dimensions in mind, you are able to reduce fear, increase trust and support, and unleash the maximum potential of every individual and the collective whole. In the chapters that follow, each dimension is identified along with the leadership practices that are used to activate leadership for effective solutions, development, and growth. In the remainder of this book I will refer to these dimensions as "Genes." While research has not yet validated that these are genes, I am proposing that when we think of the dimensions as genes, we become open to a whole new way of thinking about leadership—one that inspires us to discover our genetic code.

The Seven Vital Leadership Genes: C-H-A-N-G-E-S

Like our cellular DNA, these leadership practices always bond together in pairs. The seven "pair bonds" determine the culture of your organization, how it responds to the constant change associated with personnel, products, vendors, partners, and customers. The following table (TABLE 1.1) illustrates these pair bonds.

TABLE 1.1 Leadership Genes and Corresponding Cultures

Leadership Gene	Pair Bond	Progressive Culture
C Gene: Community	Including vs. Excluding	Instead of dictatorship, open communication where people feel included, involved in the strategy, engaged in the business, and accountable for results
H Gene: Humanity	Appreciating vs. Blaming	Instead of a climate of judgment and retribution, create an atmosphere that values uniqueness and diversity, and respects the talents of each individual
A Gene: Aspiration	Striving vs. Fearing	Instead of using overt and covert threats to meet targets, marshal the wonder of individual imagination
N Gene: Navigation	Sharing vs. Withholding	Instead of hiding the "map," ask others within teams and across divisions for guidance in making headway toward common goals
G Gene: Generativity	Wondering vs. Knowing	Instead of micromanaging and enforcing compliance with what has always been, nurture innovation that leads to inspired breakthroughs
E Gene: Expressing	Developing vs. Dictating	Instead of stifling voices in favor of one voice, encourage all to speak up, take risks, and develop themselves to develop the organization
S Gene: Spirit	Celebrating vs. Conforming	Instead of cold calculations and expectations, create an atmosphere of ongoing homage, accomplishment, and evolution so that everyone pulls together to move toward the future

Each half of the practice pairs will either lead to growth—capitalizing on change—or stagnation—resistance to change. When leaders are mindful of the power of these genes, and the positive effect the progressive half of the pair bond has, they will sustain and develop their organizations in the face of business challenges. Within each pair is one gene that, when "grafted" into meetings, conversations, new product development, and strategic business transformations such as mergers and acquisitions, will enable you to successfully manage change—instead of change managing you.

FIGURE 1.1

BENCHMARK COMMUNICATIONS, INC.

Vital Choices

Are you more comfortable excluding others than including them? Are you more comfortable criticizing colleagues behind their back than giving them feedback face-to-face? Are you more comfortable not experimenting for fear of making mistakes, or are you willing to take risks? Do you prefer to hold on to important information, or are you willing to share with others to expand our collective wisdom? Are you more comfortable telling people what to do, or are you willing to challenge them to think in new ways? What environment are you creating? Audit yourself.

Co-creating	I-centric–Protect	WE-centric–Partner
The Context We Set	Exclusive: Power-over	Inclusive: Power-with
	1. Only talk to those one level up; corner office; get my coffee	1. Senior executives discuss the strategy with employees
	2. Senior executives own the strategy; information kept close to the vest	2. Company's health, wealth, and business strategy shared with employees
	3. Using status to impress; keep the distance	3. Employees included in change process; involved, engaged, and empowered
	4. Exclusion; closed doors	4. Inclusion, open-door policy
	5. Lack of respect	5. Respect abounds

Humanizing	I-centric–Protect	WE-centric–Partner
The Relationships We Build	**Judging** 1. Critical; criticizing work; highly judgmental 2. Focuses on "what you can't do" 3. Blame; finger-pointing 4. Lack; not good enough 5. Undervalued, under-appreciated, and not trusted	**Appreciating** 1. Feedback; appreciating work; highly supportive 2. Focus on "what you can do" 3. Accountability; responsibility 4. Strength; bring talent to bear 5. Valued, appreciated, and trusted
Aspiring	I-centric–Protect	WE-centric–Partner
The Dreams We Hold	**Limiting** 1. Fear it won't work 2. Been there, done that 3. Too hard to get support; don't know how 4. Fear of mistakes 5. Don't get your hopes up	**Expanding** 1. Believe it will work 2. Bring hope, dreams, and aspirations to work 3. Rally and attract support; know how to coalesce people 4. Learn from mistakes 5. Share hopes, dreams, and aspirations
Navigating	I-centric–Protect	WE-centric–Partner
The Actions We Take	**Territorial; Scarcity** 1. Withholding; not sharing power or information 2. My territory; my power 3. Fear of giving too much freedom; restrict interactions 4. Don't cross the line 5. Don't get credit for sharing; don't share	**Share; Abundance** 1. Share power and information 2. Understand how to respect territory, to give and share 3. Give freedom for interactions 4. Open boundaries 5. Give credit for sharing; share

Generating	I-centric–Protect	WE-centric–Partner
The Ideas We Evolve	Persuading; Knowing 1. Low risk-taking 2. Same is good 3. Our way or the highway 4. "Not invented here" syndrome 5. What is, is; don't fix it; it's not broken	Generative; Wondering 1. Support risk-taking 2. Different is good 3. Experiment with new ways 4. Build scenarios 5. Break it!

Expressing	I-centric–Protect	WE-centric–Partner
The Words We Choose	Autocratic; Controlling 1. Autocratic; dictatorial 2. I'm right; know it all 3. Own the airtime 4. Show what I know 5. Tell and sell	Developing; Encouraging 1. Direct and honest 2. Listen 3. Challenge others to grow 4. Share what I know; learn from others 5. Allow positive pushback

Spirit	I-centric–Protect	WE-centric–Partner
The Purpose and Passion We Live	Compliance 1. Disconnect 2. Compliant/punish 3. This is our way 4. Top-down management 5. Dogma	Commitment 1. Connect 2. Reward success 3. Ongoing communication 4. Connect to a higher purpose 5. Spirit and passion

The progressive half of each gene is all about leading from WE instead of I:

- *Community*
  Breaking down walls and inviting others in, rather than erecting and enforcing boundaries to keep others out

- *Humanity*
  Empathy for the feelings everyone has, rather than pointing fingers to preserve your own

- *Aspirations*
  Allowing others to dream freely, rather than waking them up to "how things get done"

- *Navigation*
  Letting others set the course and share the wheel, rather than jealously guarding the compass and the helm

- *Generativity*
  Pushing the boundaries of the status quo, allowing new wisdom to emerge, rather than reverting to what has worked before

- *Expression*
  Allowing individual greatness to emerge and benefit all, rather than shouting the voice of authority

- *Spirit*
  Attaching everyone to a larger purpose and acknowledging group achievement with enthusiasm and joy, rather than pursuing self-aggrandizement

Leadership genes reside in every executive. The next section will quantify how you are using yours.

FIGURE 1.2 **Progressive Half of Pair Bond**

Communicate–Differentiate–Innovate

Leader		Culture
Inclusive	**Co-creating**	Strong sense of direction; clarity of goals and strategies; shared vision
Appreciating	**Humanizing**	Focus on strengths; high level of trust, respect, and mutuality
Aspirational	**Aspiring**	Organizational ambition; raising the bar; learn from the past culture
Sharing/learning	**Navigating**	Sharing best practices; create centers of excellence
Risk-taking	**Generating**	Continually creates and innovates; competition
Developing	**Expressing**	Leaders developing and mentoring leaders; accountability; a strong voice
Commitment	**Synchronizing**	Spirit, purpose, and communication; pulling in the same direction, toward the future

FIGURE 1.3 **Regressive Half of Pair Bond**

Dictate–Imitate–Stagnate

Leader		Culture
Exclusive	**Co-creating**	Directionless employees; lack of shared vision and purpose
Criticizing/Judging	**Humanizing**	Focus on weaknesses; lack of respect and appreciation; blaming culture
Fear Based	**Aspiring**	Lack of organizational ambition; lowering of the bar; underperforming
Silo-mentality	**Navigating**	Lack of cohesion and teamwork; lack of sharing; inner focus; failure to connect
Punish risk-taking	**Generating**	Failure to tap resources and creativity; group-think; falls behind
Dictates	**Expressing**	Failure to develop leadership, accountability; loss of voice
Compliance	**Synchronizing**	Lack of spirit; leadership and employees not pulling together

The New Leadership Lexicon

Leadership skills must evolve as technology and organizations do. When you activate the WE half of the pair bonds, and understand the concepts associated with new leadership DNA, you will transform your leadership from "power over" to "power with" and release the potent, and catalytic energy of WE. Each chapter in this book contains prescriptions for shifting from I-centric to WE-centric language and conversations. As your words shift, your environment changes for the better. People "couple" and join forces naturally. Rather than coercion, there is an energy of attraction that creates inspired engagement.

The following are "mechanisms of action" that explain how energy is released through conversations. Once you understand the mechanisms of action, you have the secret formulas for creating positive motivation in yourself and others. These are the keys for releasing vital instincts . . . and for creating transformation:

- *Knockout genes*
  Words and concepts that instill fear, withdrawal, and anger and should be eliminated from conversations

- *Gene splicing*
  Those words and practices that you should use to foster individual development and team spirit

- *Up-regulation and down-regulation*
  Those practices that maximize innovative performance and valuable contributions, and minimize fear, withdrawal, and internecine competition

- *Meta-messages*
  Implied communication that is below the surface and seemingly contradictory to words and actions. These unspoken messages confuse employees and result in territoriality and inertia

- *Junk DNA*
  Outmoded beliefs that are no longer relevant to your success today. They are "mutations" that restrict potential.

Self-Test and Scoring Algorithm

The following questions cover each of the seven vital genes and provide a mirror for your management practices, reflecting the extent to which you exhibit WE leadership DNA. There are no right or wrong answers; leadership practices exist on a continuum, and each of us typically expresses more of one gene than another. The value in providing truthful answers is an accurate assessment, using the scoring key at the end of the test, of what you need to focus on most to evolve as a leader. The bottom line? If you want to change your organization, you'll have to change yourself first.

Community

To feel included at work, employees need to have authority for making decisions, and to work co-creatively with others. Rather than being subject to positional power, they need to exercise individual discretion to connect to others. Chapter 2 focuses on how you can be inclusive and increase your power by distributing some of it.

TABLE 1.2 Culture of Inclusion

Community Question / Response: 1 = Never, 7 = Always

I promote teamwork among groups and discourage "we versus they" thinking.

1	2	3	4	5	6	7

I create an environment that honors and rewards people for finding collaborative ways to work together.

1	2	3	4	5	6	7

I enthusiastically encourage others to work together.

1	2	3	4	5	6	7

I set a positive tone by behaving in an inclusive way.

1	2	3	4	5	6	7

I model how to create a culture based on a shared vision.

1	2	3	4	5	6	7

I work with others to clarify the mission and strategies and help the organization align around common goals.

1	2	3	4	5	6	7

I seek collaborative win-win solutions whenever possible.

1	2	3	4	5	6	7

Humanity

To feel appreciated at work, employees need to be valued, based on healthy conversations. Rather than be subjected to blame, they must be encouraged to contribute their unique talents and abilities. When you are judgmental of others, you fail to benefit from your human capital. Chapter 3 focuses on resolving conflicts and maximizing everyone's personal and professional growth, uplifting all to new levels.

TABLE 1.3 Culture of Appreciation

Humanity Question / Response: 1 = Never, 7 = Always

I create an environment where people feel respected, appreciated, and valued.

1	2	3	4	5	6	7

I support open communication to resolve conflicts.

1	2	3	4	5	6	7

I create an atmosphere of personal and shared accountability.

1	2	3	4	5	6	7

I raise uncomfortable issues openly and directly.

1	2	3	4	5	6	7

I encourage the giving and receiving of feedback, and accept feedback openly and nondefensively.

1	2	3	4	5	6	7

I openly share my assumptions and invite others to share theirs.

1	2	3	4	5	6	7

I create an environment where the truth can be told at all times.

1	2	3	4	5	6	7

Aspiration

To be unafraid at work, employees need to have dreams about their future. Rather than trying to avoid mistakes and retribution, they should feel free to pursue the possibilities they envision for themselves. Chapter 4 focuses on how you can eliminate the swings of fear that employees react to with disengagement and reduced commitment.

TABLE 1.4 Culture of Striving

Aspiration Question / Response: 1 = Never, 7 = Always

I encourage others to be positive and actively seek new ideas and possibilities.

1	2	3	4	5	6	7

I inspire people to focus on goals that drive successful business results.

1	2	3	4	5	6	7

I encourage others to stretch beyond their comfort zone while supporting them in taking risks.

1	2	3	4	5	6	7

I create an environment that focuses on a quest for productivity.

1	2	3	4	5	6	7

I clearly communicate the purpose and direction so that others can understand it and contribute to it.

1	2	3	4	5	6	7

I set clear expectations and let people know when they are performing well and how they need to improve.

1	2	3	4	5	6	7

I encourage people to set high standards for their performance, and set high standards for my own.

1	2	3	4	5	6	7

Navigation

To grow as individuals and organizations, employees need to explore, learn from others, and be exposed to diverse resources and ways of thinking. When you put up walls and barriers, you create silos and divisions instead of campuses and networks. Chapter 5 focuses on how you can open your environment for the free exchange of knowledge and wisdom, resulting in the best practices that benefit everyone.

TABLE 1.5 Culture of Sharing

Navigation Question / Response: 1 = Never, 7 = Always

I engage others in the decision-making process, giving appropriate authority and freedom to act.

1	2	3	4	5	6	7

I foster cooperative relationships with and among others.

1	2	3	4	5	6	7

I am skilled at enlisting contributions from people in the organization.

1	2	3	4	5	6	7

I give credit to others for contributing and sharing information.

1	2	3	4	5	6	7

I create a learning environment within my team and cross-functionality.

1	2	3	4	5	6	7

I engage people from different departments, teams, and groups in knowledge-sharing conversations.

1	2	3	4	5	6	7

I work to break down barriers and silos to achieve synergies and create value for the organization.

1	2	3	4	5	6	7

Generativity

To be alive with wonder at work, employees need to be genuinely challenged. When you demand compliance with the status quo you reinforce what was, and restrict what could be. Chapter 6 focuses on how your environment can thrive on novelty and innovation, wonder and curiosity.

TABLE 1.6 Culture of Wondering

Generativity Question / Response: 1 = Never, 7 = Always

I make sure people are recognized for their innovative contributions.

1	2	3	4	5	6	7

I reward people for continually asking "what if" questions and testing out "what if" scenarios.

1	2	3	4	5	6	7

I encourage people to challenge the status quo and to continually look for better ways to do things.

1	2	3	4	5	6	7

I create an environment where people can bring out their best ideas.

1	2	3	4	5	6	7

I ask "What can we learn?" when we get results we did not expect.

1	2	3	4	5	6	7

I encourage and reward creativity and innovation.

1	2	3	4	5	6	7

I encourage experimentation and testing of new ideas.

1	2	3	4	5	6	7

Expressing

To build confidence and develop professionally, employees need to voice their ideas and opinions, and be heard. When you are conflict-averse and avoid confrontations and difficult conversations, you hamper individual progress, your own development, and corporate growth. Chapter 7 provides you with direction on how you can benefit from creating environments where conflict becomes the fuel for the growth of multiple perspectives.

TABLE 1.7 Culture of Developing

Expressing Question / Response: 1 = Never, 7 = Always

I encourage people to speak up when they have ideas to share.

1	2	3	4	5	6	7

I encourage people to take action when they feel strongly about something.

1	2	3	4	5	6	7

I encourage people to challenge my point of view.

1	2	3	4	5	6	7

I give people lots of room to make their own decisions.

1	2	3	4	5	6	7

I challenge people to make tough decisions.

1	2	3	4	5	6	7

I inspire others to stretch beyond their current ability.

1	2	3	4	5	6	7

I provide feedback to others to help them grow.

1	2	3	4	5	6	7

Spirit

To be excited and joyous at work, employees need to know they are part of something bigger than themselves, something important and purposeful and evolving, and to experience celebrations—both large and small—of individual and group accomplishments. Chapter 8 focuses on how you can build esprit de corps so that everyone evolves together and with your corporate brand.

TABLE 1.8 Culture of Reinvention

Spirit Question / Response: 1 = Never, 7 = Always

I celebrate accomplishments, recognizing people regardless of level or profile.

1	2	3	4	5	6	7

I inspire enthusiasm and loyalty to the company and brand.

1	2	3	4	5	6	7

I help people learn to recognize and achieve milestones.

1	2	3	4	5	6	7

I enable people to see how their efforts connect to the organizational goals.

1	2	3	4	5	6	7

I focus on ongoing improvement and development toward evolving priorities.

1	2	3	4	5	6	7

I help people take ownership of results, holding themselves accountable.

1	2	3	4	5	6	7

I encourage a commitment to excellence, even in the face of difficult challenges.

1	2	3	4	5	6	7

Scoring and Assessment

Scoring: Add up your scores in the individual genes and enter them in the spaces provided, then add the individual scores to arrive at a total Leadership DNA score:

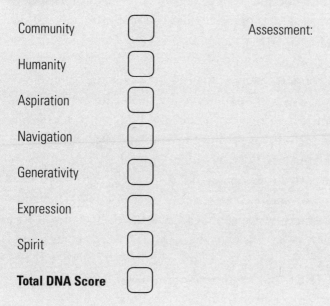

Community ☐   Assessment:

Humanity ☐

Aspiration ☐

Navigation ☐

Generativity ☐

Expression ☐

Spirit ☐

Total DNA Score ☐

Individual Gene Score:

40–49	You express WE
30–39	You have heightened awareness about WE
20–29	You are progressing toward WE
7–19	You need to strongly address this dimension of WE

Total DNA Score:

280–343	You embody WE
210–279	You usually practice WE
140–209	You are aware of WE
49–139	You need enlightenment about WE

Your positive tone in conversations enables connection with others at levels that are not always obvious. The more your interactions are trusting, positive, and supportive, and the more you keep an eye toward the future, the better your ability to catalyze positive change.

Far beyond what your conscious mind can imagine, when you set a progressive tone, the impossible becomes possible. In environments where executives *tell* people what to do, dictate *how*, and oftentimes do it themselves, they artificially limit what is possible. Environments where employees work by the book, laden with rules and regulations about what can't be done, rather that what can be done, are not attractive to people full of spirit seeking to make their mark on the world. In such places, executives wonder why they have a stodgy atmosphere, or why people call in sick all the time, or why people don't seem to be enjoying their work. It all becomes quite evident when they pull back the curtain and see what they themselves have created. Command-and-control workplaces are more than what is found in a corporate handbook; it's a way of life.

Leaders who express the negative half of a gene spread environmental toxins that trigger territorial instincts and interfere with positive and innovative connections among others. Each gene has a poison that pollutes its own space and limits what is possible:

- **In the community space:** Positional power is the toxin that prevents co-creativity.
- **In the humanity space:** Judging is the toxin that discourages people and reduces their feelings of self-worth.
- **In the aspirational space:** Explicit and implied threats are the toxins that keep imagination from thriving and shatter dreams.
- **In the navigational space:** Suspicion and lack of trust are the toxins that prevent people from sharing what they know, sharing best practices, and synergizing each other.

- **In the generativity space:** Focusing on the past and dwelling on problems and things that didn't go well are the toxins that disable creativity, experimentation, and innovation.
- **In the expressional space:** Conflict aversion, resulting in telling, not listening to others, is the toxin that prevents individuals from feeling vital and making their greatest contributions to the organization.
- **In the spiritual space:** Compliance and control are the toxins that prevent people from believing in, and committing to, the larger purpose.

Positional power, judging, fear, internal competition and distrust, focusing on the past, not listening, and coldness all close down the channels through which we interact, learn, and grow. They trigger fatal and territorial instincts that slow down or stop the healthy evolution of your brand. When environmental spaces are filled with these toxins, they cause us to disconnect, and they disable our natural creative energies and distract us, causing us to worry about worst-case scenarios. They disable us from using our incredible imaginations for inventing the future. We are triggered into behaviors we don't prefer, but which enable our survival: fighting for control, blaming others, judging and criticizing, and giving lip service to old beliefs.

Understanding Your Cultural Fingerprint

After reading each chapter, you will be able to see the impact each gene has on your culture. Within each of these dimensions you will learn to apply the new leadership lexicon, become equipped to assess your "cultural fingerprint," and have new insights for creating environments that realize the potential in your organization. You will have the tools to help you reshape your culture through the power of inspired conversations, inclusive strategies, and appreciative experiences with others that successfully tackle critical business challenges and build a stronger sense of "we're in this together."

Consider your own culture, the atmosphere surrounding your teams, and think about ways in which you contribute to impacting the psychological environment in which you work every day. The following assessment tools will help you on your journey:

- **Individual 360°s:** assessments conducted on an individual that draw upon the feedback from a minimum of four peers and/or direct reports, along with one or more bosses
- **Aggregate 360°s:** the collective 360-degree assessments conducted on a team, division, or entire organization, resulting in a bigger picture
- **Discovery interviews:** interviews conducted with individuals to uncover insights, perceptions, feelings, observations, and dynamics at play; topics can be products, a team, or company
- **Web-based profiling assignments:** profiling that utilizes the Web, making it much quicker and easier to create aggregates and see how different dynamics interact (With technology it's possible to slice and dice the data to see patterns and impacts.)
- **Focus groups:** data collections facilitated by someone with specialized training (The goal is to gather unbiased feedback from a group, e.g., customers, employees, or others whose feedback is vital during a major change.)
- **Interaction scans:** designed to identify special areas in an organization where there is a higher level of conflict, territoriality, and breakdowns that are negatively impacting the health of the organization; the conflicts identified usually fall under the following areas:
  - **Territoriality:** division-to-division conflicts
  - **Interpersonal conflicts:** friction between individuals, usually because of differences in communication or personality styles

- **Relationship breakdowns:** situations that cause people to turn to defensive behaviors such as fight, flight, or appeasement
- **Relationship triangulations:** when two people are having difficulties communicating and one or both turns to others to complain without the intention of working things out

Getting accurate and timely information, and using it properly, demonstrates that you do not have the corner on all knowledge and solutions. As you work with the concepts and ideas in this book, imagine that you are learning a technology for unleashing the energy for reinvention and change in your workplace. New practices described here will enable you as a leader to:

- Create a space where people can honor the genetic code that is resident in the culture—the programming that taps the best from everyone that is yearning to be expressed
- Create a space where people coach each other when negativity and problems arise—recognizing that criticism immobilizes the growth of a brand
- Create a space that encourages experimentation and discovery—where people ask "What if?" questions to discover new solutions that are always needed
- Create a space for making mistakes and exploring ways of building on what is already good—learning and adding to the base of knowledge
- Create a space where people can be vigilant about noticing and eliminating beliefs and practices that short-circuit growth and development—hearing all voices in the chorus
- Create a space where people can challenge the status quo—discover and share so that best practices emerge
- Create a space that allows people to discuss their intuitive feelings about the business and where it's going—how we are going to get there together

FIGURE 1.4

BENCHMARK COMMUNICATIONS, INC.

Balancing the Dynamic Tensions

As you reflect on the dynamics of your organization, you will see that everything changes—nothing in life stays the same. Understanding that the dynamic tension between protecting what we have and creating what we aspire to is the primary dynamic in shaping organizational life. Understanding the pushes and pulls of these dynamic tensions gives you a better handle on driving energy in positive ways and reducing the negative pull of downward spirals. Identify where your culture is on a scale from 1 to 10. Circle the number that represents where you are, and then circle a number that represents where you want to be. Focus on how you can narrow the gap from current reality to your desired reality.

C   Competitive/Exclusion   **Co-creating**   Community/Inclusion

1	2	3	4	5	6	7	8	9	10

H   Distrust/Judging   **Humanizing**   Trust/Respect/Appreciation

1	2	3	4	5	6	7	8	9	10

A   Stagnant/Limiting   **Aspiring**   Growth/Possibilities/Expanding

1	2	3	4	5	6	7	8	9	10

N   Withholding/Silos   **Navigating**   Sharing/Exploring

1	2	3	4	5	6	7	8	9	10

G   Competing/Persuading   **Generating**   Wondering/Innovating

1	2	3	4	5	6	7	8	9	10

E   Dictate/Control   **Expressing**   Encouraging/Developing

1	2	3	4	5	6	7	8	9	10

S   Compliant/Resistance   **Synchronizing**   Spirit/Commitment/Creating

1	2	3	4	5	6	7	8	9	10

Your Organizational Assessment

When I ask my clients questions about how their space "feels," they describe it quickly. An organization can feel toxic, territorial, or dysfunctional. Or it can feel like a family where people really care. The organizational culture explains the experiences we have every day.

Your answers to the seven following questions will provide a snapshot of what DNA is being expressed in your company (circle the appropriate number on each continuum, and total you score: 1 = Never, 7 = Always):

QUIZ 1.1

1. To what extent do executives in your organization lead from positional power and control, rather than seeking and honoring the contributions and power of employees to create the future?

	Excluding			*Including*		
1	2	3	4	5	6	7

2. To what extent do executives lead by power over others versus power with others?

	Judging Others			*Uplifting Others*		
1	2	3	4	5	6	7

3. To what extent does fear drive employee efforts versus the nurturing of dreams, aspirations, and possibilities?

	Fear			*Hope*		
1	2	3	4	5	6	7

4. To what extent do people feel trapped in silos and by boundaries versus being encouraged to exchange ideas and best practices with others?

	Territoriality			*Connectedness*		
1	2	3	4	5	6	7

5. To what extent are employees holding onto the past versus being encouraged to let go and embrace possibilities for the future?

	Convention			Innovation		
1	2	3	4	5	6	7

6. To what extent do leaders tell others what to do, rather than hear what they have to say and contribute?

	Tell			Hear		
1	2	3	4	5	6	7

7. To what extent do executives impose interpretation and conformation on others, versus attaching everyone to a larger purpose and celebrating achievement often?

	Scarcity			Abundance		
1	2	3	4	5	6	7

Total Score:

Organizational Culture

Your total score for the previous quiz provides a sense of the atmosphere that exists around you in your workplace, and the degree to which you should apply the information contained in the remainder of this book:

Range

40–49   Your company embodies WE
30–39   Your company is well on its way to WE
20–29   Your company shows signs of WE
7–19   You work in an I company

The Air We Breathe

Organizations have personalities that we can sense when we walk in the door, in the way the environment is designed, and in the way we are greeted. Every act, every thought, every feeling, and every person adds to the atmosphere and the experience. Leadership DNA is about the psychological environment we create and how it impacts our ability to grow, expand, and contribute abundantly to ourselves and our teams, and to our organization's future. By changing the boundaries in our organizations, and expanding the space for people to develop, we ensure corporate survival and growth.

Progressive companies today are experimenting with new organizational designs, shifting how work gets done, how people get rewarded, and how to involve every layer of the organization in decision making. They break through limitations, and activate and exercise spirit in the workplace. Look around your workplace. See who is in the experimenting mode, testing the waters for new ways of doing things. See who is challenging the status quo. You'll find valuable employees triggering the vital genes that are indispensable for companies that want to thrive.

We can stimulate growth by focusing on how to create environments that break from the past and allow connectivity to flow and new possibilities to emerge. Learning how to open and keep open all of the corporate spaces is the focus of the succeeding chapters. It is about how to create highly innovative work environments that elevate individual and team ability to achieve incredible results; to transform the way in which reality is viewed and to shape it into the reality that is desired by all. Ultimately, it's about instilling a culture where change is created collectively with a spirit of challenge and enthusiasm for what we can create together.

You may want to believe that success will come from your deep understanding of finance, or from your exquisite knowledge of marketing, or from your discovery of a new way to obtain energy from waste. The truth is, the healthiest thing you can do is know how to stay engaged with others in a positive way. It's easy to get pulled toward protecting yourself when your ego feels threatened, or when you are in fear of losing something of value. However, more often than not, you make up more in your head than what is really there. Lead with the positive intention that involves others. Lead from a desire to connect to others for mutual benefit.

Leading with others in mind provides a new way to face the frustrations, fears, and anxieties of being out there alone. It's the proven power of WE.

Chapter 2

The *C* Gene: Community

"There is no power for change greater than a community discovering what it cares about."

—*Meg Wheatley*

CO-CREATING CULTURES are those where the leaders, along with the employees and stakeholders, all play a part in building the organization from its values through to the realization of its deepest aspirations. People work together to create a sense of "we're all in this together." The community lives and works through a "power-with" philosophy, not "power-over," and the end result is not compliance but rather commitment to create a future together that taps the best talents of the community toward the greater good of all.

The focus is creating value together, and as a result, there is a great sense of shared ownership and accomplishment. Co-creating cultures work to include, not exclude. They focus on engagement, involvement, and participation, and they work to reduce territoriality, ego, and fear of rejection.

Co-creating cultures build "pull energy" through their unique focus on engaging with others in creating the future they want. Pull energy is like energy of attraction. People are pulled together because they desire the same outcomes. The alternative is push energy, and this often creates resistance, while pull energy creates desire. This energy extends from the company and envelopes the relationships they build with customers, alliance partners, and others wanting to share in the excitement of creating value together.

Innolect, Inc.
A Co-Creating Success Story:
We Have to Start Meeting This Way

In the early 1980s, Kittie W. Watson was a college professor who wanted to keep a foot firmly planted in the "real" world while preserving her independence. From the time she began teaching full-time, she took on high-level organizational consulting assignments that interested her and fit into her pedagogical schedule. At that time, Debra Jacobs was an internal trainer and consultant with a southern utility company. The two met when Kittie was brought in to partner with the internal team on a major initiative. They became fast friends.

Over the next several years, Deb and Kittie took on projects at different companies, but occasionally subcontracted to each other as consulting projects warranted deeper bench strength. Their friendship grew as their business experiences broadened.

In spite of the geographic distance created when Deb moved to another state, Kittie and Deb stayed in touch. They were experiencing many of the same client challenges and, more important to their future together, they shared many opinions about what they had witnessed—including a nagging desire to change the zero-sum game prevalent in many organizations.

Deb and Kittie respected healthy competition, but they struggled with the challenge of working in organizations that allowed colleagues to succeed at someone else's expense, whether by sabotaging another's work to advance one's own, or by outright lying. Furthermore, they had great respect for those who took pride in the quality of their work and those who went beyond the scope of their assignments—always doing more. They were concerned about those who were distracted by trying to please a boss or struggled to "fit in."

Kittie and Deb knew that the underlying explanation for such behavior among people who were supposedly working toward common goals was fear—fear of losing status, money, or the job itself.

Both women had been successful working in these environments, enjoying growth in reputation and revenue, but they found
this "normal" way of doing business more and more dissatisfying,
both personally and professionally. Sure, project deadlines were met,
some positive changes were effected, and paychecks were deposited,
but there seemed to be something missing for both the women and
their clients.

Kittie and Deb would implement a management development
program or conduct a stimulating visioning session, but client
benefits would remain compartmentalized, rather than distributed
company-wide. They wanted their efforts to result in a system-wide
impact, and were frustrated when clients lost time and incurred additional expenses if they decided later to duplicate the positive results
throughout their organizations. A world where people worked at
cross-purposes was just not a culture they wanted to work in. Drastic
change was needed. Kittie and Deb longed to create a different kind
of organization.

Late in 1999, Deb approached Kittie about exploring a new way
to work with clients. By June 2000, Deb and Kittie joined forces
and created a new firm where consulting engagements "took on the
whole system" to address the larger cultural challenges in client organizations. They created a brand that was defined by innovation and
collaboration, and by the contribution of each person's genius to a
greater community. Together, they developed a new way of doing
business. Innolect, Inc.—a new kind of business intelligence combining innovation and intellect—was born. Not only would their
own company operate differently, but Deb and Kittie were determined to harness the courage and innovative intelligence of every
client system that hired Innolect.

Some were skeptical about what they were trying to do, but years
of dialogue had crystallized their vision. They knew that leaders had
to have persistence and the courage of their convictions to be successful. More than having their own ideas written in stone, Kittie
and Deb had a great leadership awakening. They understood that

the growth template for their company had to be co-created rather than a top-down vision they imposed on others. Through the process of ongoing conversations with their associates, and through wrestling with the challenges together, Deb and Kittie recognized that their leadership style was not going to be the old-style "charismatic" one, but rather a new type that held open the space for engagement and participation.

They realized that this was a radical shift from traditional thinking, but were determined that it would become the pillar of the Innolect community moving forward. They knew they did not have all the answers for the complex issues facing organizations in the twenty-first century, but they would create a blueprint for success with their community of associates, which they called "the Five Community Agreements":

1. Lives Innolect values
2. Develops innovative intelligence competencies
3. Dazzles clients
4. Contributes to Innolect enthusiastically
5. Achieves business development results

These agreements serve as the foundation for Innolect associate engagement, are measured annually, and provide a road map for realizing potential—individually and as a community of practice. Innolect community engagement provides opportunities for co-creation, continuous learning and growth, the gift of challenging work, and ongoing feedback and recognition.

Once they confirmed in their minds that associates were equal players in the co-creating process, Deb and Kittie affirmed the community by acknowledging that it was held together with a rich foundation of shared values and beliefs. The "glue" consisted of key practices that have been evolving over almost two decades—long before Innolect formally came into being. By making their values and practices more explicit, they became the life force that held the community together. Innolect competencies were simple, but world-changing:

- *Clarity:* deeper ways to know self, others, and the business
- *Courage:* wiser ways to engage with others and create synergies
- *Creativity:* more creative ways to innovate, operate, and excel
- *Collaboration:* higher-integrity ways to mobilize resources and take action

These competencies formed the underpinnings of the co-creating community Deb and Kittie established. The belief was one of abundance: a lot of talent was needed, and there was plenty of achievement, reward, and ownership to go around. Everyone was free to showcase him or herself without threatening another. Outside of paid client engagements, individuals could elect to partner with associates of their choosing to work on "contribution initiatives" that were meaningful to them and that would also help to build the business. Lessons learned were shared with the community so that other associates could grow and benefit without the competitive spirit getting in the way.

Kittie and Deb believe that when each person lives in a place of wonder and curiosity, the community will evolve and grow. The future of the company depended on that belief. It also depended on operating seamlessly as a virtual organization. These women realized the importance of "building and nurturing" community members. In addition to using obvious communication channels (e-mail, voice mail, and teleconferencing), they built opportunities for associates to congregate face-to-face throughout the year by having client debriefs, professional development sessions, and by hosting an annual meeting at a private, customer-centered location.

Getting to know each other's talents, strengths, and passions created bonds of friendship and fellowship—a spirit that nurtured the Innolect community and extended into client projects. Associates who learned so much about each other through shared contributions, were able to recommend colleagues to join them when their unique talents would benefit the client. A climate of "mutual reciprocity" emerged.

The future strength and health of the company depended on it being protected from those who weren't like-minded. But instead of building walls and moats, the women installed mechanisms for self-monitoring and self-examination to ensure that they themselves exemplified the Five Agreements at all times. Kittie and Deb believe that leaders have to examine themselves first to lead co-creative organizations.

When they expanded the ranks by adding associates with the diverse talents needed to fortify the collective, a few interesting dynamics took place. Those who were accustomed to being solely in charge opted out of the new company. Those who stayed were excited by the opportunity to collaborate, and embraced reciprocity. And as long as they were willing to learn and didn't feel as if they had already arrived, Deb and Kittie welcomed new associates into the company.

"What we experienced in building our staff was that brilliant people are often the most humble. They know how much they don't know, and come across as if they are just trying to figure things out like everyone else. They have much to offer, and make a tremendous impression with clients because they come from a place of wonder and curiosity. As a result, they don't waste a lot of time on ego gratification," says Deb.

Another dynamic resulted from their vision. Once clients experienced Innolect's thriving community and witnessed firsthand how collaboratively team members worked, they wanted to mirror the Innolect culture. The company grew geometrically as a result.

Today, there are over forty associates with the firm, and orientations for new associates are offered as needed. Revenues have steadily increased, and the company is drawing interest from prestigious consulting firms that would like to acquire it.

▷ LEADERSHIP PRINCIPLE
Inclusion vs. Exclusion

Leaders like Deb and Kittie consciously pay attention to their leadership. They understand that everyone in the community can influence, creating more of what works and discarding what doesn't. They changed the DNA of their culture and their lives by instilling new patterns of engagement in business relationships. They focused on building and sharing wisdom, and they applied it by redesigning the feel of their workplace. They support their team's learning journey toward new knowledge and insights that can be shared and replicated with others.

What Kittie and Deb knew instinctively years ago—that a great leader values and harnesses collective intelligence and imagination above any one individual's—they put into practice in their firm and encouraged with their clients.

I-Centric vs. WE-Centric Leadership

I-centric leaders are fearful of confrontation and avoid it, find comfort in dictatorial control, and are not receptive to group contributions to decision making. They often lack the patience and skill for conversations that flesh out the real interests of those involved. They demand consensus. The downfall is that those who agree with the consensus often feel they have given up what they wanted just to go along, have a low level of commitment, and may even work against the direction others are taking.

WE-centric leaders appreciate the worth of every individual on their team, and value open and honest communication above all. They know that, regardless of how difficult some conversations may be, having them is more valuable than avoiding them. They encourage people to come together to co-create, they encourage engagement, and understand how to create uplifting experiences while tackling business challenges together. They are incredible listeners, and ensure that people feel that their participation will lead to expansive abundance for the organization, their teams and themselves. WE-centric leaders think collectively and create thriving organizational spaces where individuals exchange ideas, build understanding, and develop innovative solutions. Commitment is high when everyone has a piece of ownership in the project.

INTENTION ———————————————— **IMPACT** ———•

Leader Story: Failure to Include Others

"I don't exclude people; I just don't involve them until I'm ready."

Jane became VP of a *Fortune* 100 Company when her organization was acquired by a larger company, thus creating a new company of over 100,000 people.

Prior to the acquisition, Jane managed $150 million in sales as a VP and team leader, with five people reporting directly to her and a total team of forty . She was well-respected for her leadership. In fact, it was her consistently stellar performance reviews that positioned her to become VP of marketing when her company was acquired and merged into the larger pharmaceutical company. In her new position she had an entirely new team, with 7 direct reports and a team of 250 people. The acquisition raised her profile, as well as the expectations for her leadership impact in the larger company. Her sales targets were also increased threefold in the new position.

Jane was determined to succeed. She knew how to be a leader, and she wanted to integrate herself and her team into the new company as quickly as possible. Jane held meetings with the new team to get to know them and to give them direction.

Her new direct reports asked lots of questions about where the company was headed, what the new merger would mean, and what would change for each of them. She told them that once things settled down, she would have vision meetings to keep people in the loop.

Time passed quickly, and six months after the integration took place the team became anxious. Jane was often called into meetings with her boss, and she was on the road frequently. She would send e-mails out to everyone to let them know she would get back to them later.

Jane really thought she was communicating effectively. In her regular weekly meetings (whether by teleconference or in person), Jane had a well-thought-out agenda from which she directed people to take on tasks she felt they should be doing. She was tough, direct, and strong. She guided people to move quickly to get things done and to show that they were moving the integration forward. Jane told people what to do, yet provided no clues as to why. When people hinted that they felt out of the loop, she was not receptive. Her job, she thought, was to just make it happen.

Jane was engrossed in her priorities: figuring out what "integration" meant, understanding her mission, and making sure she started off on the right foot with her new boss. Within a short time, the team felt disconnected from Jane and from the new organization. Jobs had not been clearly defined; instead, tasks were assigned without context. Everything team members did was linked to Jane's agenda and not to roles they thought they should fulfill. Hushed one-on-one side conversations were common as Jane became known as the absentee leader who couldn't be trusted.

An environment of fear and distrust emerged, and counterproductive behavior resulted. Employees banded in smaller circles to get into "a loop," even if it was not Jane's loop. Territoriality arose whereby employees competed for Jane's attention and recognition. There was brown-nosing by some, which caused people on the team to resent colleagues, feeling they were trying to steal the show.

Out of frustration, team members talked to people outside the department, but were still unable to get reliable information about what was going on. Worst-case scenarios were imagined throughout the team. Her employees' fear manifested itself in other detrimental behaviors:

- Creating concentric circles of communication with others, building personal strongholds
- Sending out resumes in search of other jobs
- Proliferating e-mail trails to ensure they would not be held accountable for mistakes

The situation degenerated to the point where the entire team's performance declined, Jane felt let down by her staff, and her anger increased as she felt people were not committed to their jobs. Ultimately, project due dates were missed, expenses rose, people left, and it was no surprise that there was a negative impact on the bottom line. By acting exclusively—especially to those critical to her own success—Jane was responsible for what happened. Without realizing it, she had sent mixed messages to her team.

Fear of Rejection/Being Left out of the Loop

Leaders who demonstrate a high level of excluding behavior fail to understand how that fear triggers territorial behaviors. When we feel we are not included, we exhibit I-centric protecting behaviors. From this internal state, we focus on self-preservation and surpassing others. Our conversations tend to be competitive rather than collaborative. We fight for airtime rather than concentrating on making contributions, and we stir the we-they waters, causing others to retreat into protection as well.

When we are left out of the loop, or feel that we are, we perceive others as foes, not friends. It triggers fear of rejection, which causes us to act out to get back in the pack or leads us to reject others.

Fear is a natural response to a concern about the future. Fear is woven into the fabric of our existence, sometimes invisibly, and, when poorly managed, sets into motion a chain of consequences that seem undeserved or unjustified. Employee fear becomes the ever-present fabric when people in positions of authority are suddenly behind closed doors, speak in hushed tones to other leaders, communicate primarily via memos and e-mails, and refuse to address rumors head-on. This form of indirect communication, ironically enough, communicates a very direct message to staff members: you're not included. And that engenders harmful fears that are stoked by:

- Lack of shared focus, purpose, and vision, thus creating confusion
- Lack of company-wide communication that opens the door to paranoia (the ultimate fear response)
- Lack of personal communication and, consequently, a lack of positive emotional connection
- Lack of respect for others within the organization, thus causing resentment and undermining security
- Failure to tap a person's unique inner talent and creativity, which causes deeper isolation and fear
- Failure to develop team agreements, strategies, and decision-making policies
- A self-serving approach on the part of management
- Negativity and complaining, which are both the cause and effect of fear
- Low morale because of leadership's unwillingness to share the truth

When people feel out of the loop and are in fear of their future and their livelihood, it stands to good reason that other things are profoundly affected. Understanding how unspoken fear of exclusion is affecting your business will have an immediate bottom-line payoff.

As a leader, one of your most important jobs is to ensure that fear does not consume your workplace and degrade the performance of your work force. A leader's ability to manage fear of change and of the unknown is integral to staff performance. Great leaders are able to put themselves in others' shoes and interpret events for them in a straightforward and truthful way. In doing so, they create a sense of calmness and control that in turn creates a sense of forward movement, purpose, and security.

Real security is knowing where you stand, accepting reality, and being okay with it. There are ways to deal with fear effectively so that it doesn't undermine success. Leaders who understand how to turn down fear and turn up clarity in communication, who include rather than exclude, create workplaces where employees thrive.

FIGURE 2.1

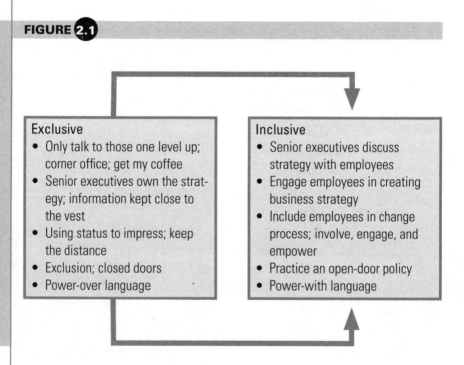

The Excluding Meta-Message

When leaders say they care about keeping people in the loop, yet fail to do so, they send a meta-message. When they talk at employees and give directives but do not explain why or do not ask questions to clarify employee understanding, they are setting an exclusionary boundary, another meta-message. Meta-messages cause employees to think one thing while the leader is saying something else. The result is confusion. These mixed messages create a metaphoric moat, and employees don't know which side of the water they are on. Without the security of knowing where we stand, we cannot do our best. A retreat into fear and protective behaviors is inevitable.

Leader Profile

Let's look at Jane's profile through a number of lenses:

How she communicates: Jane turns to only the top leaders in the company for help with business challenges. When she speaks with employees below the top ranks, her voice becomes loud. She's insistent on her point of view. She often drowns others out, speaking over them. She makes highly authoritative statements and does not ask questions—specifically, questions that indicate that she's genuinely looking to learn something new. The words she chooses are often harsh and critical, as are her tone and mannerisms. She doesn't realize that her presence, especially when she's impatient, easily intimidates people.

How she motivates others: Jane throws out challenges to people; she often gives the same challenge to many people and sets it up as a win-lose. She has people competing and undermining each other rather than working together. She believes that tough competition brings out the best in one's performance. She got to the top of the organizational leadership ladder that way but doesn't realize that her I-centric behavior stifles information sharing, hogs credit, and makes it appear as if she is sacrificing the good of the team so she can curry favor with her bosses.

How she listens or doesn't: Jane listens to judge. She critiques others' ideas and opinions, looking to disagree, rebut, or dismiss them. Her mind is so quick she may not realize that others need more time to formulate their views. In her haste to make a decision, she doesn't allow much space for others to contribute to discussions. She demonstrates disrespect for people when they don't respond quickly enough. Discussions need to get to the point, fast, because there's a job to be done and time is of the essence.

How she uses or abuses power: Jane is a power-over leader with little interest in sharing her authority with others. Her primary belief is that she is to lead and others are to follow. She overrides others when she feels her position is not being supported or is at risk. Her position gives her final veto over everything. Because she believes that a leader's job is to be an authority, have all the answers, and to give strong direction, she asserts herself through power-over energy: she is the boss and the holder of the vision. When she does ask for opinions, she does so to confirm her point of view. Then she states her mind.

Too often managers live inside of an I-centric view of leadership and feel they are right and others are wrong. They hide behind positional power and feel justified in doing so. Jane was trapped within the poor expression of gene dimensions and got results that were the exact opposite of what she wanted.

The Negative Ripple Effect

Jane failed to engage her team and peers to accomplish objectives. Instead, she rebuffed those who tried to contribute in meaningful ways. She felt their resentment, which confirmed the mistaken belief that it's not appropriate for employees to participate in strategy. The dance of disempowerment began. Employees felt Jane didn't know what she was doing; Jane thought her employees couldn't do anything right.

I-centric waves of exclusion push people away. The cascading impact is that people feel:

- Left out and disconnected from the overriding corporate vision, values, and purpose
- Envious of others
- Not good enough—of lesser value
- Resentful toward the leader and uninterested in showing loyalty toward her
- Resigned to low morale and putting forth less effort
- There is no use in trying, so they should opt out of participation at every opportunity

Junk DNA: Leadership Mythologies

Many of us have been brought up with the notion that under pressure, leaders need to become highly autocratic and give people commands and orders. We have crafted a vision of the leader as someone who is strong, invincible, and able to take tall leaps with a single bound. This vision defines a leader with an outmoded strain of DNA. It encapsulates a leader who believes that:

- Having a strong vision is enough to create a strong culture
- Asserting strong values will create a community
- Having followers makes one a good leader

How can you tell if you or your organization's managers are embodying this? There are red flags, or "mutations," that indicate a leader is expressing old DNA that limits the potential of others:

- Blind followership/ready acquiescence
- Fear behaviors
- Excuse-making/finger-pointing

- Lack of esprit de corps
- Unwillingness of employees to attach themselves to project outcomes

To evolve, you need to break the bonds of old DNA and connect to new beliefs. Research shows that top-performing companies are not led by charismatic leaders who are self-centered; they are shepherded by leaders who build collaborative organizations that are collectively focused on achieving audacious goals. Such leaders help their organizations discover, experience, and perpetuate co-creativity.

When Jane lost more staff than could be attributable to attrition, human resources came in to do their due diligence on her area of responsibility. When they determined that her leadership style had alienated almost everyone below her, executive coaching was recommended. To her credit, she was receptive to an assessment of her performance, acknowledged her shortcomings, and added new approaches to managing others. Within a couple of months, she had begun to regain the trust of those in her charge, and the hemorrhaging head count and bottom line stopped, and things began to turn around.

▷ THE LEADERSHIP STEP
Re-Create Yourself First

The co-creating leader understands that fear of exclusion triggers territorial behaviors. The essential ingredient for diminishing fear is direct and clear communication that eliminates meta-messages. People are less fearful and more secure when they know where they stand at all times. They become less afraid to ask the awkward questions and they are less intimidated when having difficult conversations.

Evolved leaders know that meta-messages can travel with any communication and they strive to create clarity and understanding over all else. How can you build an environment where people feel safe, engaged, and clear about what is going on? Instead of allowing the meta-messages and worst-case scenarios to take over your work-place, set the context for inclusion.

The Twenty-First-Century Leader Can *See* the Way to Include

To build a co-creative environment, you should reach out to every-one at every opportunity to prevent the loss of unique talents and abilities that could solve problems and formulate effective strategies. While exclusion instills fear, inclusion engenders excitement and optimism about what the future holds. There are three leadership practices that bring everyone into the fold.

Share Power and Perspectives

Innolect partners gave up part of the ownership—not necessar-ily of company stock, but of ideas and accomplishment. They made a concerted effort to get past their own egos. "We give feedback on how our people push a selfish agenda. Some people have been good independent contributors but have not brought people in to collabo-rate, and have missed experiencing what this is about; they missed an opportunity to grow our business. We don't feel we have clearly communicated until everyone gets this."

Practices for yourself:
- Inspire inclusion so that employees want to engage with oth-ers to take ownership for achieving the organization's goals.
- Value diversity of thought and essence. Value people with dif-ferent backgrounds.
- Listen to include, not exclude.
- Admit to not knowing all the answers, and invite others into conversations about how to grow the business.

Practices for your staff:
- Ask others to take the lead, and trust that they will succeed.
- Ask employees to bring others into their assignments for new perspectives and expertise.
- Create an environment where you and your employees work through tough issues together.
- Don't be afraid to talk with your people about change even if you haven't figured it out yet. Conversations about "work in progress" create a safe environment so they know that you are there for them.
- Ask open-ended questions in an effort to understand underlying concerns.

Establish an Equal Playing Field

Senior leaders at Innolect made a concerted effort to make income and compensation transparent, enabling everyone to know how each person is rewarded for his or her level of responsibility and performance: "We don't have secrets here—we are transparent. People who do more, earn more, and we put a lot of attention on helping each associate do more. We focus on growth and development for everyone."

Practices for yourself:
- Be committed to leaving every conversation a smarter person.
- Be sure reviews are realistic and targeted to each person's specific and clear job responsibilities, so that every person knows exactly where he or she stands at all times.

Practices with your staff:
- Create transparency on vision, strategy, and compensation.
- Ensure equal access to the principals to give everyone a fair chance to be successful on an engagement.

- Help others see hidden land mines: share things that may be happening inside a client project that might impact them.
- Don't leave people on their own; everyone has a responsibility to help others do their best work.
- Allow everyone to have an equal voice and allow for different opinions to be heard.
- When people are silent, help them to speak up by reframing the context. Ask for input from everyone so that all voices are heard.

Encourage Participation

All the employees at Innolect know their value to the company, and they are regularly urged to work on projects that may be out of their immediate comfort level so they can learn and achieve more. The managers at Innolect remark, "We have no interest in forcing; we influence. We tell someone that we need him to step up and do this or that. We all have a responsibility to help each other to do our best work."

Practices for yourself:
- Rather than dictating down-the-line, create space where employees can come together to have conversations about common and shared challenges.
- Communicate openly, honestly, and with boldness.
- Become genuinely interested in hearing what others have to say in order to learn from them.
- Realize that resistance to your ideas is an opportunity for learning rather than a trigger for intimidation.
- When having conversations about the future, minimize misunderstandings by repeating what employees say and asking questions so that you uncover hidden implications that may be embedded in the words.

Practices with your staff:

- Create a "big picture" view—a context for where the organization is going and why.
- Establish ways in meetings to invite participation in organizational issues, and enable each person's ideas to have equal hearing regardless of his or her position in the company.
- Encourage joint problem solving and collaboration wherever possible. Team people up to work on seeking solutions.
- Address misunderstandings quickly.

There is strength in numbers—but only if individuals are present in mind and spirit as well as body. Recognize those who are not engaged and from whom contributions are infrequent or nonexistent. To benefit from the synergy of the collective, be sure all members of your team are present and accounted for.

FIGURE 2.2

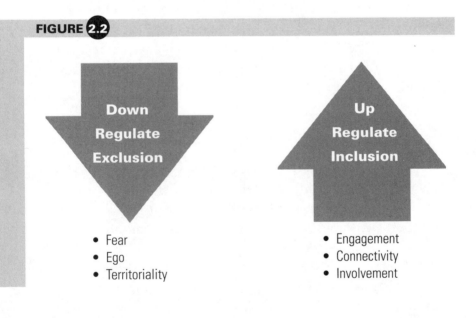

Down
Regulate
Exclusion

Up
Regulate
Inclusion

- Fear
- Ego
- Territoriality

- Engagement
- Connectivity
- Involvement

Up- and Down-Regulating

We can't completely discard competition and exclusion. It's built into our DNA as part of our survival mechanisms. What we can do, however, is express WE leadership DNA by minimizing those things in our environment that trigger fear of rejection, and maximizing those things in our environment that enable all to feel included, valued, and appreciated.

When leaders lead from a top-down mindset, they put into place controls and "regulations" that actually impede the growth of a vibrant, nourishing culture. Throughout *The DNA of Leadership* we will refer to a concept called "regulating." This concept is similar to the way we regulate hot and cold water to get the right temperature. When it's too hot we can down-regulate the heat and up-regulate the cold. In the same way, leaders need to learn to down-regulate the impact of fear in the workplace, and up-regulate the sense of support and community. As leaders become more sensitive to the dynamics at play, they will be in the position to create an inspiring and life-releasing culture, one that enables the emergence of its own unique Leadership DNA.

Down-Regulate

When you feel a sense of urgency to accomplish a mission, you must guard against the behaviors that push away those who are vital for your success. How you act and how you permit others to conduct themselves determine whether your team will pull together or in separate directions. Resist the temptation to close ranks in the face of challenge; instead, create an alloy that is strong enough to withstand the pressure of business demands by tempering destructive ways.

Fear

The natural response to a threat is to withdraw or lash out. In a business organization, such behaviors lead to a significant loss of productive man-hours and, possibly, the loss of valuable employees. Reduce perceived threats by drawing people to you instead of driving them away:

- Respond rather than react—acknowledge employee issues and other points of view.
- Listen actively and often so that you can respond meaningfully, and employees see that you really heard them.
- Walk the talk—say what you mean and *mean* what you say so people will know they can trust you.

Ego
Know-it-alls can be as off-putting as fear. People will not be motivated to do more than the bare minimum if their contributions are dismissed. You let the air out and let others breathe when you:

- Avoid making assumptions and drawing conclusions before staff input—they may be erroneous
- Are willing to acknowledge that you don't have all the answers
- Solicit, acknowledge, and accept staff feedback about your performance, and take responsibility for the impact your communications have on others

Territoriality
There are barriers—literal and figurative—that keep people out and prevent them from bringing ideas and solutions to the table. You encourage everyone's participation, to everyone's benefit, when you:

- Set the example: open door, open mind, open sharing of knowledge, and decision making
- Find things in common to break down we-they barriers
- Make guarded behaviors transparent as soon as they occur

Championship teams utilize the entire roster, from the star player who performs remarkable feats every day to the utility player who sees occasional action. Relegating anyone to obscurity in day-to-day operations will have dire consequences when everyone is needed in critical moments to produce victory.

Excluding language that is part of the Junk DNA in your culture:

- "I'll let you know when I need you."
- "We'll share that with you when the time is right."
- "Just do as you're told."
- "I'll find out who's responsible for this mess."

Up-Regulate

Embracing others allows you to create a cohesive family in your organization. No matter how talented and accomplished you are, you won't always know where the next innovation will originate or who will be credited for it. Be conscious of the following dynamics that create a productive work environment:

Engagement

Assess attachment to the mission, and ensure that is applies to everyone by:

- Sharing details about changes that are taking place
- Asking for input on how people are reacting to change so you can understand employee concerns and their "need to know"
- Keeping an open mind even if you disagree with what is being said

Connectivity

Sometimes people need to be reminded that they are all in this together. Lighten individual loads by references to the group's mission:

- Be honest about progress and milestones with others, even if you are not close to an endgame in your plan of action

- Hear both the logic and the emotion in communication—convey that you hear what is being said on all levels and how it relates to others
- Demonstrate understanding that corporate goals depend on every person's goals

Involvement

Some people readily join in; others need an invitation or encouragement. Gather stragglers into the fold by:

- Drawing people in to quell worst-case scenario thinking
- Asking for individual input on the direction you and the company are taking to attach everyone to organizational goals
- Assigning special tasks to nonactive team members, much like a teacher calls upon a student who never raises a hand to answer a question

As you build community you will see how others embrace it. They feel safer, and will step up to take on existing challenges while being confident about handling future ones. As a result, your brand becomes stronger and perpetuates itself.

Language that supports inclusion in your workplace:

- "Whom can we ask for help on this?
- "How do you feel about what is going on?"
- "Why don't you decide?"

Inclusive Conversations

For every action there is an interpretation of—and reaction to—the action. That is how communication works. People who feel involved in the strategy are engaged in the business and perform at higher levels of productivity. They are more able to include others and to contribute to a trusting, safe community. As a leader, managing communication effectively down-regulates the fear factor and up-regulates the inclusion factor. This is pivotal to your success as a leader, and your approach should include the following practices.

Shared Strategy

From the first orientation to the last meeting, be open about plans. Create teams to develop ways to translate strategy into practices. Experiment with different ways to make strategy come alive through everyday conversations. Ask: "How are we achieving this goal? What are you doing to move this initiative forward? What's working and what's not?"

Honest Reporting

Share the truth about the business—good, bad, and ugly. When people speak up, reward them so others know that forthright communication is valued. Also, allow people to give feedback on behaviors that are counterculture or negatively impacting the health of the organization—even if it's the boss's. Reward those who are courageous by giving them more plum assignments. Honest reporting and feedback become a way of life. Ask: "How am I doing? How are we doing? What can we do differently?"

Communal Contributions to Change

Leverage the enthusiasm that comes from shared work and shared success. Find a business issue important to the success of your organization, for example, how to become more customer-centric. Post this on your Web site, or create a Web log or "communal room" online. Invite contributions to this challenge. Provide creative ways for people to add their ideas. Turn their contributions into shared strategy documents that you and others can build upon in meetings. As people touch the project they become co-creating authors. Ask: "What are our biggest leadership challenges? What ideas can give us a breakthrough?"

Open Minds and Open Doors

Take notice when people are having trouble with specific challenges, such as when they exhibit territoriality or resist collaboration. Give these people the assignment of researching the challenge and making it an area of study, then of sharing their learning with others. Open your door and make yourself available for conversations so people can talk when they need to. Use symbols on your door so that people know when they are welcome, and also know when you need your own space. Ask: "In what areas would you like to grow? If the word competition were not in your vocabulary, what would life be like? How do you create a world without territoriality?"

Use Power-with Language

Commit to using WE language (power-with) as often as possible, rather than power-over language. Say: "I may have a meeting with a client, but WE made it happen."

Knockout Genes

Be sensitive to exclusive language on your part and on the part of others. The following phrases represent knockout genes—communication that is destructive to healthy organizational DNA:

- "I'll handle it myself."
- "You don't need to know."
- "You can't help."

Gene Splicing

Your words can close doors—or open them. Organizations, like the cells in the body, need a healthy template to follow. The following phrases can be used to promote co-creativity:

- "How would you handle this?"
- "What resources do you need to get the job done?"
- "What impact is this going to have on you? On others?"
- "Where would you like to be a year from now?"

Too often we think that language only involves giving and receiving information. We think words are neutral and just a means to convey facts. However, language is subject to interpretation. Words trigger emotions, which generate reactions. It connects one to another, and it can be either an umbilical cord that provides life, or a high-tension wire that delivers a devastating shock. Twenty-first-century leaders use words that build communities where everyone is nourished.

▷ A CULTURE OF INCLUSION
Community

"A community is like a ship; everyone ought to be prepared to take the helm."
—*Henrik Ibsen*

After securing food and shelter, socializing is next on the hierarchy of human needs. Everyone strives to be included and employees want to be part of a winning team. When individuals feel left out, they fight to get back in. That is how subcultures, gangs, and cults are formed. They are made up of people who feel estranged from the larger community, yet need to connect. Leaders who are mindful of the importance of building a co-creating community are more apt to build inclusion practices into their day-to-day management routines.

Rites of Passage as Told by Cave Drawings

Starting with the Neolithic period, communal ceremonies gave people a frame of reference for the culture to survive and thrive. With these rituals, societal norms became a way of life and people saw how they fit into the overall community.

In prehistoric times, when a boy turned thirteen, he was welcomed into his community with a formal ceremony that began when he was escorted into a cave. An elder held the boy's hand as they left the sunshine, with only a torch to guide their way. Inside the cave, the elder cast light on the natural rock canvas to show the boy the drawings by his ancestors, images that illustrated the rituals that the boy needed to learn to become a part of the community.

The images were explicit and spoke about the hunt and catching food. They spoke about protection from harm. They spoke of spirits and gods who were there to protect and provide sustenance. They spoke of working with others to build their community. They spoke of thwarting outsiders who could become communal threats. And they spoke of birth and death.

During the ceremony, the boy experienced psychological shifts; he was asked to take on new responsibilities, and to become part of the community—to share in the wisdom of the culture. He learned about group aspirations, and his whole frame of reference shifted from I to WE. He saw and understood the framework that would guide him from then on. When he accepted this, he was considered an adult and he assumed new responsibilities, accountabilities, and an obligation to carry on community traditions.

Replicating Organizational Inclusion

Ancient rites of passage have their modern counterparts in myriad religious and civic celebrations. In business, leaders must learn and pass on inclusive behaviors to perpetuate a thriving organization. In the business community, inclusive behaviors must be ritually performed to perpetuate a thriving organization.

Once you notice the dimension of inclusion and exclusion, you will start to see it everywhere. It's a dynamic tension that lives inside of all the decisions we make, from choosing who to include on an e-mail list to how to answer people at a meeting. The basic rule is that those who feel excluded or outside of the community react against the organization; those who feel included support the organization. To create and sustain a top-tier organization, you need to ask yourself some questions:

- How can we shift from a competitive and stagnant environment to a collaborative and growing one?
- What behaviors and actions support innovative contributions from all?
- How can we coach one another for personal growth?
- How can we grow our brand together?
- What do our customers value? How do we meet their needs better?
- How can we create the future we want?

Imagine that you have the ability to shape and craft your environment in the same way an artist can sculpt a piece of clay. Focus on the practices you can introduce into your everyday life that will help you up-regulate and down-regulate as called for, and, when necessary, knock out whatever is getting in the way. Get rid of the junk DNA that is floating around in conversations, and eliminate beliefs that do not serve the journey you are embarking on. Be diligent and fanatic about getting the results you want. Leadership is about taking the high road and seeing the magnificent possibilities on the other side.

You can replicate inclusion throughout your organization, and ensure that it is ongoing, by incorporating community gene leadership practices to create a culture where people feel involved and engaged at all times.

Meeting Strategy: Town Hall

Invite everyone to participate in company business. Do not allow fiefdoms. Seek the next situation where you can include employees in an important discussion about strategy. Bring all employees together regularly and let them know what important topic you want to discuss with them. Explain the situation completely, including the problems, and how you have been thinking about it. Ask employees for their ideas about how to handle it. Assign roles at the meeting: designate a flip-chart person to capture the ideas in writing; a timekeeper; and a facilitator, someone to help make sure that all the participants have a chance to add their ideas. Capture the best ideas and thinking, and let them know how you are going to use the suggestions. Keep an open door on the subject so employees can be an ongoing part of the situation as it evolves.

Communication and Organizational Engagement: One Company, One Conversation

Make sure that everyone gets the same message. News America Marketing (NAM), the most profitable division of News Corp, offers consumers coupons in newspapers to buy products on specials in stores. Every Monday morning the senior team and CEO have their strategy and update meeting at 9:00. Then, at 10:30, these executives run their own meetings with their direct reports. At 1:00, the direct reports run their meetings with their direct reports, and this continues until everyone is in the communication loop about what is happening.

Orientation Programs: Onboarding

Personnel should feel welcomed into the community as soon as they join the company. Cisco Systems has a very intricate orientation program for new employees. It is one-year long and unfolds in phases. First, the new employee works with a counselor, then with a team of other new employees. They then sign up for classes and training, and finally they are introduced to a Web-based knowledge-sharing site, which contains all the information a new hire needs to know in order to become part of the organization.

Nike also has an extensive orientation program for all employees. The first part is a cultural immersion, where employees learn about the founders and origin of the company. Most important, they learn of the philosophy of winning and of competition. Nike has always competed with other shoe companies. Sometimes Nike has been number one, and other times they have not. The corporate philosophy is built on "recovery and comeback" from defeat—and new employees embrace the spirit of winning through their orientation process.

Team Challenges and Journeys

Take time out of your everyday routine and go off-site. Create some high-adventure activities that require your team to work together as one. Raise the level of trust by raising the level of team connectivity. Raise the level of risk to raise the level of collaboration and synchronization. Team journeys are opportunities to have group participation on a very complex issue that cannot be tackled by only a couple of people—when the challenge is too big; it crosses over different departments, or it is not clear enough to assign. Take your team away to wrestle with the issues and problems. Structure the meetings around community discussions.

Individual Development Programs: All for One and One for All

As a "call to action," add inclusion activities in your leadership development plan. Identify situations where you can do these activities. Project out for the year what you would like to up-regulate and what you would like to down-regulate. Notice what changes occur on your teams and in your organization. Track you success. Celebrate your success.

Your Community Chest

The organization is a container that holds the potential of a community. Sometimes the organizational space becomes too closed for the collective energy to emerge:

- When management gets upset with colleagues because they haven't delivered results
- When employees and team members lose faith in one another and stop taking risks because they fear the consequences
- When the competition is fierce and old practices cause territorial instincts to dominate, filling the space with toxic behaviors that negatively impact performance, distract people from getting work done, and put out the flame of passion for work

Your job as a manager and a leader is to remove the toxic impediments to co-creating and establish a context for growth and development. When individuals visit a business that operates like a community, the energy is enveloping. It stirs their desire to want to be a part of it. It's like a wonderful aroma that activates their dream states and enriches their own visions for the future.

Leaders who create community discover that work becomes easier—for themselves as well as for their teams. People want to be heard, and voluntarily step up beyond expectations. Contributions become commonplace and generate more contributions. People give because they know they get back more. Sharing becomes a way of life, and competition is for fun, not for vanquishing an opponent. The internal culture of community naturally extends outside to customers and clients, and they love to do business where they are a valued part of the whole.

WE-centric leadership defines your thoughts, beliefs, and feelings. Co-creating communities are like having a bank account that continuously compounds interest. In such a place, you can draw upon a steadily growing principal—even when the market is in a downturn. Your "community chest" never stops paying dividends in terms of reduced attrition, budget control, met deadlines, and client retention.

Community is the first gene that comprises your new leadership DNA.

Chapter 3

The *H* Gene: Humanizing

"The deepest principle of human nature is the craving to be appreciated."
—*William James*

HUMANIZING CULTURES are those where leaders believe, "We are all in this together." Rather than seeing coworkers as competitors who vie for limited resources, twenty-first-century leaders foster a spirit of partnership and demonstrate how this leads to greater abundance for all. They teach their people that by working to honor, support, and appreciate each person's unique talents, capabilities, and contributions they can prevent turf issues and detrimental power stances. When we work as true partners we can be honest, talk about difficult issues, and grow from feedback that is delivered in a developmental way.

Humanizing cultures value diversity and encourage honesty. Giving and receiving healthy feedback and developing talent are part of the fabric of the community. Leaders in these environments work to reduce blaming, victimizing, and criticizing, and support open, honest communication and respect for others. They have a strength-based focus.

Humanizing cultures build "pull energy" by acknowledging the inherent worth of every individual. This energy extends from the community and envelopes customer relationships, alliance partners, and others who want to share in the excitement of personal growth.

VeriSign, Inc.
A Humanizing Success Story:
In the Company of Equals!

Who would have thought that a preschool Little League team would have brought together Dana Evan and Stratton Sclavos? Thanks to their children, they first met in 1992 and three years later had one of the most important conversations of their lives—one that led to the launch of an Internet security company.

"No one knew how big the Internet was going to be at the time, yet our intuition told us it was going to be a fundamental sociological change agent and security was going to be at the forefront of that evolution," says Dana, the CFO.

With the Internet becoming a public place for commercial transactions, there was a need to embed a security system into browsers to enable authentication, thus making it possible for people to feel secure doing business and communicating on the Internet. VeriSign became the first company to provide digital ID products and services for the electronic commerce. Since its inception in 1995, VeriSign has held a singular mission: to enable and protect electronic interactions. The focus has transformed itself along with the growth of the Internet and intersection with telecommunications. From its humble roots in Internet security, VeriSign has evolved into a leading provider of "Intelligent Infrastructure Services" for the Internet, telecommunications, and converged networks. These services enable businesses and people to find, connect, and transact securely across any network, anytime, over any device.

"In 1995 we had twenty-six employees, one small office, and our revenues were $400,000 for the year," says Dana. "We processed 49 million Web 'lookups' and we were selling digital certificates. Ten years later, we are still all about enabling electronic interactions, but now we do it with our Intelligent Infrastructure Services, 4,000 employees in forty-five offices in sixteen countries, and twelve network operation centers. Today, we process over 14 billion Web and e-mail 'lookups,' 3 billion telephony signals, and $100 million of e-commerce—every day—and our revenues are over $400 million per quarter."

Like other companies, VeriSign experienced dramatic fits and starts as the technology industry and the stock markets struggled to sort out this new paradigm and understand the role the Internet would play in every facet of our lives. VeriSign came out a winner in the competitive flurry because it's focused, adaptable, and resilient, and the company is shaping its culture for the long term, with the help of all of its employees.

"We've seen adversity and we've experienced successes," explains Stratton, the CEO, "yet when you put it all together, our triumphs come from remembering four things:

- "*Speed is everything:* The faster we move, the more responsive we are to our customers, the more quickly we take action, the better the results are.
- "*Business is personal:* Everything is about people; people make businesses and strategy work. If we're not in front of our customers we're not doing business. Personal relationships and interaction make us successful.
- "*Hearing is seeing:* Listen first, to our customers, to our competitors, to our employees, and to our investors will all tell us how to execute our business.
- "*Teams win:* Every success we've had is when everyone pulled together across boundaries and business units. When we work as a team toward common goals we win. When we do it this way anything is possible. From the sales rep to the person who builds our code, we work as one and the customer feels it."

Dana and Stratton use "old-style" management when it comes to handling finances. But they use a new way of thinking to create a strong employee-based culture. Dana and Stratton exhibit passion about building an incredible team, and they hire people with the same passion and drive who can roll up their sleeves and have a high level of integrity.

"At the end of the day, you need to hire people with your values," says Dana, "or you can't build the culture you want. We are the same people that we were when we started our business. We still work hard every day. We're not a hierarchical culture; everyone is held accountable for executing and delivering results. People from every level in the company can talk with us. It may be hard to get on our calendar, but it's not an ivory tower at the top."

"Our values are what hold us together. We didn't invent them," Stratton clarifies, "we discovered them. Rather than impose a set of values on our organization, we brought out the best from our employees and made that our identity. We call our set of values 'RAPID'.

"RAPID stands for Respect, Accountability, Passion, Integrity, and Drive, and the acronym has become part of the everyday language at VeriSign used to describe people's motivations and behavior. Employees say, 'That wasn't very RAPID,' or 'The way you treated that person was not very RAPID,' or "That e-mail you sent was very un-RAPID because it was dismissive.

"Our values represent who we are," Stratton continued. "Our DNA comes from our humble beginnings. We don't take anything for granted and our growth is a by-product of our success. We surround ourselves with people who are smart and driven and who feel the same way. Fundamentally, there is no strategy in the world that can replace having great people, all pulling together as one team, with a passion to win.

"We talk about our DNA as 'Secret Sauce.' We've focused the last few years on our leadership development. Similar to the process we used to identify our values, we extracted our leadership success profile from key exemplars throughout our own organization. That profile is now the foundation of our human resources platform. We're developing our leaders by teaching and by leading through example. We have a commitment to excellence and we demonstrate our commitment to our core values. And we love to win!" Stratton enthuses.

Every company, no matter how solid its numbers, strategy, and culture, hits some bad times. VeriSign experienced the 2001–2003 meltdown in the market. "It was really hard," says Dana. "Some of our businesses were either not growing or shrinking. We had to learn to exercise muscles we never had to use before, based on operational rigor and discipline. That instilled a new sense of responsibility in people. We coined a term and launched a company-wide initiative around 'Operational Excellence' at the time so we could focus on operational discipline to drive maximum productivity and efficiency. We had to work hard at it, and we adopted the maxim 'when the going gets tough, the tough get going.' We focused inward because we were unable to change the outer environment. We focused on what we could control. We closed offices, cut back across-the-board, and came out of it much stronger."

"We still talk about it," Dana continued. "In our recent satellite conference broadcast across the world we talked about our great quarter, but I stressed that it didn't mean we can lose our discipline. Because when things are good it doesn't mean we can stop focusing. Now we say, 'when the going gets good, the good get tough!'"

On April 22, 2005, its tenth anniversary, VeriSign celebrated a year of 75 percent revenue growth and earnings growth of close to 80 percent. Revenues had increased from $1.1 billion to $1.7 billion, and they attribute the growth to the ability to execute against their strategy (to deliver results) and to the ongoing passion of its leaders and all employees.

George Haddad, EVP of human resources, shares the leadership enthusiasm: "We are part of a team of people helping to enable and protect interactions over the Internet and voice networks," he says. "We have built a sustainable and profitable business—and a strong global brand."

Stratton believes you first need to define your brand, which is essentially the expression of your vision and mission, company positioning, and cultural values. Then you build the leadership team to further shape it. Last but definitely not least, you encourage employees to embrace it, for they will become your best brand evangelists. Fostering brand spirit in everybody is important to Stratton and why he believes in branding from the inside out. "Before we could bring our brand to our customers, we needed to know it and feel it inside our company, so we started our brand campaign with our employees first," he explains.

"When we held our company's brand launch it enveloped everyone," says George. "We created a song about our brand and sang it in different locations while a film crew made recordings. Then we edited together segments from Japan, Geneva, South Africa—all over the world—so we could all see the breadth of who we were: One Brand, One Voice, and One Company. It was awe-inspiring when we showed the final film to employees; there was a collective feeling of pride about who we were and what we've accomplished together."

VeriSign is on a 100-year journey that is propelled by Stratton's energy and vision. Its mission has been articulated to analysts, customers, and employees, and it identifies major milestones that extend out one, three, seven, fifteen, and up to one hundred years so that everyone knows what the long-term vision and short-term goals are.

What is extraordinary about the company is its focus on individual leadership in building a culture of humanity. Values are not an afterthought; they're a forethought. Respect, integrity, passion, accountability, and drive encapsulate the thinking of everyone from the CEO to the new employee. For employees to develop to their fullest, they must be committed to growing their leadership profile.

When George joined the company, Stratton asked him to build a world-class leadership program. Stratton stretches employees outside of their comfort zones and in doing so, taps their unique abilities and potential. Stratton is a learner himself, and he wants others to learn with him. He sees learning as a two-way street.

"Every leader casts a shadow on the company," explains George, "and Stratton's shadow is about learning and teaching others to deliver value that moves us forward on our journey to 'build transformational infrastructures that are indispensable to society.' He worries sometimes about success breeding complacency and the loss of our edge. He doesn't want us to linger in a comfort zone too long because it will take our eye off what we need to be doing to continue our leadership journey.

"Teaching is a combination of substance and style," George continues. "We now evaluate leaders not just on the results they deliver, but on how they deliver them. At VeriSign, it's about living our values, not just espousing them."

"Our success hasn't come without challenges, yet we are here because we always wanted to build a company that will last," says Dana. "We made it a point to say to employees that where we are is not the end, it is a starting point."

▷ LEADERSHIP PRINCIPLE
Appreciating vs. Criticizing

Leaders who focus on creating environments where employees are developed, establish cultural norms that lead to healthy relationship-building among employees and between employees and management. People feel honored and supported in their growth, and are valued, respected, and held in high esteem. Leaders who focus on appreciation create a culture of acknowledgment. People work at higher levels of productivity and collaboration when they feel honored and respected. Such humanizing leaders think WE, not I.

I-Centric vs. WE-Centric Leadership

I-centric leaders are judgmental and critical of others; thus it is hard to be oneself when around them. They watch with a critical eye how others handle situations every step of the way, for fear someone will make mistakes they can't recover from. They believe mistakes reflect negatively on their leadership, and so they often criticize or get involved long before truly necessary. They work off of the assumption that most people don't have what it takes to be stellar, and they are quick to bring in outsiders for help. I-centric leaders are not sensitive to others. They express anger easily, and often. Ironically, they usually get what they fear; in the end, scrutiny produces underperformance.

WE-centric leaders appreciate others and recognize the importance of their self-awareness. They strive to grow and develop greater insight in themselves and others. They are sensitive to inferences. They do make assumptions about people, but they assume that people have incredible potential they can draw upon. Rather than seeking power over others, they form uplifting relationships and create power with others. They see people as equals, which energizes relationships throughout the organization, creating a positive ripple effect of appreciation. WE-centric leaders think WE and create organizational spaces where individuals and teams work together to support one another's growth and development.

INTENTION ———————————— IMPACT

Leader Story: Failure to Honor and Appreciate

"I don't evaluate people; I tell them the truth."

Beth was ecstatic when she was promoted to lead the marketing communication function in a large paper company. She now reported to the EVP of all strategic communications services and was one step away from reporting to the CEO.

In her new role she had five times more people reporting to her. Some of her former peers were now her direct reports, and she knew this was going to be a challenge. Beth thought about the two managers she had had while working in the company, both of whom were not very good at coaching and giving feedback. They only provided direction at the time of her year-end review—never during projects. When her performance was great, she got a pat on the back and a bonus. When her performance failed to meet her manager's expectations, she left the meeting without a clear game plan of what to do and how to meet her goals more effectively.

Beth decided she would do everything she could in her first three months to make the transition smooth. She had lunch with each of her new reports and talked about the new roles each had. She set up team meetings and had what she called "a team launch" to redefine the direction the department was going to be taking. There were urgent projects coming up and she wanted to prepare everyone for the expanded amount of work they would be doing.

Within a few months the company started a new acquisition. Between the due diligence that was required and her employee lunches, Beth's calendar was full. Since she knew her former peers well, she had confidence they would handle their key assignments. She would just send e-mails asking them to let her know if anything needed her attention. She felt quite good about herself.

Her boss called her into his office one day to say that two field projects that were being managed by one of her direct reports, Maureen, had caused some problems. There had been a heated union meeting that got out of hand, and some local people were upset. Maureen hadn't informed Beth about the problems that had received coverage in a local newspaper with a very negative paragraph about the company.

Beth's manager came down hard on her and she left feeling angry, embarrassed, and ready to fire Maureen. Beth stormed into her office, shut the door, and started ranting. "Let me give you some constructive criticism," she yelled at Maureen. "That was a very unprofessional thing to do, and I expect more from you. Don't you realize that union issues are usually challenging, and to let this go for so long is just not right. You should have brought me into the loop. What were you thinking?"

Maureen, already upset about the town issue, was now embarrassed and began defending herself. Rather than being a discussion of the facts and details, the conversation elevated to a higher emotional outburst from both parties. Beth left the room, slamming the door, and Maureen sat there stunned by what had just happened. She felt demoralized and ready to quit. She hurried into her colleague's office to vent about Beth. "She is just not ready to be a manager," she said, and the two started a story about Beth's failure to lead. Gossip spread around the department through hushed conversations and secret e-mails.

Beth internalized the problem and justified why she was right in lashing out at Maureen. While she remembered that she hated it when her managers gave her such "constructive criticism," she didn't want to look back on her decision.

Beth's action created a chasm between her and her team. Respect for Beth became an issue, and she found it harder to give direction to the team. There was much resistance to her and she found that the team:

- Seemed to be communicating with looks and expressions that made her highly uncomfortable
- Started to come late to meetings
- Often made decisions independent of her wishes
- Criticized her leadership in public

Over time, the problems became exacerbated. Beth was beside herself as her effectiveness began to be challenged. She resorted to defensive behavior and focused less on providing direction and clear communication and feedback to her team, and more on covering up her own performance.

In her former positions, Beth had resented not receiving constructive feedback from her managers. In her new position, she had made a concerted effort to involve employees in the mission and to coach them on their individual responsibilities. But at the first opportunity to show respect, she acted out and harshly criticized someone who needed support in a time of crisis. Without realizing it, Beth had sent a mixed message to her team.

The Fear of Being Unfairly Judged

Beth wanted her employees to get it right, yet by giving Maureen harsh criticism she broke trust and respect, and caused Maureen to doubt her own talent and leadership instincts. Leaders who criticize their employees shove them into defensive behaviors rather than into leadership action. This dynamic impacts both the leaders as well as the employees. When teams face challenges they need a leader who has confidence in their potential. Criticism triggers fear of performing. Rather than motivating people to greater heights, it actually causes them to doubt their own talents and they underperform to avoid judgment.

Beth's lack of supportive coaching during a predicament caused the team to fear being judged unfairly. This engendered secondary fears:

- Fear of bringing challenging issues to the table
- Fear of sharing brutally honest facts
- Fear of making bad judgment calls

When people fear they are going to be unfairly judged or harshly criticized, they will avoid making decisions and taking action. They will blame others when things are not going well. Consequently, they create a psychological space that is unsafe—and paralysis when it comes to moving the business forward.

As a leader, you must ensure that fear of judgment does not become a dynamic in your workplace. A blaming culture results when speaking up about the truth, or challenging interpersonal, personal, or business issues leads to harsh criticism. A leader's ability to create an open environment for respect is vital and essential. Without this, people cannot work together in a high-performing way. Tough challenges get pushed aside, and the team's overall performance is reduced to the lowest common denominator.

You dramatically shift how you build your teams and relationships by setting the norm for open communication, where it's okay to speak up about the challenges people are facing without fear of rebuke. High performance doesn't come from pointing out mistakes people make; it comes from supporting strategic thinking and ability in direct reports. You can help employees expand their judgment, anticipate options, and stretch well beyond what they are capable of today by creating an environment in which employees are not judged and criticized, but instead are challenged to focus on new ways of thinking through the business challenges they face.

FIGURE 3.1

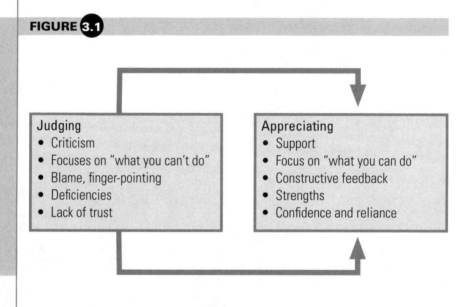

Judging
- Criticism
- Focuses on "what you can't do"
- Blame, finger-pointing
- Deficiencies
- Lack of trust

Appreciating
- Support
- Focus on "what you can do"
- Constructive feedback
- Strengths
- Confidence and reliance

The "Constructive Criticism" Meta-Message

When leaders allow others to work independently, but harshly criticize when something goes awry, they send a meta-message. When leaders promote harmony but ignite altercations, they cut off productive communication—another meta-message. Leaders who do not respect the dignity of every individual send a clear message: "You're not worth much." Employees react with avoidance behaviors, precluding solutions to problems or delaying their execution.

Leader Profile

Let's look at Beth's I-centric profile through a number of lenses:

How she communicates: When Beth's expectations are not being met, she displays anger and high emotion. Her tone of voice implies judgment. She sends reminder e-mails to move people forward, but their tone is one of disappointment.

How she motivates others: Beth uses criticism because she believes that she is being candid with the employee, and therefore operating out of integrity. She believes that not telling the employee what she is thinking would mean she was failing as a leader. Her style is authoritative and direct. To mitigate her bluntness, she often uses the "criticism sandwich," which is to say what she likes first, then what she doesn't, and then ends with what she likes.

How she listens or doesn't: Beth listens to judge. She often makes assumptions and interpretations about the potential of a person. As a result, she does not ask questions to clarify, nor engage in discussions about how to deliver on projects. When people do deliver, however, she shows acceptance and favoritism. Then her style of listening is different: she becomes more curious than judgmental.

How she uses or abuses power: Beth is a power-over leader. In times of crisis, she wields the hammer. When people challenge her, her answer is, "Because I say so." In her mind she is doing that to protect her job and keep her distance from the people who used to be her peers, but her staff feels discounted and disrespected.

The best leaders follow their own emotions. They recognize that others share feelings—such as pride and self-worth—that they have themselves. They are sensitive to the fact that they are dealing with people, not automatons.

The Negative Ripple Effect

When Beth was promoted she stepped into positional power. She felt conflicted at times about how to lead. She knew that she wanted to remain friends with the people she had grown to know so well, yet in her new role as their leader, she was unable to hold on to the personal closeness and at the same time be a manager who could help her people grow.

Leadership is a constant exercise in building and maintaining relationships. Successful relationships rely on freedom of expression and the presence of trust, respect, and an investment in a shared future. Regardless of a person's technical merits—in this case, Beth's marketing savvy—followers stop following when they feel shut out and abused. Strong relationships can weather stress. People will be forgiving of mistakes. Beth went over the line, however, when she persisted in justifying her emotional reactions and insulated herself from the concerns of those on her team. She put the results she was seeking ahead of relationships and became insensitive to the impact of her angry remonstrations. Beth began operating as an I-land unto herself.

Beth had replaced her people sensitivities with a new attitude of authority. This change in her created a change in her team. Not only did her former friends push away from her, but they also started to talk negatively about her leadership. Blame developed on both sides.

Beth's I-centric leadership created waves of fear that drowned others. The cascading impact was that people felt:

- Unable to relate to her
- Unsure of how to—or if they should—ask for help
- Incapable of meeting expectations
- A lack of respect for her in her new position

Junk DNA: Leadership Mythologies

As a leader steps up into a higher level of leadership, the challenges multiply. When you move from managing a team of 10 to managing a team of 100, you are responsible for many more interactions and conversations. Staying connected to your people and sustaining relationships while driving for results across a larger and larger employee base is a fundamental hurdle. Having personal interaction or figuratively "touching" everyone is not easy to do. But being able to create an environment where communication is personal, not positional, is at the heart of the H gene.

When we buy into a view that leaders need to be almost inhuman as they move up the corporate ladder, we accept an old view of leadership. We become leaders without heart, and we relinquish our ability to remain sensitive, caring human beings. We create distance with others rather than bond with them, and we make it more difficult for our employees to tap into what we can offer them—our world of experience—and what they can offer us—their best efforts. This view defines a leader with an outmoded strain of DNA who believes that:

- Positional power supersedes personal power
- You can't get performance from employees without criticism
- Getting too close to people weakens leadership power

There are red flags, or "mutations," that indicate a leader is expressing old DNA that limits the potential of others:

- Perpetual deference to authority
- Blame, accusation, and lack of shared accountability
- Avoidance behaviors

To evolve, you need to break the bonds of old thinking and connect to new beliefs. Leaders who develop relationships create environments where people are confident being themselves. Respect abounds and people thrive. Coaching is a way of life, and it's designed to challenge people to their next level rather than judging their past.

Fortunately for Beth, her boss had not lost his humanity as he rose up the ladder. He realized that her talents as a leader were being masked by the challenges of her new role. Her boss became her mentor and coach, and he helped her tap back into her deep sensitivities for others. They shared ideas about leadership and about what people need to grow.

Ultimately, Beth learned that power as a leader comes not from hubris but from humility. She understood that mentoring and coaching were important skills that would enable her to lead through teaching, not by judging.

▷ THE LEADERSHIP STEP
Embrace Your Humanity

Being tough is not being a leader. The leader who leads through personal relationships rather than by positional power creates an environment for open, honest communication where people support and learn from each other. Bringing your humanity to work is essential for twenty-first-century leadership.

Humanizing leaders believe that long-term success is built on inclusiveness and respect, and on the cultivation of healthy relationships with and among people. Constant attention is given to discovering better and more valuable ways of working together. Leaders with this gene believe in the inherent value of conversation and its capacity to help people be successful. They are always concerned about employee development and they aim for a mix of hard work and serious play. They relish the challenge of finding ways to stimulate people to go beyond their preconceived limitations. This is not an exercise in altruism; it's done for the sake of transformation so that the enterprise can go beyond where others have taken it before.

Fear of being judged and misunderstood is always in the background when there are relationships between managers and direct reports. No one wants to disappoint a boss. Feedback and coaching are essential for diminishing the fear of making mistakes and for exploring and learning in the workplace.

Leaders who create environments where individuals are honored and valued, communicate that it's okay to be human, to be who you really are, warts and all. When leaders relate purely through position, people become fearful of being judged, fearful of retribution and blame, and fearful of being wrong. Most of all, they become fearful of putting their tough business challenges on the table or sharing their concerns for fear that they will be looked upon as too weak to be on the team.

Humanizing leaders create environments where people are respected for who they are, where business is personal, where listening is nonjudgmental, where communication is open and honest, and where people feel motivated to work through tough issues with others. No one has all the answers, and gaining the perspective of others is vital to see the way to new insights.

How can you build an environment where people feel safe to be who they are and grow into who they can become? Instead of allowing meta-messages to hinder personal development, create an environment that thrives on the humanity that is in all of us.

The Twenty-First-Century Leader Can *See* the Way to Appreciation

To foster an environment where all are held in high esteem, you should acknowledge each individual within the collective. Everyone has feelings, opinions, and ideas. And everyone is entitled to honesty and trust. Though the ultimate responsibility for decisions remains with you, everyone must be given a fair opportunity for expression and making a contribution to preserve one's self-image. Respect for each person creates a bond to everyone that strengthens your DNA.

Share Feedback

At VeriSign, coaching and feedback are developed as leadership skills. Organizational values and leadership behaviors are embedded into the culture, and into ongoing conversations. The culture is transparent, and how leaders lead is transparent, which makes it easier to work with others toward common goals. There are measures for behavior so employees can see what behaviors will be rewarded and what will not.

Consequently, feedback is embedded into the culture. With information from peers, managers, and others, an employee can adjust and redirect behavior and stay on track with others.

Practices for yourself:
- Remember that relationships are the building blocks for success.
- Stay true to the "power of shared purpose" in your interactions with your team.
- Be able to identify where you and the team are right now relative to your goals.
- Where there's a gap, ask yourself, "What's missing, and what's needed now?"
- Mine the gap: "How is it an opportunity rather than a problem?"
- Catch yourself criticizing people.
- Make it a habit to find what can be appreciated in every person.

Practices with your staff:
- Point out things people are doing well.
- Cultivate an environment where it's safe for people to speak honestly and openly with one another.
- Be specific about the feeback you're giving others.
- Be timely with your feedback, and sensitive to its impact.
- Give coaching in private.

Establish Self-awareness

At VeriSign, self-awareness is a critical factor of a successful leadership profile. Without it, it's easy to become a blaming leader. By focusing on self-awareness for himself and others, a leader ensures a constant state of learning and growth. Knowing strengths enables a leader to move projects forward by leveraging the best each person brings to the table. Rather than people feeling that they have to conceal their shortcomings, they will boldly exhibit their strengths.

Practices for yourself:
- Be a role model for your team.
- Notice your own degree of receptiveness to feedback.
- Notice your reactions to receiving feedback.
- Give feedback rather than criticism.
- Coach through your personal power, not positional power.
- Be candid but not harsh.

Practices with your staff:
- Make giving and receiving feedback a regular practice.
- Assess developmental opportunities with all of your staff.
- Leverage the talent on your team on critical projects.
- Develop a rich vocabulary for acknowledging people.
- Encourage a culture of coaching—peer coaching as well as your own.

Encourage Nonjudgmental Listening

At VeriSign, listening without criticism is a way to gain new perspectives on challenges and opportunities. When we listen nonjudgmentally we become more perceptive to what is happening around us in our relationships, in our business, and in the world. VeriSign knows it is important to be a listening culture and that priority emanates from Stratton Sclavos. Leaders pay attention to what employees think. For example, they are in the process of collecting data to align their Total Rewards program—a comprehensive compensation and benefits package—over the next several years. The goal is to ensure that the elements perceived to have the highest value are properly emphasized.

Practices for yourself:
- Be conscious of how much time you spend listening versus speaking.
- Ask questions; listen to learn.
- Learn to distinguish between facts and beliefs, explanations or interpretations.
- Press for accuracy; that is, get factual information versus opinions about something.

Practices with your staff:
- When you encounter resistance, ask "why" questions to learn more from people. Find out what is important to others.
- Brainstorm ways to continually educate people.
- Give your staff opportunities to share their learning with one another.
- Turn these occasions into developmental opportunities so that they include instruction and coaching.
- Test your team's listening skills with the aim to teach and learn.

Leaders and employees share more than a mission; they share their humanity. Emotions, desires, and hopes may vary from person to person, but everyone has them. Leaders who appreciate this strengthen the connection to and among others and motivate all to work together to achieve the goals they have in common.

FIGURE 3.2

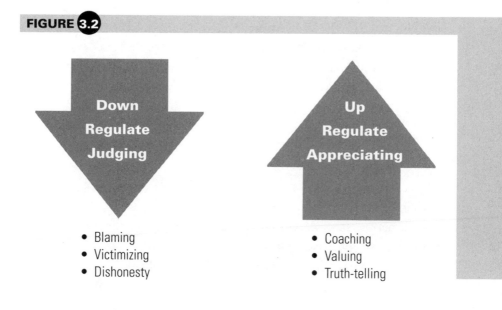

- Blaming
- Victimizing
- Dishonesty

- Coaching
- Valuing
- Truth-telling

Up- and Down-Regulating

WE leadership DNA is expressed by shifting the overall feel of the environment from judging (devaluing) to appreciating (honoring). When leaders listen and communicate judgmentally, they are coming from ego, from I-centric thinking. When they are coming from a state of honoring others, they put ego aside in order to bring greater collective value into the world. They are not coming from power over others; they are coming from power with others, from WE-centric thinking.

Down-Regulate

In your efforts to preserve your own feelings, be careful not to disregard those of others. Resist defensive reactions that alienate employees and don't deflect responsibility for problems that arise. Shared burdens are lighter ones, so reduce the load for everyone by reducing the weight that comes with the following territorial behaviors.

Blaming

People who don't make mistakes aren't trying hard enough to advance themselves or the organization. Display zero tolerance for behavior that is a waste of time and harmful to productivity:

- Pointing fingers at others
- Scapegoating
- Sneering

Victimizing

All people struggle, and even suffer, at times in their work environment, but martyrdom has no place in organizations. Be vigilant about attitudes that not only lead to the loss of the person who has them, but also infect others with malaise:

- Seeing oneself and others as subject to positional power
- Accepting weakness as something that limits personal growth
- Feeling that making a mistake or not having the skill to accomplish something is a wound to carry forever

Dishonesty

Insincerity, fabrication, deceit, and outright lying are cancers that spread throughout an organization and destroy the healthy tissue that connects people. Excise the following wherever they occur:

- Covering up problems or mistakes
- Pretending one has the answers and failing to ask for help
- Avoiding the truth about a situation, seeing the world through rose-colored glasses even when the world is not rosy

Differences can be used to drive people apart, or they can be seen as the diversity necessary for your organization to differentiate itself and survive and thrive. The opportunity for growth increases dramatically when destructive behavior among individuals is reduced.

Judging language that is part of Junk DNA in your culture:

- "You are just not cutting it."
- "That was not good enough."
- "I can't see how you can pull that off."
- "I made a mistake in thinking you were the right one for this job."

Up-Regulate

Frequent "touching" of others reinforces connections. Regardless of personal strength, everyone needs affirmation. You can acknowledge individuals with the following practices:

Coaching

Knowledge is multiplied as it is shared. Successful leaders duplicate themselves and other valuable staff members by:

- Encouraging open dialogue and communication
- Challenging people to take on assignments that stretch their abilities
- Starting from a place of appreciation and support, not blame
- Acknowledging the importance of how things get done, not just what needs to be done

Valuing

Genuine appreciation for every individual's abilities and contributions assures that they will be forthcoming—without being pressured to do so. Demonstrate a high regard for others by:

- Showing respect for diverse experience and points of view
- Anticipating potential in others
- Assuming positive intent
- Conveying genuine respect for the diversity of thinking of others through your tone of voice and facial expressions
- Encouraging people to share their feelings and concerns

Truth-telling

Honesty, which is not to be confused with mean-spiritedness, is not something to be feared or, worse, avoided. It leads to accurate assessments, worthwhile change, and breakthroughs that benefit all. Frank leadership:

- Shares the brutal facts about the business—people can handle it
- Sets the context for truth telling—personal and business growth
- Reinforces the connection between truth-telling and the organization's values

As you spread a feeling of humanity throughout your organization you will see it grow. People consider their impact on others and self-regulate words and actions to accomplish objectives with concern for the feelings of colleagues. As a result, your "family" stays together for both the short and the long haul.

Language that supports the emergence of appreciation in your workplace:

- "Let's look at the facts together so we can figure out where to go from here."
- "Let's talk about how you've been able to do it in the past. Perhaps you can apply some of the same wisdom to this challenge."
- "Share with me what's really creating the bottleneck—the root cause—so we can find a better way."
- "I don't have all the answers. I'd really like your perspective on this."
- "I won't be angry if you put the real issues on the table—we're in this together."

Appreciative Conversations

Not being able to speak openly and honestly about business, concerns, and fears is oppressive to people and to relationships. When we feel we can't be forthcoming, we protect ourselves. Feeling we will be judged or criticized for speaking the truth causes us to stop speaking up to those with whom our conversations are most important and vital. When this happens, communication gets foggy, unclear, full of innuendos, assumptions, and interpretations that do not reflect what is happening.

Leaders can clear their environmental air by fostering and valuing truthful communication. Listening without judgment is a critical component. Leaders who listen to find blame create a more stifling environment. Leaders who listen to find solutions and answers create an open and thriving environment where trust and respect flourish.

As a leader, creating an open, communicative environment is pivotal to your success. Practices and attitudes should include:

- **Supportive feedback:** Ask yourself how often you give feedback to others in a way that brings out their greatest potential.
- **Positive teaching moments:** Ask yourself how often you share your own learning and insights through personal stories as opposed to judging others for not having the answers.
- **Shared responsibility for learning:** When faced with big challenges, do you consult with others to unearth the root causes and work together to find solutions?
- **Individual worth/value:** When listening to others, are you communicating back that you value what they bring to the table, or are you communicating back judgment and criticism? How you listen determines how others feel.

Knockout Genes

Be sensitive to language that causes people to recoil from open communication:

- Candid—used to pass judgment
- Faults—pointing out weaknesses or shortcomings
- Blame—avoiding ownership of problems

Gene Splicing

Creating environments where people feel they can be open and honest is essential for building trust and respect. Graft the following into your conversations:

- "I believe in you."
- "I trust you are being honest with me."
- "We can't get caught up in ego."
- "If I hear you correctly. . . ."
- "How would you feel if. . . ."

Language can either bring out the best or the worst in others. Words can uplift, drawing people closer together, or demean them and drive them apart. When we are wounded, we shrink from contact and focus solely on self-preservation—which diminishes others in the process. When we are cherished, we are emboldened to strive and achieve more. Twenty-first-century leaders use words that foster environments where no one is afraid to achieve greatness.

▷ A CULTURE OF APPRECIATION
Humanizing

"Leadership is not magnetic personality—that can just as well be a glib tongue. It is not 'making friends and influencing people'—that is flattery. Leadership is lifting a person's vision to high sights, the raising of a person's performance to a higher standard, the building of a personality beyond its normal limitations."
—*Peter Drucker*

"What we have done for ourselves alone dies with us; what we have done for others and the world remains and is immortal."
—*Albert Pike*

Chair Ritual of the Babemba Tribe

The Babemba Tribe in South Africa has a unique solution to deal with transgressions in their society. When a member of the tribe acts irresponsibly or unjustly, he or she is seated in the center of the village alone. All work stops and every man, woman, and child in the village gathers in a large circle around the accused.

Each member of the tribe takes turns telling the transgressor all the good things that the transgressor has done in his or her lifetime. There is only one rule: no one can tell anything that is not true. No one is allowed to fabricate, exaggerate, or be facetious about the transgressor's accomplishments or personality. They speak of every incident, every experience that can be recalled with detail and accuracy. They speak out loud about his or her talents and gifts.

The ceremony continues until everyone runs out of positive comments about the person in question. At the end of the ceremony, the circle is broken and a joyous celebration takes place, and the person is symbolically and literally welcomed back into the tribe.

Replicating Organizational Appreciation

While drive and achievement are a must for a business to be successful, humanizing leaders have discovered that people drive harder for results when they are respected. Humanizing leaders also know that we all need help in reaching our goals—sometimes it's through coaching, and other times it's when we need to be stretched to think beyond the limits of what we now know.

Great leaders are both coaches and learners. They set the tone for personal and organizational growth by being in a learning mode along with their direct reports. In this way, when they are coaching, it comes from a spirit of mutual gain. In fact, they anticipate that while one person is learning, another is, too.

When employees fear being unfairly judged or criticized, their performance suffers. They may turn to blaming others when challenges arise because they don't want to look bad in the eyes of their manager or other peers. Humanizing leaders take the fear out of hierarchical relationships and replace it with a desire to be open, to learn, and to honor others.

Managers who are openly critical of employees instill constant fear of being the next target for a boss' frustration and disappointment. To create and sustain an appreciative organization, you need to ask yourself some questions:

- How can we shift from an environment where people fear being judged and criticized to an environment where people feel valued and respected?
- What behaviors and actions support the encouragement of open communication?
- How can we coach one another to bring our real selves to work and be supportive of one another's growth?
- How can we constantly acknowledge one another?
- What are our customers saying?

You can replicate appreciative communication throughout your organization, and ensure that it is ongoing, by incorporating humanizing gene leadership practices to create a culture where people are comfortable speaking up, sharing the truth, and supporting each other in finding solutions to tough challenges.

Meeting Strategy: High Touch

Leaders at VeriSign apply the concept of high touch (lots of robust, open and honest, yet caring discussions) in their interactions with employees to reduce misinterpretations and misunderstandings, and to be transparent about what is important.

When we do not have regular contact with others, especially our supervisors, we tend to imagine worst-case scenarios—which can instigate a cycle of fear behavior. Frequent "high-touch" interactions, including the use of personal storytelling to express vulnerability, replaces fact-based reprimands.

VeriSign employs other practices to connect with employees:

- **Leadership circles:** They bring in the top 100 leaders to participate in addressing issues in the short- and medium-term, allowing leaders to provide input for the long-term direction of the company.
- **Extended executive seminars:** These gatherings contain far more than status reports; they are specifically called every six weeks to identify roadblocks and to enlist everyone's contribution to meet challenges. Stratton reviews his "Worry with me" list, and puts all of the difficult issues that keep him up at night on the table for all to understand and address.
- **Quarterly all-hands meetings:** These bring strategic and operational updates to employees on a regular basis and allow them to ask questions of the executive team.

Communication: The Brutal Facts

At VeriSign, Stratton started a process of talking openly about "brutal facts" to avoid a culture of blame. He insists on knowing what's not working. Teams follow his lead and put the brutal facts on the table. Sometimes it's hard because there are egos attached to a problem that needs to be dealt with.

This process encourages people to admit when they are having problems that need to be addressed. And that ties back to their emphasis on self-awareness about what's working and what's not. Self-awareness is not just being aware of what you are great at—it's also being aware of what you are not great at, so that you can work on it.

Coaching

The emphasis at VeriSign is on development, learning, and teaching, not on criticism. The latter focuses on the evaluation of past performance with an emphasis on shortcomings and short-falls—failure. The former is future-oriented and refocuses abilities and strengths in anticipation of future success.

Developmental coaching acknowledges a common humanity, the mistakes we all make, but it stresses the necessity of making mistakes for learning and growth. This results in employees challenging themselves to take on bigger goals rather than shying away from risk. Employees are less self-conscious and more effective.

A Teachable Point of View

Leaders at VeriSign focus on creating a Teachable Point of View (TPOV), a concept introduced to them by Noel Tichy, that ties one's personal life experience to the business journey at hand. All leaders incorporate a personal reflection with an example of how they've integrated the RAPID company values in how they lead and manage. As part of the executive leadership program at VeriSign, each participant develops his or her TPOV as a platform from which to lead, teach, and grow his or her team. This process engages people and makes them more aware of one another's goals, and how they tie back to the company's goals and values.

Reweaving the Leadership Network

Many companies grow through acquisitions as VeriSign does. In the face of diverse cultures coming together it is important to establish processes for integrating cultures in a way that appreciates what each one adds to the whole. VeriSign brings together leaders from different geographies, businesses, and functional groups to discover how to learn together and solve real business problems over a sixteen-week period. Without being directly involved in one another's work, people become linked to, and actively supportive of, each other's missions.

Meetings of these networks are sessions that increase company-wide awareness and lead to completely objective opinions and recommendations that often have high value.

Raise Emotional IQ

VeriSign's leadership programs contain segments and modules to teach the principles and practices of relationship intelligence. The framework of STEPS serves as the backdrop to the program, with each participant going through a 360-degree process where feedback is supplied from managers, peers, and direct reports. Leaders overcome an initial reticence to such an approach when they see how it provides tremendous insight into development needs, blind spots, and insensitivities to others that negatively impact performance. Feedback is a gift to a leader. These 360-degree "letters from home" generate action plans that VeriSign leaders use to improve their business.

Your Shared Humanity

Human beings have always faced the same issues: how to survive, how to be happy and live a joyful life, how to be part of a community, how to be known for good things and attract good people, and perhaps how to make a difference and leave a legacy. These themes run through all of history, all of literature, and all of religion.

Competition with others and challenges that threaten us—conflict—can be win-lose propositions, or wonderful opportunities to display concerted effort to everyone's benefit. Recognition of how much we have in common with others is the key to overcoming our differences. When we struggle and fall short of expectations, there is great support in knowing not only that others experience similar travails, but in knowing that others are also the source of help.

Great leaders lead from humility, not from egoism. Awareness of the humanity we all share—imperfections and talents, fear and courage, hopes and dreams—is the source of that humility. Humility is the tie that binds; your humanizing leadership gene is the humble thread that keeps everyone bound together with a shared purpose.

Chapter 4

The *A* Gene: Aspiring

"Great ideas, it has been said, come into the world as gently as doves. Perhaps, then, if we listen attentively we shall hear amid the uproar of empires and nations a faint flutter of wings, the gentle stirring of life and hope."

—Albert Camus

ASPIRING CULTURES are those where leaders, together with employees, strive to achieve audacious goals. Aspiration means to breathe. Leaders who tap into their A gene infuse environments with healthy air for the inspired conversations an organization needs to thrive. Aspiration is when everyone supports each other by breathing hope into fear, and by creating an environment where optimism trumps pessimism.

Aspiring cultures are characterized by a high level of learning, of taking one step after the other, and when opportunities arise, being aware and seizing them. Aspiring people have a heightened awareness about their environment. They focus on the future, rather than on past mistakes. They encourage their teams to learn from experience. They reduce fear of change, fear of making mistakes, and fear of blame, and focus on challenges, opportunities, and possibilities.

Aspiring cultures build "pull energy" by focusing on releasing hopes both at the individual level (careers) as well as at the organizational level (brand). This energy extends from the community and envelopes customer relationships, alliance partners, and others who want, and need, to dream to live and to live to dream.

115

Gordon Brothers Group
An Aspiring Success Story:
Dare to Dream

One hundred years ago, Gordon Brothers Group (GBG) was in the jewelry business. Fifteen years ago, it was in the liquidation business. Today, Gordon Brothers consists of eleven businesses from liquidation to merchant banking. Each business evolved out of a rich combination of instincts for the marketplace, incredible leadership, and a well-honed ability to thrive inside of change. In fact, GBG creates change.

There is a pace of excitement inside the GBG offices. Big talent, but with tempered egos. People are brought into projects to contribute their unique ideas, and everyone learns from someone else. Risk-taking is essential to the expression of their DNA, as is courage. It's never about making mistakes; it's about figuring out what's next.

GBG leaders live in the trenches with one another, working hard and taking the risks along with everyone else. "I think success is due to leadership plus hard work," says Michael Frieze, past CEO and current vice chairman who was brought into the business by his grandfather. "You just can't get anywhere without hard work. If you're not working hard, how can you expect the people on your team to work hard? It's a very competitive world, and the ability to win in that world is getting progressively more challenging. You have to work really hard to get there. A leader has to set the right example, and give up responsibilities.

"When I first joined GBG, I had a difficult time," Michael continues. "I didn't feel I was making a difference, so I left to go to Harbridge House, and then later to start my own company with friends. In this latter venture, we were losing money and Linda, my wife, who was a social worker at the time, supported the two of us. She stopped working after her eighth month of pregnancy, and my grandfather, sensing we were having financial trouble, said the business really needed me and asked me to come back. I knew that wasn't really true, but I went back, close to broke and humble.

"The day before I came back, my grandfather went around to everyone in the business—only nine people at that time—and told them they were not to tell me anything, that I had to learn on my own and make mistakes as fast as possible. He was a philosopher, and so much of what Gordon Brothers is today is built on his beliefs, which I now share. It turned out we were a lot alike.

"My grandfather wanted me to really understand that you have to make mistakes in business. If you are afraid of making mistakes you will never be a leader and you will never get to where you want to go. I teach that to everyone who comes to Gordon Brothers. I want to encourage them to grow, and not feel there are boundaries that inhibit them; and to ensure that they feel this is a place where they can develop their career, and that this is not a place where they need to be afraid that people will point their fingers at them and say, 'Hey John, you made a mistake.' Rather, you want to create an environment where you come to John and say, 'That didn't work out the way we had hoped; let's do a postmortem and see why that happened.' You have to create a learning environment and allow your people to grow," explains Michael.

That is the essence of Gordon Brothers. People there might not be as ready as they would like to be to take on additional responsibilities, but executives feel if they are not given responsibilities, they won't find out what they are made of. The Gordon Brothers environment is one where people are less inhibited than in most other environments about giving someone something to try, and watching what happens. They know this is the way you create stars. It also gives people the confidence to explore new opportunities with more comfort. They are not afraid of making mistakes when the boss sends them out on a hunting expedition to try pioneering things.

When new employees come to Gordon Brothers, Michael participates in the interview process and the new-employee orientation process. He explains the business so people understand that it is a hybrid of retail and deal making which they call "merchant banking." Employees learn from day one that they are going to win some and lose some, and that's just part of the process. The same philosophy applies to their careers—win some, lose some. But at Gordon Brothers, career growth is not only in the hands of an immediate manager; it is in the hands of mentors, other managers, and the employee.

Michael is a third-generation leader at Gordon Brothers. His son Ken is also in a company that "used to be a family-owned business, but now is a business with family," Michael says. "You don't get kudos here for being a family member. You need to perform or you don't get your next promotion, no matter who you are. That is not usual in a family business. Here, people really believe in the concept of three intertwined circles: work, family, and community."

They believe and promote all three, and it starts with family. Work is important, but they also want their people to think about community. They raise money as a company for Children's Hospital, and they give a community service award every year to an employee so that people understand that they care deeply about how the rest of the world is doing and that they can make a difference.

"People want to come to work here because we care about them and because we treat people with dignity when change is thrust upon us," Michael says. "We help develop their careers.

"Change is the only constant in life and in business. Businesses that embrace and welcome change have a greater chance for success than firms that don't. If we don't have the resources in place to deal with change, we go get them. We operate with a hub and spoke concept. We have incredible administrative resources in our hub that support the businesses that are the spokes. This structure enables us to handle many different enterprises, whether it's real estate, equity, inventory, debt, international operations, appraisals, or fixed assets, and to add new spokes to the existing hub as change occurs.

"People move around in our company a lot, which is part of how we handle change. They move within a business or among other spokes while they take on new challenges, grow their careers, and grow the company in the process. Our incentive system is a combination of how well they do in their own division and how the company does as a whole. If I'm helping someone and he or she is successful, I'll benefit," says Michael.

He explains how GBG deals with change to evolve: "How do you step into new businesses you don't know? Sometimes it happens by accident. The next time it might be planned. For example, you are asked by a bank, because you are a liquidator, to appraise some inventory. You understand the bank is lending on that inventory, and you realize you have a capital base, so why can't you lend on inventory? Then you realize you can lend on other assets, so you develop a real estate or a fixed-asset business. You realize you can be a provider of wider services without giving up the core," says Michael.

People at Gordon Brothers take risks and step out. New business ideas are harvested through a multistep process—and the culture is built to support the growth of these new business development efforts. This process turns the fear of failure into a platform for courageous action. According to Michael, "It works because people are good and because mediocrity isn't accepted. We expect people to be great. But greatness doesn't mean you can't make mistakes. We learn more from failure than we do from success."

Champions of ideas are encouraged to spread their wings and take a chance. What is most fascinating about the GBG culture is that it replicates a process that Walt Disney used to turn visions into reality. Disney labeled rooms in his house Dreamer, Reality, and Critic, and as he developed his ideas he physically moved from room to room. While in the dreaming room, he imagined what could be. While in the reality room, he tested the idea. And while in the critic room, he evaluated it.

And while the term *failure* generally connotes a negative result, failure is an important path on the road to success. "Whether an individual fails or succeeds, the bottom line for us is making sure we have created an environment where ideas can germinate and opportunities abound to cultivate learning experiences. Inherent in this is reinforcing the message that risk-taking is essential, both for the personal growth of the employee and the growth of the company. If we have done this, we will be successful," says Michael.

> ▷ LEADERSHIP PRINCIPLE
> **Courage vs. Fear**

Aspiring leaders like Michael Frieze recognize that for a company to thrive people must have dreams but at the same time have the courage to put one foot in front of the other when heading down a new road. Aspiring leaders find it intriguing to see what will be next, to find the door not yet open, to seek opportunities at every turn. There is inquisitiveness about what could be rather than an adherence to what is. They further recognize that it's their job to create opportunities for the next generation to become opportunity-seekers. Such leaders embody and encourage hope for—not fear of—the future. Aspiring leaders think WE, not I.

I-Centric vs. WE-Centric Leadership

I-centric leaders fear the future, so they react to the normal ebb and flow by reprimanding people for not performing. Because they become afraid under crisis, they are less supportive, and say, "I told you so." Rather than trying to exceed norms, they merely produce what is expected. I-centric leaders lose the support of their teams. They retreat, avoid, and convey disappointment. They create an atmosphere of discouragement, low enthusiasm, and constricted imagination.

WE-centric leaders recognize the importance of encouraging people to unleash and follow their aspirations. Aspirations are the fuel for growth. Rather than allowing fear to drive out hope, aspiring leaders imagine the best-case scenarios and encourage people to make the impossible possible. WE-centric leaders create organizational spaces where individuals and teams test limits, test reality, and take risks to expand their horizons on projects that are larger in scope and more challenging than usual. They instill confidence, and know that talent develops through the process of realizing dreams.

INTENTION ──────────────── **IMPACT**

Leader Story: Fear of Change

"I don't yell at people; I encourage them to be better."

Mark was the best real estate salesperson anyone had ever seen. He was someone others wanted to have on their side, at their meetings, and on their projects. He was a winner. When the company he partially owned was purchased by a larger holding company, Mark cooperated with the sale and became the EVP of Sales, with a responsibility for all salespeople in the United States.

Mark was charming, good-looking, and an incredible extrovert. He was someone who openly cared for the business and its success. Management loved him, and they wanted Mark to stay on to mentor the next generation of salespeople.

The goals for business growth were enormous. The new company's strategy was to add salespeople—and so the staff expanded from 250 to 450 almost overnight. It was up to Mark to instill the new talent with a sense of purpose and direction. He was anxious to rise to the challenge. He wanted to prove that he could deliver results for his new firm. Mark was now on the road supervising and overseeing the onboarding process for 200 new salespeople. However, he was also a new father. His position dictated that he travel during the week, and be home only on the weekends. He became tired and stressed by the demands of his new position.

On the trips he really got to know each person as much as he could, and would individually mentor and coach them to drive more business. Over time, the pressure mounted. When he fell short of the ambitious targets that were assigned to him, he changed from a great coach to a screaming boss, from a people person to a "need to deliver" dictator. Six months passed, and Mark's personnel retention rate plummeted. Once proud of the fact that he could keep talent forever, he was now spending significant time replacing talent he was losing.

Mark's end-of-year review clearly defined him as a boss who was tough on people. He was known to yell to get results, and would chastise people for not delivering. He was seen as someone who didn't care about people and would push for results at all costs.

Approached by his boss, the CEO of the parent company, for his leadership deficiencies, he was defensive. Mark had not internalized the fact that he had changed. He still thought of himself as the great leader and mentor of others.

Mark had blazed a trail of accomplishment in the old firm, but stifled in others the very initiative that had been responsible for the firm's remarkable achievements. Without realizing it, Mark had sent mixed messages to his new sales staff.

Fear of Change

Leaders who react to new responsibilities by retreating to previous patterns of personal success restrict the ability of others to capitalize on change. People who work for them who used to feel secure in their approach to doing business will start to doubt their own talents. When a boss yells at an employee to do more and deliver more, without going through the process of helping his or her staff figure out how to get more from their own talents, relationships disintegrate, frustrations take over, and no one is able to find new ways to deliver desired results.

The resultant fear in the workplace causes everyone to question whether new growth goals can be achieved. Deep inside, everyone wants to deliver on performance goals. Yet when tensions get high and leadership direction is unclear, performance remains flat or declines.

Mark's behavior exemplified the insensitive fear-based boss. While in the past he was great at people building, he was now seen as someone who favored a few and beat on many. He felt he had little time to spend with each person to bring them up to speed with their territories. So he chose to just demand results and see who could deliver. Some people, whose territories were rich with new opportunities, were able to come through. Others felt the heavy hand of their boss. This led to secondary fears:

- Fear of disappointing the boss
- Fear of failure
- Fear of competition among peers
- Fear of the future

Mark's fear of personal failure created an attachment to the past, to his old ways of doing things, and to his fear of change. In the past, being macho was revered. He was part of the old-boy network and there was a sense of power that came from that. In the new world he had stepped into, he had to move from a fraternity spirit to a mentoring spirit. In addition, his role and responsibilities expanded beyond what he had been used to in the past. Mark had succeeded with his personality and now he had to succeed with his strategy. He was being challenged on the way up the mountain and felt a loss of oxygen along the way. His old way of leading was just not the answer.

As a leader, you must ensure that fear of change does not stop you from growing and seeing the opportunities ahead. Mark wanted everyone to succeed and yet he failed to stop and see what he needed to change to help his team get there. He later admitted that he had had a golden spoon in his mouth most of his life and the challenges never took him outside his comfort zone before.

Leaders must be able to manage their own ability to change and grow if those around them are going to have the opportunity to step up and become leaders as well. Great leaders are able to get inside of change and see that they need to create an environment where others can grow to meet that change on their own terms. Leaders need to see change as an opportunity for everyone to be a part of creating the future. Leaders who instill a sense of hope set the tone for greatness to emerge.

You can help employees—and yourself—by encouraging them to step into change with a desire to learn and grow. Leaders who reach out for feedback set into motion the ability for others to gain confidence during change. Leaders who make change a friend help others embrace change with hope for realizing aspirations.

FIGURE 4.1

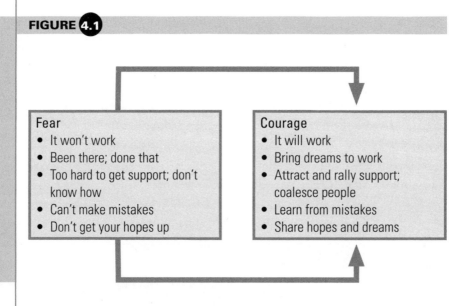

Fear	Courage
• It won't work	• It will work
• Been there; done that	• Bring dreams to work
• Too hard to get support; don't know how	• Attract and rally support; coalesce people
• Can't make mistakes	• Learn from mistakes
• Don't get your hopes up	• Share hopes and dreams

The Threatening Meta-Message

When leaders say that they are on your side and believe in you, but yell at you for not performing, they send a meta-message. When leaders believe they are driving for results, but fail to support people in the throes of growth, they indicate that they don't believe people have what it takes to perform—another meta-message. Leaders who fail to mentor others, who don't allow others to visualize and achieve their dreams, send a clear message: "There is no hope for you." The result is loss of employee and corporate potential.

Leader Profile

Let's look at Mark's I-centric profile through a number of lenses:

How he communicates: Mark comes across as intense yet very people-oriented. He is a driver and expects that he can demand what he wants and get what he wants. Those who deliver are in the inner circle; those who do not are failures to be shunned. He does not accept mediocrity, just results. As a result, people who are struggling feel they cannot turn to him for help.

How he motivates others: He hires successful people for their talent and expects them to produce as usual. He does not see that his role is to develop his staff. He demands a tremendous amount from people and does not have the time or inclination to train them. He likes to be seen as someone who has a cadre of the best under him; people should be honored just to be part of a winning team.

How he listens or doesn't: Mark is so overwhelmed that he just can't be there for everyone. While he might want to, he can't, and therefore stopped trying. He has to get through his long to-do list and when people put personal demands on him, he withdraws to protect his sanity. He is treading water and getting the best results he can. People complain that he is not there for them.

How he uses or abuses power: Mark knows that he knows sales and he is one of the best in the industry at closing deals. Leading and managing a large staff of people are outside his comfort zone. He's tough on others to sustain his personal winning streak. He yells and screams to get others up to the level he expects. He demands results.

He engenders fear attached to failure to produce results and he knows that he can push that button to sort out the winners from the losers.

Managing others is far different than managing oneself. Leaders who strive to meet their goals without helping others to satisfy their inherent hopes and dreams unnecessarily handicap themselves and their organizations. Trying to force results by using threats threatens both the attainment of short-term goals and risks long-term success.

The Negative Ripple Effect

Mark had a great reputation as a salesperson. People loved to be around him. New responsibility created demands on him that were beyond what he was able to accomplish without making changes. Even though he wanted his people to be successful, he didn't understand the role he had to play in mentoring and in creating the right psychological environment for his people's success. The old style of "beat them to succeed" was not working, yet he did not see another way. Inspiring hope in others was turned off in his genetic code. He instilled fear in the sales force, and rather than inspiring others to reach for the stars he made them fearful of making mistakes.

Mark caused his team's performance to go into a holding pattern. His failure to create an environment for shared support in taking on new challenges in the face of the new ownership caused good people to leave and others to stop growing. He had become an I-centric leader who created waves of fear that drowned everyone. People felt:

- Unable to approach him about how to tackle the markets
- Unable to let others know they were struggling
- Embarrassed about appearing incapable
- Discouraged and dismayed
- Fearful about their future

Junk DNA: Leadership Mythologies

Many of us have been brought up with the notion that our job as a leader is to set high expectations for others, whip them into action, give them big bonuses when they succeed, and let them know when they've failed. This is the performance cycle we have all experienced and we carry it forward into the next generation.

Over time, this framework creates an undercurrent of fear about making mistakes, taking risks, hiring people smarter than we are, being bold, and most of all, dreaming big dreams.

Fear-based performance techniques do not create better performance. Instead, they create underlying worry and anxiety that keeps everyone on edge. Having deep awareness about how much it takes to succeed is healthy; having fear about our performance is not. Such fear erodes our self-esteem, causes us to be overly cautious and sensitive, and puts a strain on our relationships with others.

When we buy into the notion that we need to frighten others into performing, we become a power-based leader. Research has shown that punishment for failing to perform does not stop people from performing poorly; it only reinforces the fact that they are nonperformers. When we see the leader as someone who wields carrots and sticks, we reinforce an old style of leadership. This outmoded strain of DNA reinforces old beliefs such as:

- Punish mistakes and they will go away.
- Be tough on others and they will become tough.
- Setting high expectations is enough to get high performance.

There are red flags, or "mutations," that indicate a leader is expressing old DNA that limits the potential of others:

- Emphasizing results at the expense of relationships
- Devaluing the ideas and input of others
- Blaming others is more prevalent than honoring others

- Failing to take personal responsibility for the atmosphere and climate of the environment
- Making demands and not giving people room to explore options
- Mistakenly believing that people are motivated from the "outside in"; that is, that they'll respond best to extrinsic rather than intrinsic motivators.

To evolve, you need to break the bonds of old DNA and connect to new beliefs. Top-performing companies create environments where fear does not own the organizational terrain. Leaders intentionally focus on creating safe environments where others realize that change is constant, where having the courage to step out and experiment is good, and where they are not punished for making mistakes. Leading, at all levels, becomes part of the fiber of the organization. Such leaders make change natural and help their organizations connect directly to what success can look like for themselves and for their customers. As a result, they grow exponentially in the face of change.

When Mark's team gave him some very critical feedback during a 360-degree process of evaluation, the human resources department discovered that Mark's heavy-handed style of pushing too hard on people was causing performance to drop.

Executive coaching was recommended for Mark, and he was very responsive to this process. Feeling the pressure for success himself, he welcomed new insights into how to be tough yet gentle, how to create motivation for winning yet do it with support, and how to make himself available to be a great mentor for others. He admitted to his coach that he held a very old view of leadership that was passed along to him by his previous bosses. He knew inside that it was not a good model, yet didn't know how to break the cycle alone.

After six months of coaching, the organization saw the positive impact he was having on others. The energy in the team was outstanding, and more stars started to shine. The business was back on track and Mark was promoted again.

▷ THE LEADERSHIP STEP
Aim to Dream

The aspiring leader understands that fear of change and making mistakes causes individuals to resort to the primitive fight-or-flight reaction. The essential practice for diminishing this fear is to take risks, knowing that each step will be a lesson for learning. By creating an environment where people can stretch, try new things, dream, and dare to take risks, there is psychological safety in learning to step into a new level of greatness.

Aspiring leaders give people room to learn and grow. They take the edge and anxiety out of stretching beyond a comfort zone and enable people to experiment and discover their own potential without fear of punishment or retribution from the boss. Doing so eliminates the meta-messages that cause fear of change in others.

Evolved leaders know the damage that meta-messages cause: performance anxiety, fear of making mistakes, insecurity, and mediocrity. How can you build an environment where people push their limits, stretch outside of what they know, and dare to dream about what they might achieve? Instead of allowing meta-messages to reduce the potential that resides inside of the organization, set the stage for exponential growth.

The Twenty-First-Century Leader Can *See* the Way to Courageous Effort

To build a thriving environment where employees can realize their dreams, you need to be the beacon that leads the way into new territory. Instead of implying by words and actions that the future is something to be feared, remove restraints that chain employees to the present—or the past.

There are three leadership practices that untie the binds and unleash innovative energy.

Share Dreams for the Future

Dreams are an investment in the future of your people and your brand. New ideas are created by cultivating, at an organizational level, the capacity to dream. People need time and space to imagine what could be. Wise leaders create environments where people are encouraged to dream, and where no dream is too foolish to share.

Leaders such as Michael at the Gordon Brothers Group have borne witness to the extraordinary power of shared dreams. Michael wants to make sure that ideas, no matter whom they come from or how unrealistic they may appear to be, capture the imagination of his cohorts. He has created a culture where he and others around him listen for any kernel of an idea that might be worth pursuing. Part of the success of the leadership at GBG is their ability to draw people out so that they share their hopes and aspirations publicly. This involves creating a culture of trust and safety.

Practices for yourself:
- Be future-based. Rather than looking at the current conditions, project yourself into the future and freely speculate about what is possible.
- Make room. New dreams need a way to emerge. Review your existing commitments and eliminate those that don't support your goals.
- Consider your impact as a leader and role model. Ask yourself, "What behaviors of mine support, and which ones inhibit, the dream-creating potential of my staff?"

Practices with your staff:
- Schedule downtime together away from the pressures of the office.
- Consider using a trained facilitator to promote a free and open dream-creating session together.

- Plant seeds. Use "What if. . . ." questions to catalyze people's imagination. Ask, "What if there were absolutely no limitations on what we can do to succeed?"
- Engage your people from the perspective of your customers. Ask, "As a customer, what would I really want?"
- Listen with authentic interest for what's possible rather than for what's not.
- Comingle your dreams with others. Listen for something, anything, you can take away and use. Shuffle or combine ideas.
- Consider using alternative, right-brain methods, such as music, storytelling, movement, meditation, or poetry to stimulate people's imagination and spark their dreams about the future.

Establish a New Way of Thinking

While new employees are selected to join Gordon Brothers because they are smart, they are also selected because they are adaptable and open to experimentation. Those who imply during interviews that they "know it all" are not looked upon as good matches for a culture that is in a state of constant learning and seeking new ways of thinking.

At Gordon Brothers, there is also a willingness to recognize one another's blind spots. We see what we want to see (or don't see what we don't want to see). We may be in denial about something rather than face up to a threat or problem. Or, we'll downplay the importance of something likely to occur in the future rather than acting to address it now before it becomes a crisis. We also have a tendency to stand by a belief that the cause of a problem lies "over there," rather than face up to our own role and responsibility.

At Gordon Brothers, value is placed on having direct conversations without a need to find fault or assign blame. Meetings can be tough, intense, and challenging. People know not to step around the proverbial elephant in the room. They address the real issues face-to-face, however uncomfortable that may be, so, at the end of the session, each member of the organization comes away more equipped to raise the bar on performance the next time around.

Another key to success in the Gordon Brothers culture is the ability to "reframe." Leaders reframe mistakes as lessons learned; challenges and obstacles are opportunities for learning. Reframing is a way to ensure that fear does not erode talent, nor the culture.

Practices for yourself:
- Listen for when you are defensive or are too emotionally invested in your position.
- Regularly ask yourself, "How have I helped contribute to stagnation—through what acts of commission or omission?"
- Remember your breakthrough moments. Be able to answer, "How in the past have I created space for new ideas to emerge?"
- Turn opposition and conflict into an opportunity to harvest new thinking.
- Learn to explore why others are saying what they are saying or thinking—rather than rejecting it.
- Regularly review what has and hasn't worked and mine those answers for future benefit.

Practices with your staff:
- Be aware how others respond under pressure. Distinguish between responses or thinking that arises in the heat of the moment versus the more opportunistic responses that come from the imagination.
- Encourage people to leave the space open for new listening, not just "I know it" listening.
- Encourage divergence and nonjudgmental listening where different points of view can have life; interrupt patterns where people jump to quick conclusions.

- Set the table for rigorous dialogue, where there is time to sift through different points of view and explanations so you can see how to connect up resources with new ideas.
- Open the space for brainstorming. Create a break from the past, allowing the future to emerge.
- Keep people focused on what they're for rather than on what they're against.
- Continually review and renew. Review your actions for vital lessons learned and use them as an opportunity to renew your commitment to your goal.

Encourage Risk-taking

At Gordon Brothers every change represents new challenges and opportunities. Leaders encourage risk-taking and know that it is the pathway to build the business. There is constant encouragement to experiment and try new things, albeit in a prudent manner. In considering risks, active consideration is given to the upside and downside potential of that risk, in terms of what serves the customer and the business. Risk-taking is coupled with postmortems (lessons learned) so that risk in the future is mitigated.

Practices for yourself:
- Demonstrate your own willingness to take risks. Set an example for others.
- Clarify your standards to establish what is or isn't a risk worth taking.
- Notice when you shy away from risk. Don't defend or justify your behavior, just notice it.
- Be aware when you adopt the "Monday morning quarterback" role and how this affects a climate of risk-taking.
- Be clear! Make declarative statements so that you and others know what you're committing to. Don't waver.

Practices with your staff:

- Share how you arrived at your own accomplishments so that others can learn from you.
- Explore the difference between "playing to win" and "playing not to lose," and adjust attitudes and behaviors accordingly.
- Promote sensible risk-taking. Share what disappointment you would be willing to risk.
- Befriend disappointment. Have the rate of learning be what you measure.
- Conduct an "appreciative inquiry." Ask others about specific times when they took risks because of something they believed in. Acknowledge the qualities they displayed.
- Interview one another and create a composite picture of what things would look like if your different dreams were realized. What would be possible then?

Courage is not exhibited in the absence of fear; it is exercised despite it. Fear can paralyze, or it can mobilize. Successful leaders acknowledge its natural presence but refuse to let it impede progress; they marshal the adrenaline it generates and channel it into forward movement.

FIGURE 4.2

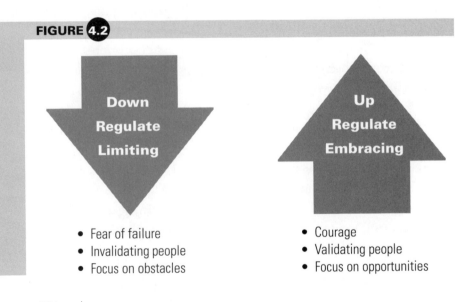

Down Regulate Limiting

- Fear of failure
- Invalidating people
- Focus on obstacles

Up Regulate Embracing

- Courage
- Validating people
- Focus on opportunities

Up- and Down-Regulating

WE leadership DNA is expressed through harvesting the imaginations of individuals and helping them realize their potential. When leaders create an environment of intimidation or fence people out based on job title, lack of seniority, educational level, or some other restrictive factor, they underscore an I-centric mode of thinking. When they express genuine interest in the potential contributions of others, they signal their receptivity to a free-spirited exchange of ideas, hopes, and dreams. Aspiring leaders reinforce a culture where ideas are circulated and collaborated upon.

Down-Regulate

During times of stagnation or crisis, you might be tempted to take over the reins and control events. It is precisely at those times that you should release the pressure and allow others the room to learn, grow, and do their jobs. Reassure your team that you have faith in its ability to weather the storm by curtailing restrictive lines of behavior.

Fear of failure

Falling short of expectations is not a pleasant occurrence for anybody, but that should not restrict future attempts to make progress. To motivate others to keep trying:

- Remove worry about trying new ideas.
- Eliminate threats related to unsuccessful efforts.
- Prevent the adoption of a doom-and-gloom mindset.

Invalidating people

Diminishing others precludes bold action on their part and lowers morale. Vigorously guard against behaviors like the following that belittle:

- Engaging in water cooler conversations and gossip behind people's backs
- Sneering and rolling your eyes, when someone's speaking
- Reprimanding people in front of others

Focus on Obstacles

Overcome impediments to progress such as the following by ignoring them, removing them, or going around them:

- Physical barriers such as walls and partitions within the office that impede the flow of ideas and conversation
- People jealously guarding their creative thinking
- Concentration on reasons why an idea won't work
- Performance appraisal systems that foment competition rather than nurture collaboration

Progressive leaders know that they do not have all of the answers and regularly call upon employees for their knowledge and abilities. Rather than waiting to see which way the wind is blowing, they set sail with all hands onboard doing what they are capable of doing.

Language that is part of Junk DNA in your culture:

- "That's too pie-in-the-sky. It'll never work."
- "Why bother? They never have anything worthwhile to say."
- "This better work, or else!"
- "Yes, but. . . ."

Up-Regulate

Set a positive tone for a proactive approach to the future by taking risks yourself and by getting out of the way when others are willing to do so. Guard against assigning blame or chastising when attempts fall short or don't work out. Instead, reinforce mistakes and failures as learning experiences that add to knowledge and can lead to success later on by demonstrating bold leadership.

Courage

While fear itself cannot be eliminated, its harmful effects can be neutralized by leaders who:

- Create an environment where it's safe for people to explore new possibilities.
- Dare to share ideas that seem far-out or far-reaching.
- Question current ways of doing things.

Validating people

Individuals make worthwhile contributions to the collective when they feel they matter. To acknowledge the importance of everyone:

- Make a conscious effort to include everyone, especially the quieter people and people across various departments or divisions of the business.
- Cultivate appreciation of one another. Recognize others openly, and make it known why you are acknowledging them.
- Consciously encourage people who have made mistakes. Credit them for daring to go into uncharted waters and with providing valuable knowledge.

Focus on opportunities

Cast challenges and setbacks as occasions to demonstrate the best that everyone has to offer. Draw out value from crises by:

- Listening for whatever idea may hold even a sliver of promise
- Listening for dreams that encompass the customer's viewpoint
- Listening for ways to build on one another's dreams so that the process becomes a collective one

As you free others to explore the paths that they wish to embark upon, you will find new avenues that lead to solutions and growth. Employees who aren't afraid to dream awaken entire organizations to possibilities and unexpected achievements. As a result, your company's collective imagination will take it far beyond what can be seen on the horizon.

Language that supports the emergence of dreams in the workplace:

- "I really like the part of your dream about. . . ."
- "Who else has a dream or a wild, crazy idea they'd like to share?"
- "If our customer could have absolutely anything at all, what would it be?"
- "Let's create a sense of excitement and ambition around this issue and see what emerges."

Aspiring Conversations

Some people have the mistaken notion that aspirations and cold, hard facts are mutually exclusive, and that when people dream big dreams they are removed from reality. Put another way, they think that if people knew "the truth," it would be depressing and would stifle creativity. In actuality, people must know the current conditions in which they're doing business. They must know what's working and what isn't. It's against that background—for example, understanding the financial condition of the company—that people will concentrate their thinking and do their best brainstorming. In organizations where people feel and operate like owners, they will respond to the challenge, even if the circumstances are difficult. They will think in novel ways because they know that the future of the business (and their own career) may well depend on it.

It's also important that people receive timely, critical feedback about their own performance. In some environments, people are not challenged, or may not challenge themselves, to raise their level of performance. Or they may not even know that more is possible. They and their organization might have settled for standards that are below what they could be.

Aiming for greater levels of excellence will often create a breakdown. This is a kind of breakdown you should welcome. You'll move people out of their comfort zone. You'll provoke the question, "How do we get from A to B?" The answers may not be obvious. They may not be easy to implement, either. However, this is where the A gene causes leaders to discover new pathways to growth. Harnessing the motivation to learn is the A gene in action and sets an example for others to follow. When the A gene is replicated, and people recognize the essential value of continuous learning, you establish a learning enterprise where the dividends keep paying off.

As a leader, creating an aspiring community is foundational to success. Practices and attitudes should include:

- **Being grounded in reality:** Don't flinch from the facts. Inform everyone who has a stake in the future of your organization about them, and then get to work on inventing new possibilities.
- **Believing in the power of community:** Envision your organization as an orchestra that is highly talented, synergistic, and committed to playing magnificent music together by drawing out the best from each and every member.
- **Giving and receiving feedback:** People who aspire to improvement want to know how they're doing and how they can better their performance. Keep kindling people's hunger to learn and grow through a mix of positive and critical feedback, and be receptive to checks on your own behavior and performance.
- **Creating a mood of ambition:** Be especially vigilant when you sense yourself, and others, beginning to coast. Be on the lookout for new ways to challenge yourself, and identify new goals to reach for.

We may see ourselves as adults who have stopped growing. While this may be true from a physical perspective, the reality is that the human spirit is dynamic and the need for evolution is constant—and unremitting. An organization must also grow to survive, and its heart and soul reside in the people who strive to advance individually as part of a progressive whole.

Knockout Genes

Support the inclination to strive for fresh, new innovations with a careful pruning of unnecessary work or a tendency to hold onto the status quo. The following are words and phrases to strike from your vocabulary:

- "It can't be done."
- "This is a waste of time. Let's get to the bottom line."
- "Yeah, right, like that'll really work."
- "Let's not bite off more than we can chew."
- "So far, I haven't heard anything worthwhile."

Gene Splicing

You set an example for others. People constantly base how they should work on what you do and say. To stimulate the kind of culture that invites people to think and act in bigger, more creative ways, focus on the following in your conversations:

- "Let's see how we can. . . ."
- "What if we. . . ."
- "What's really possible?"
- "I want to hear more. . . ."
- "Imagine if we could. . . ."

Language can open doors or slam them closed. When you communicate an acceptance—and expectation—of bold thinking and actions, and back it up with your own daring, crises and challenges are seen as nothing more than opportunities to excel. Twenty-first-century leaders use words that create a culture of high performance.

▷ A CULTURE OF HIGH PERFORMANCE
Aspirations

"I have had dreams and I have had nightmares, but I have conquered my nightmares because of my dreams."
—Dr. Jonas Salk

Every time you pioneer into new territory, you face fears, challenges, and things you don't know. Working together to down-regulate fear and up-regulate courage makes change something everyone can embrace and look forward to. Too often, we allow fear of change to limit what we do and in doing so, we often spread our fear to others—anchoring everyone firmly in place.

When groups of people work together to take on new challenges, to support each other in new explorations, and to turn mistakes into lessons learned, everyone raises skill and wisdom together. The leader's job is to minimize the fears and maximize the opportunities. Helping people reframe fear into learning opportunities and reframe mistakes into lessons learned are critical skills that allow aspirations to be realized for the benefit of all.

The Power of Shape Shifting

In *The Way of the Shaman*, Michael Harner describes a shaman as "a man or woman who enters an altered state of consciousness—at will—to contact and utilize an ordinarily hidden reality in order to acquire knowledge, power, and to help other persons." As their consciousness leaves their physical body, shamans move out into the universe. There they have access to the world of spirit and can travel back and forth in multiple dimensions. They enter a space where new life or energy can be created.

One of the powers learned by shamans is the method of shape shifting. It is possible to dream oneself into different states of being, to transform and become that which we envision in the mind. The act of imagining can create a new reality. Just as water evaporates and turns to ice or rain, its essence remains the same even though its form has changed. One of the techniques shamans use during shape shifting is merging. As they merge with an animal, plant, or person, they gain the experience of oneness. All wisdom and knowledge is accessible. They are gifted with "becoming" a tree, animal, or plant and thereby bring its unique wisdom back into the world.

Shamans teach us not to judge from a limited human mindset, but rather to see and experience wisdom from a richer and fuller perspective. They teach that life is not what we think it is; that there are a multitude of possibilities if we expand our vision. The lessons of a shaman help us release assumptions and be available for true knowledge and experience in the present moment.

Replicating Organizational Striving

Leaders owe it to themselves, their customers, and their stakeholders to tap the unlimited potential of their work force and aim for producing transformational results.

While it is intrinsic to the human experience to dream, much of the day-to-day work experience is mundane and repetitive. Plus, it's normal for leaders to focus most of their attention on the urgent tasks that confront them each day. They must consciously create room to spark the kinds of conversations that allow the new and untested to bubble up. Who really knows what solutions, projects, processes, or entire new businesses can spring forth? Who really knows what a group of stakeholders, committed to a common mission, is capable of achieving?

Creating and maintaining an aspirational culture requires guarding against the spectrum of threats that rises up to overwhelm us, often without our realizing it. Even the most visionary leaders may miss seeing these threats, especially if they're of a less dramatic nature: a slow downward trend in customer orders; slipping down a notch or two in the standings of a "most-admired company" list; or a decline in a customer satisfaction survey. Other threats, of course, are more dramatic: when a top salesperson misses getting a huge piece of new business; when a senior executive resigns mysteriously; or when issues of ethics are raised.

Threats of any nature, when mismanaged, can sap the vision from an organization in a slow, steady, cumulative way. Fear is a close relation of mismanagement. It erodes hope that tears at the tissue of an organization, one day and one conversation at a time. It continues until the organization's capacity to stretch and dream has been stripped bare.

We acknowledge that breakdowns are part of business. It's how leaders respond that makes all the difference. They can turn their breakdowns into opportunities for pulling people together and fashioning more diverse thinking, more creative engagement, and more bold "stand taking." Or they can signal that it's time to circle the wagons, gossip, turn a blind eye to blame, and just hold on.

Wise leaders look for the earliest possible clues to take actions to redirect the life force within their organizations and nurture and sustain the aspirational drive. To that end, you need to ask yourself some questions:

- How do we shift from an environment where people fear making mistakes to one where people value their dreams and aspirations more?

- What behaviors and actions support a striving environment?
- What behaviors and actions threaten that environment?
- How can we coach each other to go beyond our comfort zones?
- How can we all work together to capitalize on opportunities?
- How do we want to connect to our customers' dreams?

You can replicate a higher level of striving throughout your organization, and ensure that it is ongoing, by incorporating new leadership DNA practices to create a culture where people work together to imagine, learn, stretch, and develop.

Meeting Strategy: Postmortems

At Gordon Brothers, postmortems on projects are part of the standard practice. These are not dissections of individuals; they are analyses of deals. People who are part of that process sit around the table looking at the deal and asking what went wrong and what went right. Everyone knows who was responsible for what, but that's not the focus. The conversation centers on what went right and what went wrong, and what can be done about it. The lessons are accumulated in a database and shared so everyone can access new wisdom. Others can get up to speed on all deal-making initiatives. The following addresses how their DNA is strengthened.

Communication: We Have a Dream

At Gordon Brothers, aspirations are woven into the fiber of the organization. Michael Frieze sees the aspirational environment as one that marries opportunity with risk-taking and moves from risk-taking to business building. It starts with aspiring with the customer, where the first new breath occurs. When a customer voices a wish, the Gordon Brothers team listens and shares the dream.

From that first whisper, team members take the idea back to the company so the idea now has a life outside of a wish. Michael and his senior team identify people inside whom they believe have special talents for making that dream come to life. Then these people create a first draft of a business case/plan to start the process moving forward. With the help of other peers, the opportunity starts to take shape. Within a few months there is structure to the idea, and then meetings and conversations turn a customer wish into a real business.

To further share the dream, Gordon Brothers assigns a board to the business. Impartial outsiders can ask the right questions and sharpen the focus, so something that once was a possibility and desire becomes a living and profitable business poised for growth. Many of the GBG businesses have sustained themselves because of this process.

When this sequence is coupled with down-regulation of mistake-making, when it's okay to test and learn, there is a built-in readiness to learn from mistakes, to grow from experiments, and to give wings to wishes—customer wishes.

Individual Development Programs: Stretching

The DNA of Gordon Brothers is about expanding goals. People are asked to contribute to projects for which they may not have prior experience. This is intentionally done to challenge them and take them out of their comfort zone. This practice has lived inside of Gordon Brothers from its inception, and has been carried forward. When GBG identifies a new business they want to enter, they identify GBG executives whom they could possibly assign to the projects, knowing full well that they may have no experience within this new industry. The goal is to create a new platform for learning and to enable executives to make new contributions. Behind this strategy for growing talent, is the essential belief that they have great internal potential that needs harvesting.

Opportunism

Gordon Brothers, as well as many companies tuned into the market, believes that harvesting opportunities is the aorta of the business. Their DNA is outward-focused and they have learned how to swiftly and agilely create a team to capitalize on the opportunities that are out there.

Experiment and Institutionalize

Another dimension of Gordon Brothers' DNA is the incredible support for experimenting, even when creating a new business. The only way to move forward is to take a step at a time, to try it out, and once you've captured what works, institutionalize it. This pattern has worked for each of the new businesses Gordon Brothers has launched. Each came from a customer need, and each turned into an industry service that would be leveraged across many clients.

The Breath of Life

We all still have dreams about what we could accomplish to make us feel whole and happy and fulfilled. For each of us it's different, yet the dreaming and striving are always there.

Dreaming is essential to being human. We can dream on our own, or we can dream with others. Dreaming within organizations provides the air necessary for ongoing survival in the face of the challenges that change brings. Your aspiration leadership gene breathes life itself into others and helps them hold onto their dreams and turn them into reality.

Chapter 5

The *N* Gene: Navigating

"Sometimes our light goes out but is blown into flame by another human being. Each of us owes deepest thanks to those who have rekindled this light."
—*Albert Schweitzer*

NAVIGATING CULTURES are those where leaders work together with employees to move deftly with changes that occur at any time, with or without warning, within the company or out in the marketplace. Navigating is the highest level of collaboration in that it requires all parties to put their attention on their company, its marketplace, and the industry landscape. Leaders who use the N gene are captains who steer their people through great seas of change in technology and respond to the shifts in the needs of the consumer. Navigating is when every team member pulls his or her share while heading together toward a common destination.

In such cultures, the focus is on working through challenges as one cohesive unit. Navigation is characterized by mutual support and growth, of sharing rather than withholding. People cross-pollinate to build networks, and to exchange insights and wisdom. They reduce fears of loss of power, loss of turf, and of scarcity of resources and rewards, and focus on building trust, respect, and an abundance mentality.

Navigating cultures build "pull energy" by taking a collective stance on shaping their evolution. This energy extends from the community and envelops customer relationships, alliance partners, and others who want, and need, to have a hand on the wheel.

New Wave Entertainment
A Navigating Success Story:
I Didn't Know We Could Be so Smart

"What makes New Wave so great? Burritos on Wednesday mornings," says CFO Alan Baral, tongue-in-cheek. Yet burritos represent a lot of what New Wave Entertainment (NWE) is all about: a passionate, have fun, grow-the-talent, share-the-wisdom, share-the-rewards, support-each-other culture.

People are proud to work at New Wave, and proud to have it on their resumes. Why? It's a place where interdependence is a way of life. Today, New Wave is a brand that people know and is recognized in the industry as a top-notch diversified company that provides best-in-class entertainment marketing services, talent management, and television/film development and production.

The entertainment marketing world has exploded over the past ten years and New Wave rode with the tide because they positioned themselves to navigate changing currents. Their leaders kept their eyes open to industry shifts, found concepts they liked, talked them over inside the company, put resources behind them, and developed them. Some succeeded, some did not, but they kept moving forward with everyone aboard, learning together along the way.

Leaders responded quickly to trends and constantly spiraled into new businesses. In one of the most competitive industries, New Wave continues to attract the best talent in the industry. Is it luck or something else?

"We're in a creative services business," says co-owner Paul Apel. "We don't make widgets or any product. Our success is based on a person's impression. We have to understand what our customers want. If you do it right, you get the chance to do it again. If you don't do it right, you have to find someone who will be able to help you do better."

New Wave is the best in class in several areas. Its DVD unit is producing special features for more than 100 video releases, including some of the entertainment industry's biggest hits, such as *Harry Potter*. The Motion Graphic Design Division, popularly known as the Studio at NWE, is a top-tier broadcast design, DVD design, and titles design producer. Their work appears on major networks such as HBO, CNN, and MTV. Whether it's designing the graphics for the Super Bowl halftime show, creating the graphics for the Olympics, or creating titles for feature films, the Studio is sought after for their memorable looks. New Wave's TV Spot Finishing division has been the industry leader for years, and typically completes more than 3,000 television spots each year.

The New Wave of eleven years ago looked quite different from how they are today. They started out creating and finishing trailers and television spots, and now produce their own television shows and movies. The company has grown exponentially since 1994, and this came from the leadership DNA of Paul Apel and Alan Baral, principals. They shaped a culture of strong, creative collaboration that is incredibly supportive of the life and family needs of each individual. Employees are well taken care of from insurance to how to find and finance a house. A huge amount of energy is put into ensuring that everyone fits in. "As a result, they 'push it,' and love the challenge of pushing it!" says Alan.

New Wave finds and leverages the best talent, and brings it to clients in the best way possible. "We do not tell staff what their creative approach should be. They own the product because they do it," says Paul. "They're the ones who come up with the ideas for the show or the trailer or the DVD content. They implement this with as little input from us as possible. At any time, we have hundreds of projects going on at once. It's almost impossible to turn on the TV or go into any Blockbuster or Wal-Mart without seeing our products. We work with the biggest entertainment conglomerates in the world—something we're very proud of. We do work on every network, 24-7.

"New Wave provides an all-encompassing service. When studio executives, talent, producers, and filmmakers come into the building they are blown away. We can create the concept, write it, shoot it, offline it, online it, put the graphics to it, compose the music, mix it, ship it, and get it on air without leaving the building. These creative services are our spine, and as we grow we continue to strengthen it. Our goal has always been to create a strong brand built on a culture of creativity, freedom, interdependence, and growth," explains Paul.

The people who are attracted to work at New Wave are exceptional. They come because they want the freedom to grow, and are given that freedom. Some come in as freelancers. Others start out as interns, and then move into different divisions. The first day new employees join the company they go on an orientation tour. Often, both Alan and Paul do the orientations to ensure everyone knows what's important to the culture. Even new customers get a tour from the principals, and as they walk around the 40,000-square-foot building in Burbank or other locations in Los Angeles, they see how this creativity is birthed.

"Our clients are challenging people. They are amazingly creative," says Paul. "They love our nonhierarchical environment and they allow us the freedom to challenge them. That makes it fun.

"We operate like a family. It's no different than at home. If there is someone or something causing stress for the family, it affects everyone. You either get rid of the stress or find new ways to deal with the problem. We spend a lot of time communicating. Everyone wants the family to succeed."

They have rituals for sustaining interdependence. "We are continually learning our lessons about collaboration," says Alan Baral. "That is what holds us together. We're not a confrontational culture. People don't get angry a lot at each other. We talk things out. We ask each other, 'What's the problem; what's your issue?' Then we understand the issue, and we come to a resolution about it."

At New Wave, divisions work with one another to get the jobs done. They are one another's creative vendor pool, if you will. They negotiate with each other and have learned to work well and play well with each other.

"We are incredibly interdependent on each other, so much so that this year we're changing our monetary reward structure. We now bonus people on the company's success rather than a division's success. This way we're all shooting for the same targets," Paul explains.

Alan does not mince words about what the culture is all about: "We're in a highly creative environment with lots of egos, yet what we want here at New Wave, and what we would like to think we've created, is a very collaborative environment. It drives us crazy when one person wants to get too much credit when he touches something. When people act out of ego, or too much 'me,' others feel they are unsupportive of the organization, and no one wants to take them to meetings, work with them, or be with them. They eventually get the message that we value collaboration. Our people reinforce our sense of community.

"We encourage giving credit for contributions. But when someone demands more it doesn't fit into our culture. In a creative culture, credit is a large issue both inside the organization and also to the public at large. Getting credit means you are on the credit roll at the end of a television show or movie. The order is a big deal for everyone. People jockey for the title and position. We're constantly working on our rules, customs, and practices so that they're on the table. Everyone gets the credit he or she deserves, but it's within our sharing culture," Alan explains.

New Wave employees know their environment is fair and they know the leaders care. As the industry changes, sometimes roles get diminished. The company does an exceptional job of supporting their people to adjust to new areas of growth.

In 1993, New Wave was owned by someone else, and the original fifteen employees all worked exclusively on TV commercials and movie trailers for the Walt Disney Company. Paul Apel, Allen Haines, and Richard Kaufman were part of the original team. A deal was cut to sell the company to them. Alan Baral, a lawyer, was called in to join the group of creative talent to bring some structure and business experience to the changing company.

Shortly after the new owners took over control of the company, there were intersecting events that took place simultaneously. The company moved to larger quarters to prepare for growth, and their sole client was about to go through its own management shift. Jeffrey Katzenberg, the head of theatrical for Disney, left that company because the vision there was changing. As part of the change, Disney severed the exclusive arrangement with New Wave, and they were free to seek work from other studios and enlarge the company.

At this time of change in corporate strategy, the industry was exploding with new technologies that enhanced motion picture advertising. New Wave needed to find new digital graphics experts. Scott Williams, an incredibly talented designer, was brought onboard to launch a digital graphics division. He had to bring his own computer with him, because New Wave had no idea what equipment was needed to create new design work. The principals didn't know the digital graphics business, so they had to rely on Scott and the talent he attracted. Scott's division more than tripled the business over the next two years. He attracted more talent to work with him, people who had unique technical knowledge.

Because of the way film studios worked, Paul and Alan faced tough challenges. There was pressure on studios to launch movies in a big way. This led to the development of the superstar editor and superstar producer. A promotional services company like New Wave was no longer the relevant factor. Studios wanted specific producers or editors, and this fed egos. Talent salaries soared. At the same time, studios wanted to pay less, so overall margins dropped. "The biggest challenge for New Wave then was acquiring great talent while preserving our collaborative culture," says Alan. "We had to grow our brand in a healthy way."

How They Succeeded

"At one time," says Alan, "we didn't do it the way we do today. If a leader wasn't strong enough we would jump in and handle the problems for them. We were cutting the legs off of the leader and we were sucked into micromanagement when we needed to be working better at macromanagement. It took lots of experiences and we had lots of learning lessons around these issues that helped us understand how to do things differently."

As leaders, what Alan and Paul learned from integrating new divisions and talented people into their culture, is that they need to provide coaching to new executives so that they can function independently.

"I want people to learn, on their own, what ways are effective," says Alan. "Paul and I don't want to take over someone else's job. We hope our leaders aspire to be the best they can be. We'll get called in to help when it's needed, but we don't micromanage now. Because of that, we are sought after and our input is valued and respected.

"For example, we're delivering a TV show. There are a lot of people working on it but it runs into some difficulties. We don't get involved from arrogance. We'll come in and throw out some new ideas, but it's up to the group to turn it around. Our input is another perspective, not 'the' perspective. If it works, great; if not, people don't have to use it. If it catalyzes something else, great. We're available, not responsible, for the creative. It's different than in some organizations where the boss comes in on a project you've been working on for six months and takes over.

"People want to be challenged creatively. If they are allowed to be creative without the input from us, or use our input the way they want, they enjoy the process. At the end of the day, creativity is all about collaboration.

"For us to survive, we need to produce our best work, and that always comes from our interdependence," says Alan. All of the leaders at New Wave share the same strand of DNA and agree that they have to grow by staying connected. Under their skilled stewardship they do just that.

Sharing vs. Withholding

Navigating leaders like Alan and Paul recognize that for a company to survive, let alone thrive, people must work together to deliver what the customer wants. In wartime, collaboration means working with the enemy. At New Wave, there is no enemy. That word does not exist. Navigating leaders further recognize that it's their job to expand the boundaries, so that creative talent has the room to grow and develop. In doing so, each individual feels valued, respected, and fulfilled, and in turn values and respects others so that they can realize their potential. Navigating leaders think WE not I.

I-Centric vs. WE-Centric Leadership

I-centric leaders are boundary-setters. They feel they need to define the territory within which people can come and go, and are sensitive when people overstep the line. As a result, they establish invisible stop signs and roadblocks within and around their working space. The primary downfall is that people they work with feel restricted. Obstacles and barriers seem to be everywhere, making it hard or impossible to imagine big ideas and contribute to a company's evolution. The I-centric leader's subordinates are always politicking and looking for ways to circumnavigate the organization and its processes, ultimately wasting both time and energy.

WE-centric leaders recognize the importance of boundaries in defining tasks and responsibilities; however, they open boundaries at every opportunity so that people can interconnect for their own benefit and company growth. Rather than restrict, they encourage mutual exploration and sharing. They understand that sharing with positive intention creates best practices. WE-centric leaders think WE at every turn and create organizational spaces where individuals and teams can explore and interconnect and exchange ideas and knowledge. In these spaces, people remove limitations and blaze new trails to customer solutions. There's a passion for moving the organization forward. WE-centric leaders instill an atmosphere of abundance where colleagues feel that they create success together.

INTENTION   **IMPACT**

Leader Story: Failure to Build Trust

"I don't distrust people; I just make sure they are doing their jobs right."

Richard was one of five senior executives in a large publishing company, reporting to the CIO who reported to the president. Like many publishing companies, his organization had a big initiative to expand the Web side of the business. It was hoped that an expanded Web presence would provide greater data management, more ability to repurpose existing content, and increased ability to reach customers through different channels. It was the wave of the future, and Richard had been hired to head the new department.

In his role, Richard had a staff of five reporting to him and was also responsible for overseeing technical people from different divisions. All business unit heads were to determine how Web technology could best serve their departments and then assign the project to their IT people who would in turn work with Richard to develop and execute the projects.

Richard was extremely smart, read everything on the subject of business and leadership, and had been around the technology world his whole life. He was very savvy about new developments in the field and considered himself a seasoned expert. Richard wanted to make a good impression and ensure that people knew he was qualified to take on the challenges ahead. At the first executive meeting he met the divisional presidents, their IT manager, and was introduced to everyone as the new IT project head. He listened to how people described the company strategy and what the divisional heads were trying to accomplish. He offered his opinions about the marketplace, what other organizations were doing, and what the company needed to think about in order to be successful.

Richard visited the person in charge of IT at each business unit, and critiqued the team's progress at IT meetings. When team members would give their project updates, Richard would offer radical feedback or even make bold suggestions to change the plan or redirect the initiative. His behavior usurped the authority of the IT person who was officially in charge of the project.

It was as though a bomb had been dropped on the team. People were confused about what to do and how to do it. Richard's visits had the effect of changing previously agreed upon decisions regarding the project. After Richard would leave, the on-site IT person would have to scramble to put the team back together and create a clear direction.

Six months passed, and Richard was deeply immersed in five critical projects. On a few occasions, he was asked to visit with the CIO for emergency meetings. "These projects are not running well," she told him. "Some of the presidents are giving me feedback that there is confusion and disruption, and it appears the projects are falling behind. In addition, there seems to be some confusion over the way decisions are being made, and at times there seems to be too many bosses involved." Richard listened to his boss, and said he'd take care of everything.

However, bigger problems arose. While the projects emanated from separate divisions, the project teams worked on the same IT platforms. Therefore they had to share information as well as equipment. Part of Richard's responsibility was to orchestrate these interdependencies so that each team would get the time and resources it needed for its own part of the overall project.

The CIO fielded calls about conflicts between divisions. One divisional president called up to say that his project was behind schedule and that it would not be finished within budget. Another divisional president complained that there were e-mails shooting back and forth about projects being redirected and about tensions among the various divisional IT heads. A once calm and productive company was now abuzz with politics. Critical projects that would shape the future of the organization and its reputation in the marketplace were being derailed by confusion and infighting.

Two of the projects went into red alert. Neither was into the alpha testing state with customers, and the division presidents felt their jobs were now on the line. The CIO was called in to troubleshoot almost every day. Moreover, the marketing people were concerned that they would not be able to go forward with their PR and marketing campaigns because the projects were not complete. The CIO's job was to deliver the projects on time, and her peers were rapidly becoming disappointed in her leadership—and the lack of results. She was determined to find out the root cause of the delays.

The CIO talked with Richard's team and learned:

- The team was not empowered to work freely with the other divisions. Richard demanded to touch every minor decision, and to make every major one.
- When people moved too quickly, Richard criticized them.
- Internal fights about priorities and timing existed on every project.
- Richard was preoccupied with assigning blame.

Everyone on Richard's team wanted the problems to go away and had repeatedly turned to Richard to fix them. They felt only he had the authority to settle disputes. Divisional heads felt their teams lacked capability and came down hard on them. However, when their teams pushed back, the heads looked closer, but they were unable to pinpoint the origin of the problems. Territoriality and we-they behaviors were at an epidemic level, but the finger always seemed to point at people other than Richard.

Richard never thought he was responsible for the chaos. Under heightened scrutiny, the finger finally pointed to him. He was now center stage. His arrogance, micromanaging, and lack of respect for the input of others was the cause of the mess. He had substantial knowledge that could solve complex technical challenges, and showed it off to everyone. But he refused to allow others the freedom to decide how it would be best implemented. Without realizing it, Richard had sent mixed messages to everyone.

Fear of Losing Power

Leaders who have a fear of losing power and importance are overbearing and want to be perceived as the ultimate authority figure. They feel they are invaluable to any important conversation, and insert themselves so their presence will be known.

Leaders like Richard start a cascade of insecurity in their environments. People below them who used to feel secure feel like imposters, and they worry that everyone will find out they are not up to the job. This resultant fear in the workplace causes everyone to question what is real and true, the veracity of information given, and eventually themselves. Individuals begin to resort to blaming and finger-pointing whenever they fear they will be picked on for not delivering. It leads to underperforming teams.

Richard talked about others doing their jobs, and then stepped in to do them, making people feel less competent. Richard's behavior exemplified the "all-knowing" boss. He withheld information to remain the voice of wisdom. He overstepped his boundaries, did not respect the authority of others, even of those in his own peer group. He overrode decisions others made.

In doing so, he caused others to feel less trusted and skeptical of other team members, thinking they were part of a we-they internal battle. He was not very good at team building or getting people to work together through major tradeoffs and decisions.

Therefore people felt they had to defend themselves against the "other team."

This led to secondary fears:

- Fear of crossing an invisible line
- Fear of retribution
- Fear of accountability
- Fear of owning a decision
- Fear of sharing information
- Fear of challenging the boss
- Fear of making mistakes
- Fear of reaching out to others to discuss situations

Richard's fear of losing power created an environment where others also felt a loss of power and, therefore, were driven by a need to preserve what little they could. Territorial behavior resulted, and people imposed their power over others whenever possible. They fought back for what they felt they had lost: acknowledgment and respect.

As a leader, you must ensure that fear of losing power and respect does not consume your work teams and cause your staff to feel they need to fight for survival. Our sense of respect and power is profoundly affected by how we are encouraged to work and play with others, and by how much freedom we have to learn, grow, and nourish our souls at work. A leader's ability to manage fear of losing power, and feelings of incompetence, is integral to creating environments where all employees contribute to problem solving, innovation, goal attainment, and growth.

A great leader puts his or her own ego aside to develop an environment where others comingle, collaborate, and develop interdependencies. Such a leader inspires people to give their all and to build brands and wonderful products and services for clients and customers. Leaders who instill a sense of freedom set the tone for greatness to emerge.

You can help employees—and yourself—by encouraging them to knock down silos and cross boundaries, to share information and wisdom, and to seek collaboration in the face of very big and often complex business issues. Collaboration is something that comes easily to people who feel they trust each other and who feel that each has the other's best interest in mind. Employees openly share when they feel that they are working toward the same organizational goal.

FIGURE 5.1

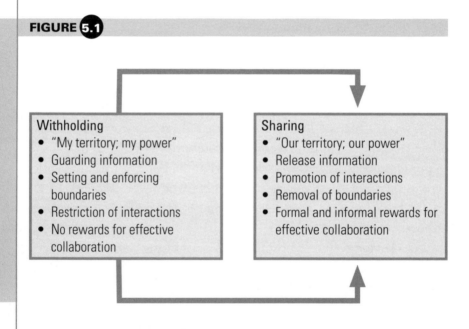

Withholding
- "My territory; my power"
- Guarding information
- Setting and enforcing boundaries
- Restriction of interactions
- No rewards for effective collaboration

Sharing
- "Our territory; our power"
- Release information
- Promotion of interactions
- Removal of boundaries
- Formal and informal rewards for effective collaboration

The "Your Voice Doesn't Count" Meta-Message

"Life is a perpetual instruction in cause and effect."
—*Ralph Waldo Emerson*

When leaders say that it's important for everyone to do his or her job, but micromanage, they send a meta-message. When leaders believe they are driving for overall harmony, but drown out other voices, they limit fruitful interaction—another meta-message. Leaders who do not establish a culture of free exchange where employees set priorities and work out the dynamic challenges send a clear message: "I don't trust you." Employees react by looking up for answers, not all around, where effective help is close at hand.

Leader Profile

Let's look at Richard's I-centric profile through a number of lenses:

How he communicates: Richard comes across as arrogant, intrusive, and disrespectful of the talents and opinions of others. He is caustic when people seem upset with his intrusion, and he communicates nonverbally that they are crossing his line of authority. In other words, he conveys through words and actions that his voice counts more than others. As a result, he sends confusing messages: He wants people to do their jobs, but implies he could do it better.

How he motivates others: Richard doesn't think about inspiring others. He feels that people need to motivate themselves and that he has little to do with it. He expects people to respect authority and to do their work. He likes to be seen as someone who knows what the industry is all about and how to get things done. And that should be enough for others to just do what he tells them to do.

How he listens or doesn't: Richard seems to hear everyone, yet when it comes to following up on what was discussed, he leaves a lot to be desired. Either he didn't really listen, or what others said meant little to him. Either way, he is in his own world.

How he uses or abuses power: Richard is a power-over leader. He is arrogant, intimidating, and he violates boundaries instead of crossing them. He does not demonstrate respect. He sets up people to blame others as a survival technique. He is not a team player, and therefore ignores group authority.

Turf does not have to be protected to be respected. Leaders secure their own territory and that of others when they provide free access to knowledge and expertise. Opening borders opens up a wealth of opportunity where everyone can access help, learn, contribute, and develop. When employees explore new territories they discover new resources, and companies expand as a result.

The Negative Ripple Effect

Richard lived in a shell, and wouldn't let others in. Even though he wanted the projects to be successful, he didn't understand that collaborative environments were necessary to make that happen. This part of his genetic code was turned off. He engendered competition within and between teams, and reduced the opportunities for innovative solutions to highly technical problems. Under his leadership, people became territorial and looked to assign blame. He had created an environment of fear that caused a breakdown in interconnectivity, a distrust of sharing, and a desire to get back at others.

Richard alienated himself from his boss and became an outsider to everyone else. His arrogance and projection of superiority made others feel small and powerless. He was an I-centric leader who created waves of fear that left everyone behind. People felt:

- Unable to make valuable contributions
- Unable to collaborate with others
- Unsure how to work things out
- Unsettled by territorial disputes
- Confused and discouraged
- Unable to figure out the root cause of problems

Junk DNA: Leadership Mythologies

Many of us have been brought up with the notion that our job as a leader is to be there with the answers, to step in when things are not going right, to question people's work approaches, and to make sure everyone pleases the boss. That comes from an ancestral and mythological belief that "when I grow up, I will be in charge, and others will respect my authority." That reinforces an I-centric view of leadership.

Having power is essential for survival. Fear of losing power causes us to want to fight to get back our power. If we are known for specific skills or talents, we want to leverage them. If, however, someone diminishes us or makes us feel less capable, we want to strike back. That is a part of what territoriality in business is all about.

When we buy into the notion that we need to fight to get back our power or territory, we accept both the fighting strategy and the belief that someone can take away our power. When we see the leader as someone who takes away our power, or when we see others taking our power by taking our knowledge, we relinquish our ability to act freely. This outmoded strain of DNA reinforces old beliefs that:

- Respect comes from having a title
- Leaders have the most authority
- Interdependence weakens power

There are red flags, or "mutations," that indicate a leader is expressing old DNA. Such behavior undermines people's power to solve problems and increases:

- Territorial behavior
- CYA activity
- Incidents of formal and informal complaints
- Poor morale
- Stagnant progress/missed deadlines

To evolve, you need to break the bonds of old DNA and connect to new beliefs. Top-performing companies create environments where power politics do not own the organizational terrain. They intentionally focus on enabling the talents of each person and encouraging each level of leadership to own its role in harvesting wisdom and insights. They have a robust acceptance of individual talents and contributions, and know when to step away and encourage collaboration and dialogue rather than stop it. Such leaders help their organizations connect directly to their customers and grow exponentially.

When due diligence was conducted on the IT situation at the publishing company, executive coaching was recommended for Richard. When he did not respond satisfactorily, it was clear that Richard was not a fit for an organization that needed to be highly collaborative, interdependent, and responsive to collective needs. It became apparent to his boss that they were better off without him.

The organization promoted one of its directors to lead the department. Within three months, the projects got back on track. Division presidents felt their goals would be met, collaboration reached an all-time high, and the collective teams began to reap the promised reward of new offerings.

▷ THE LEADERSHIP STEP
Never Operate in a Vacuum

The navigating leader understands that fear of losing power triggers territoriality and competition. The essential practice for diminishing this fear is to give away power. By creating a decision-sharing workplace, all can see clearly how to bring their unique talents to bear on projects and get credit for what they do, while collaborating and supporting others.

Navigating leaders break down silos where they exist and build trust by giving trust. They manage their own egos publicly, so they symbolically communicate that sharing power is essential for the health and growth of the organization. Doing so eliminates the meta-messages that cause fear in others of losing power.

Evolved leaders know the damage that meta-messages cause: increased territoriality, infighting, taking credit, and assigning blame. How can you build an environment where people collaborate to share knowledge and wisdom and feel that brand-winning is more important than anything else? Instead of allowing meta-messages to divide your employees, steer the ship using the whole crew.

The Twenty-First-Century Leader Can *See* the Way to Learn

To build a sharing environment, take advantage of every opportunity to open new channels of communication within your immediate team and across divisions. Value teaching as much as doing, and learning as much as teaching. Employees should understand that hoarding knowledge and placing a priority on personal triumph will not be viewed as favorably as mentoring and sharing credit. Internalize the following three leadership practices to advance your entire organization.

Share Wisdom and Breakthroughs

New Wave works at creating a collaborative culture where all the doors are open. They have biweekly management meetings where the heads of all the departments get together and talk about department matters, and how they are running their parts of the business. They make a point to ask: What do we need to do differently? At their meetings, those who attend rotate leadership in the sessions. Each person gets a turn to set up, make a presentation, and moderate the discussions on agenda items gathered from everyone beforehand. The meetings are varied, richly interesting, and provide a regular way to share breakthroughs and insights.

Practices for yourself:
- Think of how you can create ongoing idea exchanges with your staff and peers.
- Inspire people to challenge and be challenged to grow to the next level.
- Value learning and growing.
- Be available but not imposing.
- Openly reward people who take on bigger challenges.

Practices with your staff:
- Rather than impose your ideas on others, offer your ideas as alternative perspectives.
- Make it easy for people to get together to toss around ideas for current and new projects; value dialogue and brainstorming.
- Promote cross-departmental involvement in tasks and projects.

Establish Broader Networks

Everyone inside of New Wave is considered a potential vendor to someone else in the organization. People work on one another's projects, use one another's equipment, and bill for one another's talent. Sharing starts with the open-mindedness of leaders. They don't create islands of conflict by playing favorites. They consciously manage the "superstar diva" syndrome that sometimes shows up. They manage entitlement. They manage resentment.

Practices for yourself:
- Set the tone by crossing boundaries and inviting others into your department for assistance.
- Show trust by distributing decision-making power.
- Realize that your organization has the required resources to get any job done; your job is to foster interconnectivity so that the greatest wisdom can emerge.

Practices with your staff:

- Give employees freedom to experiment and explore ideas with others.
- Introduce outsiders into teams.
- Encourage everyone to seek individuals who can help with an assignment.
- Inform everyone about company resources and provide easy access to them.

Encourage Cross-pollination

At New Wave, when one division brings an opportunity into the company, it is assigned to a divisional team or it is passed along to another division. Cross-pollination also takes place when people are moved around inside the company from one division to another for learning and career building.

Practices for yourself:

- Set the tone by training others in your job skills.
- Communicate excitement about cross-pollination.
- Challenge yourself to open new corporate channels.
- Identify additional resources that can help your people.

Practices with your staff:

- Don't have your people do just what they were hired to do; allow them to do more.
- Make resources available for private projects.
- Create a mentoring environment where someone who has worked in the industry a long time can get together with less-experienced people to talk about approaches to projects.

People who closely guard their knowledge and experience are imprisoned by their actions. Volunteering information and being a mentor frees you to develop personally and professionally. Effective leaders steer their people toward one another and point out that everyone grows as each person grows.

FIGURE 5.2

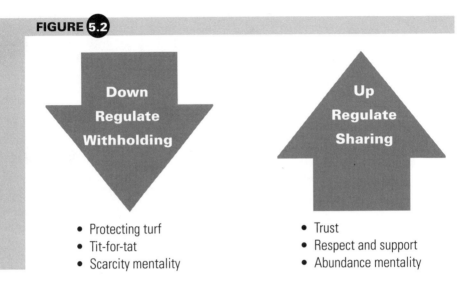

Down Regulate Withholding

Up Regulate Sharing

- Protecting turf
- Tit-for-tat
- Scarcity mentality

- Trust
- Respect and support
- Abundance mentality

Up- and Down-Regulating

WE leadership DNA is expressed by shifting the overall feel of the environment from withholding (territoriality and noncollaboration) to sharing (openness and cooperation). When leaders withhold, they are coming from ego, from I-centric thinking. When they share knowledge and power, they put learning before everything and engender trust in individuals and in the group's ability to reach its destination.

Down-Regulate

Consultants and potential hires outside of the company may not be the answer to the crises you face. The best solutions to problems are often close at hand, readily available, and cost-effective; your challenge as a leader is to ensure that they are accessible. To maximize the return from employees in whom you've invested heavily, break down the behaviors that isolate people and valuable information.

Protecting turf

A classic characteristic of stagnant organizations is compartmentalization. To avoid duplication of effort and mistakes, and to promote the sharing of knowledge and experience that can hasten solutions and progress:

- Resist playing favorites, which encourages the preservation of status.
- Disapprove an attitude of entitlement wherever it occurs.
- Stress service to others and nonacceptance of insular behavior.

Tit-for-tat

Reserve combativeness for outside competitors. Promote cooperation and teamwork by:

- Diffusing petty rivalries
- Stopping reflex reactions
- Penalizing quarrelsome behavior

Scarcity mentality

People fight among themselves if they perceive that there isn't enough to go around, whether it's food and shelter, information and equipment, or credit and rewards. Put an end to internal conflict by:

- Conveying that no one is an island, that all company personnel and other resources are available to everyone
- Making facilities available to staff during off-hours to experiment and develop ideas they want to work on
- Displaying confidence that staff skills are sufficient to get the job done

Personal feelings of insecurity can cause us to protect what we have and distrust others whose motives are uncertain. Such behavior breeds more territoriality and further reduces the sharing of vital resources and makes everyone's job more difficult than it has to be.

Language that is part of Junk DNA in your culture:

- "I'd better not fill them in about this."
- "That's my job."
- "They don't know enough to handle this."

Up-Regulate

Walls can be scaled or knocked down entirely by leaders who won't accept restrictions to progress that are erected by their own employees. Remove internal barriers to your organization's progress by building roads and bridges between and among people.

Trust

Leaders who are secure in their own abilities allow others to display theirs. You compound dividends from your staff when you:

- Create equal chances for all.
- Provide freedom and time to explore, to work with other colleagues, and to go after what they are curious about.
- Ask others to decide.

Respect and support

Leaders who honor and encourage employees are held in high esteem. You should give more than lip service to the value of others by:

- Allowing others to make substantial contributions
- Deferring to others' abilities
- Don't just hear—listen

Abundance mentality

Conveying that there is enough work, opportunity, and credit for everyone defuses internal strife and keeps the focus on group goals. You can display the bounty by:

- Rotating leadership tasks to everyone
- Employing feel-good practices often: doughnuts, bagels, pizza, picnics, softball and other games
- Spreading rewards and awards around liberally

As you open your internal highways they will become well traveled. Employees will be excited about visiting new territory, and will be accepted with open arms at every stop along the way. As a result, the road to success will be shorter.

Language that supports the emergence of collaboration in the workplace:

- "What if we tried it this way?"
- "What can we do together that will *wow* our customer?"
- "Give me your ideas about another way to say this."
- "Do you have another perspective I should consider?"

Collaborative Conversations

Micromanaging, lack of trust, and fear of power loss builds walls within organizations. Territoriality takes over when we fail to manage the egos in our workspace. Leaders can prevent hubris from taking over by removing boundaries so people feel respected and appreciated for what they contribute and are not limited in their growth potential.

When we put a small fish in a very large tank, it can grow to match the space. In organizations there is a dual challenge: How to enable the "fish" to grow, and at the same time not eat other fish.

When leaders learn how to break down silos in an organization, and give people the freedom to spread out, they find new ways to benefit the organization as well as themselves. In the process, they actually develop the ability to self-regulate their own egos.

As a leader, managing collaboration is pivotal to your success. Practices and attitudes should include:

- **Open boundaries:** Ask yourself how you can open the space for sharing while preserving individual responsibilities.
- **Open exchange of information:** How transparent are your business strategy and goals? How easy is it for people from one division to get information from another?
- **Respect for individuals:** Acknowledge the value each person brings; support the work everyone contributes.
- **Promoting individual freedom:** Create an environment where people take initiative to experiment, test out new concepts, launch individual projects, and seek out others who can contribute to the effort.
- **Giving credit fairly:** Make a point to recognize the contributions of others, whether small or large, whether they impact one person or the entire organization.

Knockout Genes

Be sensitive to language that causes people to get into territorial and noncollaborative behaviors. Make a conscious effort to remove the following words and phrases from your conversations:

- "I'm the only one who . . ."
- "What good is that?"
- "I don't trust you."
- "What in the world were you thinking?"
- "It's none of your business."

Gene Splicing

When you are aware of the impact that your words have on others and you replace words that have negative connotations with ones that offer support, you will see dramatic effects on morale and performance. Work the following concepts or phrases into your conversations:

- Team up
- Join forces
- Work together
- Pool resources
- Catalyze

Language can be a fist or a handshake; it can threaten or invite; it can stymie or guide. Communication can separate people ("Do not enter") or it can bring them together ("This way to the meeting"). Twenty-first-century leaders use words to join hands on a common journey.

▷ A CULTURE OF LEARNING

Navigating

"Coming together is a beginning; staying together is progress; and working together is success."
—Henry Ford

Working collaboratively comes naturally. Too often, we allow others to inject territoriality and politics into work relationships. When groups of people work together, it is natural that there will be issues about sharing resources, information, power, and credit. The leader's job is to minimize these issues and maximize the value of genuine collaboration. Some cultures emphasize that everyone must be connected to maintain the health of the entire culture. Creating strong families creates strong individuals.

Ho'oponopono: *Hawaiian Ritual for "Making Right"*

Like many cultures that live close to nature, the Hawaiians believe that since we are all connected, any individual problem, be it physical, emotional, or spiritual, is the result of an imbalance within the family. For Hawaiians, the concept of the *ohana*—the "extended family"—is very real. The concept of family extends not only to those related by blood, but to every living thing and even the gods themselves. These strong family links have obvious benefits and serve to keep everyone together through all the generations.

When someone is ill or if something is not going right, the entire family gets together. Each person shares any unresolved conflict or emotion that they are dealing with. It is considered important to resolve any anger or resentment since it is believed that such emotions affect the entire community. Everyone is urged to speak, until all the issues, resentments, and guilt are expressed. During the ritual, no one is permitted to leave the room. Eventually, through prayer, discussion, confession, repentance, and mutual restitution, a point of resolution occurs. The ritual is concluded and relationships are set right.

The purpose of *ho'oponopono* is to correct and restore good relationships among family members. During the process, self-scrutiny and discussion of individual conduct, attitudes, and emotions are necessary and truthfulness and sincerity are required. Confessions of error must be full and honest. All prayers and forgiving must come from the heart. Hawaiian's call this *'oia'i'o*, the "very spirit of truth." This is reflected in one of the key tenets of *ho'oponopono*—that problems can be resolved if they are approached collectively.

Replicating Organizational Sharing

In organizations, leaders must ritually steer others toward collaborative behavior. Collaboration is that wonderful experience of trusting and supporting others in the mutual pursuit of shared goals. It's when people face each other as friends, not as foes. It's when the spirit of creating something together supersedes individual self-interest. That is when individuals work together to move with the ever-shifting marketplace, which is essential for the health and growth of an organization.

When employees fear that their power base is in jeopardy, they become territorial. They become competitive and lash out at others who are perceived as threats. They become more I-centric to ensure they get the resources and recognition they need. When egos take over the organizational terrain, it adds to the burdens of leadership. Leaders may react by imposing control to get control. They might have to discipline people for acting out. Leaders might have to counter the ego dramas, and usurp contexts and situations that could be managed more effectively by their teams. To create and sustain a collaborative organization, you need to ask yourself some questions:

- How do we shift from an environment where people fear losing power to one where people feel confident that sharing will bring them greater value?
- What behaviors and actions support a collaborative environment?
- How can we coach each other to be comfortable sharing and supporting each other?
- How can we all collaborate to create innovations that expand and grow our brand?
- How do our customers want to connect to us?

You can replicate a higher level of collaboration throughout your organization, and ensure that it is ongoing, by incorporating navigating gene leadership practices to create a culture where people pursue interdependence and interconnectivity.

Meeting Strategy: Monday Morning

Companies that have regular Monday meetings are able to get into a rhythm of information sharing and updating that enables people to feel connected, involved, and aware of key decisions and projects and how to influence them. Companies that fail to establish this as a regular practice find that people feel out of the loop and are always trying to get in the know. The result can be constant anxiety and unnecessary focus on getting back in the loop—a serious waste of time, energy, and money.

Every Monday morning at New Wave people are brought into project meetings. Out of these meetings come spontaneous follow-up meetings that heighten connectivity. People share and communicate "what's next" and track projects together—they learn to navigate with each other. Meetings are the way people work and play together. They are ongoing. Because of the constancy of the communication, there is less need to do a big monthly meeting, because people are updated all along as a way of life.

Communication: Cross-functional Shareware

New Wave custom-developed a Web-based program to provide access to information across the company on all projects. The people involved in a project and those affected by its scope can find out what they need to know to manage the ramifications and success of the project from their point of view. In support of this imperative, software is capable of tracking hundreds of ongoing and sometimes interconnected projects to keep tabs on people as well as technical resources. The whole infrastructure of their business can be seen online. It provides transparency and visibility to projects, from every internal communication, to project status, to customer interactions. Feedback is real-time every step of the way so that people can be truly accountable.

Individual Development Programs: Interconnectivity

When people join New Wave, they are shown how to navigate the organization. They learn where the divisions are, how to find the right people, whom to rely on to get the support they need to make good decisions, how to complete projects, and advance their careers. People learn how to ask for projects, and to suggest projects. Doors are open from immediate supervisors right up to the principals of the company. They get performance feedback during every project session, and they can interact with senior talent to validate what they know and don't know. Consequently, employees are always able to make decisions that benefit their own individual development.

Disseminate Success Stories

At New Wave, the leaders encourage departments to share, on a company-wide e-mail basis, when something good happens. In addition, there are regular celebrations for successes, and the parties and events become shareable currencies. Products they have created for clients are displayed on walls throughout the company and are updated as new projects are completed. Representations of success are abundant, and can be seen by employees and customers alike.

Harvest Customer Wisdom

Employees are given accountability and responsibility for connectivity to clients, taking them out for lunch and visiting regularly with them to talk about ideas and concepts. Management is fully behind customer involvement, out of which come better ideas for what to create and how to do it. New customers get tours so they can see the breadth and depth of creative work, from which they may harvest possibilities for their futures. "Many harebrained schemes have turned into really valuable avenues for new business," says Alan.

Your Navigational Compass

As the adage goes, burdens shared are halved, and joys shared are doubled. Over time, the joy of collaboration may get interrupted by the need to look good, the fear of losing status by being too open, or by the notion that a friend is a foe who wants what you have. When this happens, we separate from the very people who can help us and our company succeed.

We all have the DNA for collaboration that is already hardwired and programmed for us. The N gene activates the WE state so we connect to others' needs. When we are operating out of trust in each other, ego subsides and we become open to grow, learn, and nourish one another without fear of loss. We are each more able to bring our greatest talents to the fore.

When you watch a crew work a boat in rough waters, throwing the sail back and forth as the winds change, you see a team operating out of incredible interconnectivity. People know what they are to do, and they support each other. They are doing their part and seeing the whole picture at the same time. They are responsive to unexpected shifts and turns and are able to redirect themselves when currents change. Your navigating leadership gene is the tool that keeps everyone onboard and pulling together to head the ship in the same direction.

Chapter 6

The *G* Gene: Generating

"You will either step forward into growth or you will step back into safety."
—*Abraham Maslow*

GENERATING CULTURES are those where leaders, along with employees, stakeholders, and customers work together to envision and create the future. Generativity is the highest level of collective innovation. It's the ability of individuals to "hold the space" for new ideas to emerge. It enables teams of people to live in a state of curiosity and wonder, rather than in a state of "knowing" or assumptions. In such an environment, where creativity is valued, the organization holds a tremendous potential for growth and is catalyzed by "next generation" thinking.

Generative cultures are rich with wonder and curiosity about the unknown. They focus on innovation and the creation of new operating models. Experimentation and play are standard practices, and scenario building is built into the fabric of the community. They work to reduce fear of failure and fear of making mistakes, as well as to reduce fixation on current success. As a result, the stagnation that causes companies to fall behind is avoided.

Generating cultures build "pull energy" by taking a proactive stance for shaping their evolution. This energy extends from the community and envelopes customer relationships, alliance partners, and others who want to share in the excitement of innovation.

Herman Miller, Inc.
A Generating Success Story: How Does Your Garden Grow?

When you walk in the front door of the Herman Miller design yard, one of the first things you see is a sculpture of the Water Carrier. The artwork commemorates the role of tribal elders in Native American lore. In Native American cultures, the oldest and wisest members of the tribe pass on their knowledge of rites and traditions though stories. Just as a jug of water replenishes the body, the tribal elders serve as vessels of knowledge and information that replenish the spirit of the tribe.

"One of my jobs as a water carrier here is to share our stories of success and failure," says Linda Milanowski, director of learning and development at this century-old company. "Water Carriers remind us of what made us successful, and warn us not to repeat mistakes. Another lesson from the water carrier, and one of our biggest lessons and traditions, is that we don't copy, we innovate. We don't do knockoffs. We design original products."

Being a water carrier at Herman Miller requires twenty years of service to the company. "You know, it's often said that older people don't want to change. But I've been in meetings where our water carriers, who are the longest-term employees, are the ones who say, 'It's not working anymore . . . we need to start over,'" says Linda .

One of the most significant things about the Herman Miller culture is the company's focus on curiosity and learning. There is a strong belief in the individual and especially in the creativity that each person brings to work. To encourage a wonderful sense of curiosity, leaders focus on helping Herman Miller employees experiment and take lessons from those experiments. This is such a strong part of the culture that's built into everything they do and say—it's embedded in their genetic code.

Their people are open and live "inside" the learning process. At Herman Miller, its okay to say, "I don't get it." It's okay to make mistakes in the pursuit of new learning, as long as the mistakes aren't repeated. The culture is one of "transparency and inclusiveness and engagement," and that is apparent to all employees and customers who visit. It's about listening to their customers and observing the world around them in new ways. It's about valuing the whole person and valuing relationships.

Today the culture is built upon a statement of values that they call "Things That Matter (TTM): Incomplete Thoughts about Herman Miller." These values guide their corporate community. It's understood that those incomplete thoughts about Things That Matter call all employees to constant testing and re-evaluation. TTM focuses on how employee behavior drives customer and shareholder results. Every employee knows that TTM is a working document; it is reproduced on desk mats for all to see and think about. It has clouds and looks like a doodle pad. Anyone can make suggestions for updating it. The corporate culture is a constant work in progress.

TTM speaks to the following values:

1. *Curiosity and exploration:* We keep these alive by respecting and encouraging risk-taking and by practicing forgiveness.
2. *Performance:* It isn't a choice; it's about everyone performing at his or her own best; we measure it; it enriches our lives and brings value.
3. *Engagement:* It isn't about showing up; it's about being owners, actively committed to the life of the community, sharing in our success, caring about our community, and making a difference.
4. *Design:* It is a way of looking at the world; it can require research, starting over, listening, and humility.
5. *Relationships:* We work hard to keep relationships; the ability to amplify our talent through networks of people and organizations around the world depends on the quality of our relationships.
6. *Inclusiveness:* To succeed as a company we must include all the expressions of human talent and potential. When we

are truly inclusive, we go beyond toleration to understanding all the qualities that make people who they are, that make us unique, and most important that unite us.

7. *Transparency:* It is all about letting people see how decisions are made, and owning decisions; if you can't tell how decisions are made, you've probably made the wrong choice. Without transparency it's impossible to have trust and integrity. Without trust and integrity, it's impossible to have transparency.

8. *A better world:* This is the heart of Herman Miller and the reason we come to work; we contribute to a better world by pursuing sustainability and environmental wisdom; by participating in the effort, we lift our spirits and the spirits of those around us.

9. *Foundations:* The past can be a tricky thing, an anchor or a sail, or a tether or a launching pad. The stories and people in Herman Miller's past form a unique foundation. We value and respect our past without being ruled by it. Our past teaches us about design, human compassion, leadership, risk-taking, seeking out change, and working together. From that foundation we can move forward together with a common language, and a set of strong beliefs and understandings. We value our rich legacy more for what it shows us we might become, than as a picture of the past.

Herman Miller's employees appreciate the richness of the company's history and the values upon which it was founded. In 1909, D. J. De Pree, fresh out of high school, joined a small, fledgling firm in Zeeland, Michigan, called Star Furniture Company, which was launched in 1905. D. J. was full of youthful curiosity and motivation, and he thought about how things could be done better.

In 1923, D. J. bought the company with money borrowed from his father-in-law, respected business leader Herman Miller. D. J. became president of the company, and renamed the company the Herman

Miller Furniture Company. It was in 1927 that D. J. dramatically shifted the way he led the business. It was prompted by the death of one of his employees, Herman Rummelt, who worked as the company's millwright. When D. J. paid his respects and sympathy to Rummelt's family, the widow spoke to D. J. of her late husband's talents as a poet. As D. J. listened to the incredible lines written by this millwright, it transformed the way he viewed the people who worked for him.

Are we all extraordinary and uniquely gifted? Was Herman Rummelt a millwright who wrote poetry, or a poet who was a millwright? As D. J. walked home from his encounter with Mrs. Rummelt, he answered his own question. He decided that everyone was extraordinary, and everyone had extraordinary gifts far beyond what was visible on the surface.

D. J. thought deeply about how he could create a workplace that benefited from each employee's unique contributions. In time, he drafted a clear vision statement for Herman Miller:

> *Providing products and services that not only improve the quality of life for customers, but also the quality of life for people who work at Herman Miller. The way we work together is as important as what we design, manufacture and sell to others.*

D. J.'s innovative approach impacted every aspect of the business. The company had been copying traditional furniture designs, but D. J. wanted to manufacture products that reflected his own vision. He traveled to New York to talk with up-and-coming furniture designers. He asked to see sketches of their ideas; that led to creative partnerships with many of them. In the process, D. J. totally reinvented the way he did business.

Today, Herman Miller still partners with exceptional designers to come up with new products. It may take five years or more before one produces something extraordinary. The key is to find exceptional talent and then nurture it patiently until it blossoms. Herman Miller seeks those who live and breathe problem-solving designs, those who seek to create solutions that make people more healthy, productive, and supported. Herman Miller partners with designers who have an intense curiosity and want to make the world a better place.

In 1962, D. J.'s son, Hugh de Pree, took over leadership of the company, and the business grew by leaps and bounds through its design partnerships. Hugh created a research center in Ann Arbor and gave the company the freedom to "explore anything." They moved beyond furniture to environments. They researched how people worked and lived, and explored innovative materials to create furniture that had maximum comfort and utility.

By the time Hugh's younger brother, Max De Pree, took over in the 1980s, the company had become recognized not only for modern designs but as a great place to work. Max had the ability to write, and he communicated what the company did internally to the outside world through a number of best-selling books on servant leadership. He coined phrases such as "Inclusive Capitalism" and "Sharing Corporate Wealth."

In 1995, Herman Miller had turned to a leader who was not a De Pree descendant, but he carried the water as if he were. Mike Volkema took over the responsibility of respecting the company's legacy while moving forward.

At that time, Herman Miller was still a great place to work but the company was not making any money. Revenue was good, but the bottom line was not. The company had become very decentralized, with independent subsidiaries all over the world that had their own HR, finance, and IT. The sales organization too often confused customers. Salespeople from one subsidiary approached a customer saying they were from Herman Miller, and the next week another salesperson form another subsidiary showed up saying he was from Herman Miller. There was an element of internal competition that made customers uneasy.

On the production side, it was hard for salespeople to get through internal walls. When a person moved to corporate from a subsidiary, it was considered moving to the "dark side." Mike saw that this wasn't working. His challenge was to improve the bottom line while preserving the creative culture.

Despite differences that existed, everyone did have two vital things in common: They loved the brand and wanted to be connected to it, and they had great respect for what the brand meant. Therefore, there was a lot of energy and pride in Herman Miller, the company brand. The Herman Miller logo had value and broad recognition for excellence and integrity. The respect for, and attachment to, the brand was a unifying factor. Everyone liked to think of Herman Miller as the "BMW of the furniture industry." People inside Herman Miller just needed to work and play better together.

At a time when the prevailing wisdom was decentralization, Herman Miller centralized. Mike reorganized to form one company. Everyone was recruited to help in the transformation, and nothing was exempt from scrutiny. Everyone helped to knock down walls. *I* became WE, with one set of practices, one purpose, and a common vocabulary. They launched leadership development. The process took place over several years, until there weren't any "sides" at all. People now connect across the hall or across the world.

Change can be very difficult. Herman Miller employees often ask, "How would the De Prees handle this?" This practice leads to discussions that expose fears and identify possibilities for growth that change represents. Of course, there are steps forward and steps back. But overall, there is a momentum toward a shared platform centered on customer needs rather than on individual work styles and objectives.

Brian Walker is the current president and CEO who helped Mike through the business downturn after the 9/11 tragedy. This was probably the shakiest time in the company's history. The impact of 9/11 caused the company to lose 40 percent of its revenue, and a similar percentage of its 11,000 employees. The future was cloudy and employees were shaken by the scope and duration of the downturn. At a time when all logic said not to focus on building, Brian chose a strategy to do just that. He focused on building stronger leaders in the face of this monstrous challenge.

Brian was CFO before taking on his new position, and in preparation for the new role he took the time to go into the Herman Miller archives to understand what made the company a long-term success in a highly competitive industry. He uses the same shared approach in challenges, such as international product launches, whether he is talking to the board of directors or to someone on the plant floor.

Things That Matter is more about how things are done at Herman Miller than about what they do. They will always be about problem-solving furniture design, but they will always be changing how they do it. They design much more than furniture.

Their creative culture is felt from the moment one arrives at Herman Miller. They have three key areas where customers visit and contribute to innovation. The Design Yard has an area called the Front Door, where customers provide feedback about what environments could look like in the next few years. The Greenhouse is a beautiful showroom and operations facility where customers can see award-winning chairs, like Aeron and Mirra, coming through the production cells. When you go into any area of Herman Miller, it's an environment for nurturing and growth. At Herman Miller, they design environments. Their customers don't just buy chairs; they buy a habitat where they can live and work comfortably.

Marigold Lodge, on a peninsula at Lake Michigan, is a wonderful place of corporate hospitality and renewal for customers. Company personnel spend a lot of time with customers, who share stories about what they like and don't like about Herman Miller furniture. The company has an infrastructure to manage this information: customer stories and feedback are passed along to sales and production so they can better understand how people respond to company products. It's their way to learn.

Herman Miller designs and updates their own workplace environments, the human dynamics, so that people can freely access and apply their unique genius. They create spaces inside all of their buildings where people can congregate and talk, to have meetings, and be together. For example, their marketing and sales teams are in a building called the MarketPlace. Conversations change when you are in a wonderful environment. That's who they are, and that's how their products and their company stay fresh and exciting.

Herman Miller is a 100-year-old company that is still new. It will always remain new because its culture is still based on the creative principles inherent in D. J. De Pree's original vision statement. Their creative energy connects their past with their present, and generates their shared future.

▷ LEADERSHIP PRINCIPLE
Growth vs. Group Think

Generating leaders like the De Prees and their successors recognize that for a company to survive, let alone thrive, it must continuously reinvent itself. Invention literally means the use of ingenuity and imagination to produce something previously unknown. Generating leaders further recognize that no single individual could be the vessel of all creative ideas, and so they cast the net widely throughout their organizations to catch the nourishment that could come from anyone. Generating leaders think WE not I.

I-Centric vs. WE-Centric Leadership

I-centric leaders focus on what they know and they feel they need to publicize their own expertise. Demonstrating that they have all the answers is of prime importance to them; wonder and curiosity pose a threat to them and cause anxiety. In meetings, they focus on the content of the issues, not the process. They are very resistant to change, because it means they could become less powerful or less important. Rarely do they give away what they know, because in their minds it weakens their power base. In their minds, their knowledge is power, and sharing with others results in a power drain. Their behavior causes others to "go along to get along." The primary downfall is that they don't move at the pace of change; they slow it down. Some refer to them as points of power, anchored to the past. I-centric leaders are not energy generators; they are energy consumers.

WE-centric leaders readily look for new ideas from others, test them, and spread them around. They believe that sharing shifts conversations from breakdown to breakthrough. They are catalysts for wisdom and seek to discover the next generation of thinking. They are agile, flexible, and they facilitate collaboration. They think in new ways and inspire others to do so. They look at problems innovatively with others; in fact, problems are seen as opportunities and challenges that bring together colleagues in shared experiences, releasing energy and creating excitement along the way. WE-centric leaders always think WE and create organizational spaces where individuals and teams interconnect to share their wisdom, experiences, and insights to expand everyone's horizons and exponentially multiply knowledge. WE-centric leaders are energy generators.

INTENTION ———— **IMPACT** ——•

Leader Story: Failure to Take Risks

"I don't punish people for making mistakes; I show them how to avoid making them."

Frank was one of six managing directors in a telecommunications firm reporting to the division president. His department managed billions of dollars in pension funds for the organization, and Frank prided himself on being a "best practice" executive, top among his peers. He read voraciously about good leadership and believed he was embodying these practices. He was mild-mannered and never raised his voice. He loved telling people that his team was the best, smartest, and highest performing.

Frank had four people reporting to him. He and his team evaluated outside vendors and assessed their money management abilities to decide which ones they would contract with. Frank saw himself as an authority, and thus wanted to work with others who were in authority as well. He made every decision only after extensive and thorough investigation, involving iteration after iteration until all the facts were in and there was no doubt about the right way to go. He had many vendors parade through the office until he saw them all, and then he chose those he wanted to work with.

When preparing proposals and reports for his boss, Frank had his own style of working. His team gave it a name, and referred to it often: redlining. Frank would ask one of his direct reports to create the first draft. He would go over it and redline changes. The individual would then take the document and revise it, and send it back to Frank. Frank would redline it again. This process was repeated as many as fifteen times. One of Frank's direct reports was overheard saying, "It gets down to where there are no signs of the original document, and we are making corrections to his corrections."

Frank used other teaching methods. He assigned reading on weekends and holidays; he recited past war stories and covered in great detail the tactics he had used to emerge victorious; he never missed an opportunity to point out any flaw, however minor, in someone's vocabulary, mannerisms, or choice of clothing. He was the esteemed professor who magnanimously imparted all he had learned.

In December, each managing director received a performance evaluation based on a 360-degree feedback process. In his latest review, Frank received the lowest scores of the six direct reports to the divisional president. As a result, he was called in to speak with the VP of human resources.

Unbeknownst to Frank, three of his four direct reports had visited human resources on their own in the four months prior to his performance review. One complained about the redlining process, saying that in all of his other jobs he was considered a good writer, especially when his boss was clear about what needed to be written.

He was frustrated and exasperated and felt it was a draining exercise that taught him nothing and lowered his self-esteem. Another informed human resources that his blood pressure was very high and that he was taken to the hospital the previous Friday night with an "almost heart attack." The third person related what Thanksgiving Day was like that year. Frank and all four team members were on a teleconference with a client brainstorming and planning for a presentation that they were going to make the following week. Each person was forewarned that they needed to stay on as long as it took to finish. The call started at noon and ran on for hours. Dinners started without them at their family tables.

The head of human resources learned further that the individuals felt like they were being "kept back." They felt they could not grow in their positions, and that they were being unfairly evaluated. The head of HR asked each person why he or she did not speak up before, and all three said the same thing: they felt they were the only ones underperforming, and that if they spoke up they would be fired.

The work environment had degraded to one of fear and mistrust. Frank was putting so much emphasis on "getting it right" and "perfectionism at all cost" that he had lost sight of the human beings who worked for him. They felt that he treated them as cogs in the wheel of work and that, in his eyes, they were merely "its," not individuals

Frank's team tried to survive their boss's insensitivity. However, their distress was not containable and they:

- Internalized the problem, thinking that maybe they weren't as good as they thought they were
- Took more sick days than usual
- Made many mistakes on reports that went to the president
- Started to blind cc other colleagues outside of their team

Each of Frank's reports wanted to be tough and gut it out. However, eventually their frustration hit critical mass and they gave Frank the ratings they felt he deserved on the 360-degree evaluation.

Frank thought of himself as a best practice leader. His style was driving, perfectionistic, and tough. Yet it was dressed up in a pleasant style. He was relentless and nice at the same time. Without realizing it, Frank had sent mixed messages to his team.

Fear of Failure and Making Mistakes

Leaders who create fear of failure and making mistakes fail to understand how that fear triggers insecurity about performance and feelings of incompetence. When employees think they are performing at their best but are told that they are failing to deliver, they lose confidence in themselves and in their ability to be successful in the future. Fear of failure and of making mistakes actually causes individuals to make mistakes—it becomes a self-fulfilling prophecy. Employees become afraid to push back on a tough boss with high standards because they don't want to look like they "can't do the work."

This fear in the workplace causes individuals to avoid experimentation and risk-taking. It leads them to blame others when something goes wrong so that they are not associated with the failure. It can even cause team members to point out others' mistakes, deflecting attention to anyone other than themselves.

Employees who work for a boss who triggers fear of making mistakes underperform more often than they overperform. When beaten down they lose their aspiration to stretch and grow, as well as their passion for going to work.

Frank sent mixed signals to his team. He talked about their "high performance" to others, yet he rejected their individual contributions. Frank's desire to raise the bar for his people caused him to send them home on weekends with lists of articles to read on leadership, yet when they tried to show initiative, he rejected them. When they asked him to streamline priorities, he wasn't receptive. He said he cared about them, but he treated them like he didn't.

Frank's behavior exemplified group think: he was omnipotent, and everyone had to go along with his program. This behavior engenders secondary fears:

- Fear of letting the boss down
- Fear of letting the team down
- Fear of speaking up
- Fear of giving the boss feedback about his impact
- Fear of telling the truth
- Fear of talking to your boss' boss because you may be perceived as weak
- Fear of inadvertently making career-limiting moves
- Fear of reaching out to others for help

The overall fear of employees is that others will view them as weak, stupid, or incompetent. So they turn inward, and hide who they are from others. They disassociate their personalities, assume disguises so others cannot really know them, and fragment their identity. They put distance between themselves and what they want to be, as well as distance between themselves and others.

Consequently, they lose intimacy with individuals and with a connection to a greater whole.

As a leader, you must ensure that fear of failure and making mistakes does not consume your work teams and cause your staff to withdraw from the work that needs to be done. Our sense of identity and well-being is profoundly affected by how much freedom we are allowed in order to learn, grow, and nourish our souls at work. A leader's ability to manage fear of failure and feelings of incompetence is integral to creating environments where employees contribute to problem solving, goal attainment, and growth.

Great leaders put themselves in others' shoes and have empathy for their challenges, and can give people the room to experiment, make mistakes, and learn. Leaders who instill a sense of freedom set the tone for greatness to emerge. They create fun environments where people want to come to work, learn from each other, and grow together.

You can help employees—and yourself—by encouraging them to challenge conventional thinking. High performance doesn't come from pointing out mistakes; it comes from supporting risk-taking. You can help employees expand their horizons, anticipate the future, and stretch well beyond what is possible today by creating an environment in which employees are not punished for not being perfect, but instead are able to focus on learning and creating breakthroughs in every area of their professional and personal lives.

FIGURE 6.1

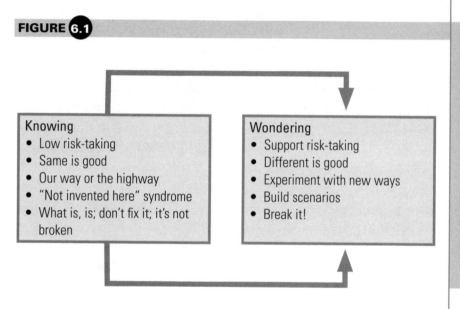

Knowing	Wondering
• Low risk-taking	• Support risk-taking
• Same is good	• Different is good
• Our way or the highway	• Experiment with new ways
• "Not invented here" syndrome	• Build scenarios
• What is, is; don't fix it; it's not broken	• Break it!

The Go along to Get along Meta-Message

When leaders say they care about their people, yet they treat them as "its," they send a meta-message. When leaders believe they are driving for perfect performance, yet focus on mistakes, they are stifling creativity—another meta-message. When leaders believe they are good leaders, yet refuse to take feedback, they send a hidden message of fear, and distress results.

193

Leaders who study what good leadership looks like, yet only project onto others without self-scrutiny, send the message "I'm okay; you are not." The reaction employees have to this message is to protect themselves: go along to get along.

Leader Profile

Let's look at Frank's I-centric profile through a number of lenses:

How he communicates: Frank does not communicate with anger or high emotion. In fact, the tone of his communication is rather modulated. Yet the words he uses suggest high pressure and drive. As a result, he communicates dual messages that are very confusing. When he speaks with his boss and other leaders above his level he appears to be towing the company line, yet when he feels he is driving toward a goal he really wants or has a different point of view, he leaves the pack and does his own thing his own way. In other words, he takes a backdoor approach to get what he wants.

How he motivates others: Frank sets very high bars and openly talks about his high-performing team. He labels it as such and is proud to speak of the team in this way to others. He likes to be seen as a boss who leads talent. Yet his direct reports feel that he does this to look good rather than because it's true. They feel he leads through fear. If they fail to live up to his standards, he pushes them to step up and does not take no for an answer. He feels he is a cheerleader; they feel he has no empathy or awareness of what others are going through.

How he listens or doesn't: Frank listens in order to evaluate the level of commitment and energy people put into their work. He favors people who meet his high standards and sends out signals of disappointment to those who do not meet his expectations. He has a hierarchical way of listening, with him on top, others below him and above or below each other, and someone on the bottom. Once he places someone in this order, it's hard for him to change his mind. When he is in a driving mode, he rarely picks up cues from others. So if someone sends help signals he does not recognize them. When he is locked into a strategy, he doesn't hear anything other than what confirms his point of view.

How he uses or abuses power: To those who work for him, Frank is a power-over leader; to those he works under, he likes to be perceived as a peer. He is tough and appears to be a command-and-control leader, mostly because he dictates to others. He believes that if he tells people what to do, they will not make mistakes, and so he protects them. In doing so, people are afraid to experiment, to test out new things, to learn and grow. His direct reports feel he treats them like junior executives rather than the senior executives they are.

Leaders who know it all get a failing grade at test time. In the end, they get a very tough lesson when they learn that they don't have the answer to every question, and that they don't even know what all of the questions are. Success and growth are a question of how the knowledge and abilities of others can be tapped. Enlightened leaders know the answer.

The Negative Ripple Effect

Frank evaluated everyone in light of his own aspirations and goals. He did not value his people for their unique potential, and failed to benefit from their creative contributions. His touting of his high-performing team was not matched with the support it needed to be truly exceptional. For him, teaching was sending people home to read rather than discussing the issues, and actively listening, in order to grow together. By creating a pressure-cooker environment, he created an environment of fear that forced everyone to march in lockstep toward his predetermined destination.

Frank had alienated his staff. They felt his desire to look good superseded everything else. His annual review determined that he did not listen to feedback, nor did he understand how to work with others to achieve collective goals.

Frank was an I-centric leader who created waves of fear that carried everyone along with him. The cascading impact was that people felt:

- They were unable to meet their boss' expectations.
- They were a constant disappointment to their boss.
- No matter what they did it wasn't good enough.
- They were not being heard.
- They were constantly angry.
- They were not valued.
- They didn't belong and wanted to go to work for someone else.

Junk DNA: Leadership Mythologies

Many of us have been brought up with the notion that our job as a leader is to protect others from harm. That comes from an ancestral and mythological belief that the hero is always there to shelter his or her progeny. Our protective nature is innate and we live it out every day. As parents, the role of protecting becomes critical to ensuring the safety of our children. If we bring this tendency to work, we create environments where fear of taking risks prevails.

When we buy into a view of the leader as hero and savior, we accept a limited role in overcoming challenges. We see the leader as more knowing and wise than we are, and we relinquish our ability to experiment for the sake of our own learning and achievement. This vision defines a leader with an outmoded strain of DNA who believes that:

- Protecting others from harm is a critical role of the leader.
- Preventing others from making mistakes is smart.
- You are better off avoiding risk-taking than making mistakes.

There are red flags, or "mutations," that indicate a leader is expressing old DNA that limits diversity of thinking:

- Blind followership/deferring to authority
- Blame and accusation
- Lack of curiosity and an unwillingness to experiment

To evolve, you need to break the bonds of old ways of thinking and connect to new beliefs. Top-performing companies push against conventional wisdom and experiment; they are shepherded by leaders who are not afraid to say they don't know and who seek to live in wonder and curiosity as a way of life. They have a robust acceptance of everyone's individual talents and ideas, and do not judge others who are different. Such leaders help their organizations emerge from status quo thinking to discovery and innovation.

When the members of Frank's team finally began to talk openly with one another to share their frustration, they looked at this "best practice" executive with new eyes and went to human resources.

Executive coaching was recommended for Frank, which he resisted. He perceived his poor 360–degree review as "just a bad year" attributable to staff two levels below him who were not able to fulfill the demands he passed down from the president.

After reluctantly interviewing eleven coaches, Frank selected one who seemed open to exploring the situation with him rather than assuming outright that he was wrong. After three months, he could not ignore the evidence that they collected and he finally owned responsibility for the impact he had had on his team. He accepted feedback about his driving style and stifling behavior. Then he embraced new training in WE-centric practices.

Within six months Frank was a new leader. One of his direct reports asked, "Where did my old boss go?" But he and his team knew that was a rhetorical question. What they really cared about was that for the first time in memory they liked where they all were.

▷ THE LEADERSHIP STEP
Keep Growing

The generating leader understands that fear of making mistakes triggers more fears and limits exploring, testing of new ideas, and learning. The essential ingredient for diminishing fear of making mistakes, and for exploring and learning in the workplace, is for the leader to make mistakes a part of growing—not acts meriting punishment. People should be less afraid to play out ideas that are not fully "baked" and willing to share early thinking before they have full proof an idea is ready to be launched. Employees will then be more open to generating ideas and feel more secure about it. They'll ask the awkward questions and freely admit when they don't understand. They will readily ask for help and be more willing to change their minds and accept another's idea.

The generating leader also needs to be more transparent about his own mistakes in order to communicate that curiosity and daring are essential for the health and growth of the organization. Doing so eliminates the meta-messages that cause fear.

Evolved leaders know the damage that meta-messages cause: loss of innovation. How can you build an environment where people feel safe to experiment, to test ideas, and most of all to make honest mistakes? Instead of allowing the meta-messages to stagnate your workplace, generate curiosity, wonder, and innovation.

The Twenty-First-Century Leader Can *See* the Way to Grow

To build an environment filled with the wonder of possibility, encourage thinking outside the usual way of doing things and convey an expectation that innovation is the new norm. Moderate parochial behavior in yourself and others; place a premium on imaginative solutions so that no one hesitates to stretch the envelope. The following three leadership practices ensure a constant flow of new ideas.

Share Unconventional Thinking

At Herman Miller, invention permeates the company. Executives speak about innovation with employees, they create unconventional workspaces, and they live creativity in all they do. Herman Miller's legacy and history was built on the relationships the company formed with unconventional designers to build their next generation of furniture. They continue that legacy by embedding unconventional thinking into training programs and in how leaders engage employees to ask questions and push back, always seeking better ways to work and to meet customer needs. Curiosity is more important than reinforcing tradition. When customers visit them, feedback is gathered and disseminated in real time to others in the company. Employees know when conventional wisdom is not working, and they are ready to examine and implement unconventional ideas.

Practices for yourself:
- Think of innovating as learning, not making mistakes.
- Inspire people to be curious and to ask questions.
- Value experimentation.
- Admit to not knowing all the answers, and to making mistakes.
- Openly reward people who are curious.

Practices with your staff:
- Ask your employees for their new and wild ideas.
- Ask them to challenge each other's ideas to come up with new and better ways to work.
- Bring together people with very different ideas.
- After every major project, get together to discuss what worked and what didn't, and what can be done differently next time.
- Bring important operational and customer challenges to the table where employees can take responsibility for brainstorming, rather than providing all the answers.

- Come to meetings with more questions than answers, such as, "How could we do this?" and "How can we change that?" Make the environment safe for curiosity and wonder.
- Emphasize creativity rather than performance.

Establish an Experimental "Laboratory"

At Herman Miller, the company keeps curiosity high by expecting and encouraging risk-taking, and by practicing forgiveness. They understand that you can't be both curious and infallible. In fact, they appreciate that if you never make a mistake you are not exploring new ideas often enough. Everybody there makes honest mistakes. What's important to them is that everyone learns from them and moves on together to a higher place.

Practices for yourself:
- Keep an open mind to alternative perspectives.
- Give up the need to be right.
- Think of mistakes as a way of learning and exploring that which you do not know.
- Practice forgiveness.

Practices with your staff:
- Create an environment where people have fun at work.
- Reward the testing of new ideas.
- Bring the outside in: send people out to the marketplace to research what others are doing to inspire innovation.
- Give individuals and teams challenges to break out of old patterns to create new ways of working together.
- Invent customer scenarios and "what ifs" to find new ways to work with them.
- Make brainstorming a regular part of meetings, and engage everyone in idea-generating sessions.

Encourage Innovation

At Herman Miller, whenever they tried to fit into a niche, they weren't successful. They succeeded by creating new opportunities and new markets, and by pioneering new niches.

Practices for yourself:
- Set the tone to make unconventional thinking a norm.
- Communicate your acceptance and approval of testing, experimenting, and honest mistakes.
- Challenge yourself to create new approaches to projects and employees.
- Reveal your own mistakes.

Practices with your staff:
- When having vital conversations about the future, ask for responses to "what ifs."
- Allocate specific times for idea generating, scenarios, and solutions.
- Make innovation workshops frequent and invite the participation of customers and others across the company.
- Team people up to work on alternative approaches to anything and everything.

The only idea that absolutely has no value or can't be used is the one that isn't stated. Take the lead in ensuring that every thought, no matter how far-fetched, has a fair hearing, and that no one who contributes an innovative thought that doesn't pan out, will be diminished in any respect in the eyes of peers and superiors.

FIGURE 6.2

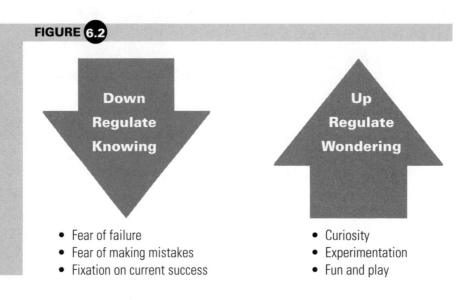

- Fear of failure
- Fear of making mistakes
- Fixation on current success

- Curiosity
- Experimentation
- Fun and play

Up- and Down-Regulating

WE leadership DNA is expressed by shifting the overall feel of the environment from knowing (the need to be right) to wondering (the need to discover). When leaders are in a state of knowing, they are coming from ego, from I-centric thinking. When they are coming from wondering, they are curious and put ego aside for generating something new and better in the world. They are not coming from defending the past; they are coming from generating the future.

Down-Regulate

In too many organizations people refrain from taking risks that could lead to phenomenal breakthroughs because they fear embarrassment, castigation, and damage to career advancement. They hesitate to speak up and ask questions in favor of taking the safer course of not rocking the boat, and expend tremendous energy trying to appear as if they have everything under control. Leaders who also act that way reinforce such behavior and spread stagnation. You can open the floodgates to new ideas by reducing impediments to innovation.

Fear of failure

Worrying too much about what might happen delays or prevents altogether the positive things that could happen. You can stop paralysis by:

- Reframing failure as a temporary breakdown before a breakthrough (The creative process often requires many attempts before finding the best solution.)
- Acknowledging the importance of how things get done, not just what needs to be done (The safe way is not necessarily the sure way to growth.)
- Rewarding original thinking even when it leads to a dead end

Fear of making mistakes

Avoiding mistakes because of a fear of personal and professional repercussions at the expense of discovering breakthroughs has more serious consequences in the long run. Leaders shouldn't treat mistakes lightly, but they shouldn't punish them, either. You can provide the freedom for discovery to your employees by:

- Redefining mistakes as "steps to get from here to there"
- Asking for and appreciating feedback from others to help you move closer to your targets and goals
- Leaving behind telling people how to do things

Fixation on current success

If you're standing still, you're losing ground. Reliving past glory and relying exclusively on what got you to where you are, sure ways to let the competition pass you by. You will mobilize yourself and your troops when you:

- Stop defending and dwelling on achievements that stroke your ego but do not stoke your energy; move on!
- Expand your learning beyond what you already know by living in the next challenge, not the past success.
- Envision what could be.

Change cannot be managed effectively by adherence to the status quo. It is addressed by being "within the change," which means altering thoughts and actions to adapt to circumstances. This will only happen across-the-board when leaders are flexible, and open and receptive to new ideas.

"Knowing" language that is part of Junk DNA in your culture:

- "This doesn't belong in the workplace."
- "You'll never get it past my boss."
- "If we were another type of company, we could do this."
- "There's no way this will fly here."
- "It's just a waste of time."
- "Leave it for after-hours."

Up-Regulate

To replace a pervasive "knowing" attitude where everyone defends his or her position by relying on the past, instill excitement about exploring the unknown and the glory that awaits all who venture boldly. Prime the pump of innovation by exhibiting and instilling a new outlook:

Curiosity
The potential for discovery breathes life into organizations, and successful ventures breed others. You can ensure a constant flow of innovations by:

- Encouraging people to go after what they are curious about
- Making wonder and curiosity an end in itself
- Asking questions for which you have no answers

Experimentation

Big rewards await those who dare, those who try something completely new. No one knows if something will work until someone takes a stab at it. Put your organization in a position to benefit by:

- Giving employees the opportunity to stretch their talents to try new assignments
- Eschewing convention (This doesn't mean giving up what you know is good; it means expanding what is possible by changing practices and policies that get in the way of progress and that are resisted by staff.)
- Embodying curiosity about how anything could be improved, from simple procedures to complex strategies

Fun and play

Work doesn't have to be all work. Leaders who inject fascination and some childlike wonder into the tasks at hand make the mundane enjoyable and the unusual exhilarating. You can unleash the child within everyone by emphasizing that:

- Play is the action or drama. Play is the freedom of movement. Play can be hunches, diversions, and improvisations.
- Play is expanding the universe, not limiting it.
- Play enables us to enter spaces we've never been before and explore them with a nimble mind.
- Since we don't already know what the answer is, we will have fun discovering it.
- Play is full use of the mind. It's about tapping into the imagination, the unconscious, and the intuitive.

As you spread a sense of wonder about possibility, employees will become more confident as they expand their abilities to solve problems. As their ideas are given credence, they accept those of others and demonstrate a willingness to develop new concepts. As a result, your entire organization changes for the better.

Language that supports the emergence of wonder in your workplace:

- "What if we tried it this way?"
- "How about suspending judgment so we can see where this line of thinking will go?"
- "There's no risk in talking about it!"
- "If we 'pilot' it and it doesn't work, we don't have to adopt it."

Catalyzing Innovative Conversations

Negativity, lack of trust, fear, dictating, and focusing on the way things have always been done, insidiously eats away at the heart and soul of individuals and organizations. Like a fire out of control, fear of failure can fill the organizational space with toxic air, and before you know it, you lose consciousness.

Leaders can avoid polluting their environments by fostering creativity. Listening to others who have new ideas can stimulate your own creativity. Human beings have the ability to unfold and evolve, unless they build or support walls that prevent generativity from taking place. The doors to creativity and expansion are always open until we shut them. As a leader, managing creativity effectively is pivotal to your success. Practices and attitudes should include:

- **Support of risk-taking and experimentation:** Ask yourself how often you fired someone for making an honest mistake.
- **Testing is good:** Everything should be able to withstand scrutiny. What is best will last.
- **Different is good:** While appreciating what we all have in

common, recognize that differences define the breadth and scope of an organization.

- **Build scenarios:** Create a container where many experiments take place at the same time. They don't necessarily need to go into production; they can just be a way to play out possibilities to see what they look like, taste like, and feel like before you make a choice. Provide room to play.
- **Break it!:** Periodically revisit who you are and what you have created. When people and companies calcify, they stop growing. Even though we strive to create and remain in a comfort zone, know that breaking it is a way to regenerate.

Knockout Genes

Be sensitive to language that causes fear and holds people back. Make a conscious effort to remove the following words or concepts from your communications:

- Failure
- Disappointment
- Letdown
- Catastrophe
- Fault

Gene Splicing

You will see dramatic effects on morale and performance when you replace words that have negative connotations with ones that offer support. Graft the following words into your conversations:

- Experimentation and daring
- Learning

- Adventure
- Accomplishment
- Achievement

Language is the oil for the pump of innovation. Words that preserve the status quo, that judge failed attempts harshly, are like worn-out lubrication that will cause an engine to seize. Changing the way you speak, using words that convey an excitement about discovery, will keep your pump well lubricated and will stimulate an adventuresome environment.

▷ A CULTURE OF LEARNING
Generating

"It is impossible for a man to learn what he thinks he already knows."
—*Epictetus*

Balinese Spirit

The Balinese believe that art represents spirit and is a representation of collective thought. From childhood, each person is trained to be a dancer, musician, mask-maker, or artist in one of the many crafts that are honored in Bali. This is done to express spirituality and creativity, rather than as a means of making money. Although many Balinese create a living from their art, it serves a more important function: allowing their culture and history to flow from generation to generation. Children are taught to be part of the collective whole, and villages have master workshops that go back for generations.

To be a master artisan, one must be able to see how each art is related to the other. Thus, a mask-maker must understand the dancer who will wear the mask. The dancer needs to understand the significance of the story in order to bring the story to life.

It is not uncommon to watch a temple celebration and see performers from ages eight to eighty working together. Members contribute all they can to ensure the success of the group. A wonderful example is the gamelan, the Indonesian version of an orchestra. Each instrument is tuned to its neighbor, making the whole gamelan a self-contained, coherent musical unit, played as a single instrument rather than a collection.

The Balanese village is completely self-sufficient. According to Bill Dalton in the *Bali Handbook*, the Balanese village is "Not just a collection of family compounds, the rural community was and is a whole series of interlocking corporations, a living organism, a microcosm of the cosmic order."

Indeed, this model of connectivity is extended to the entire Bali population. The hundreds of villages that make up the entire Balanese population are as connected as their performances are. Every village joins the others as part of the collective whole, contributing its share to the culture and economy of a thriving island nation.

Replicating Organizational Wonder

In the business community, risk-taking behaviors must be ritually performed to regenerate thriving organizations.

When employees fear risk-taking, innovation and creativity are dampened. They avoid making mistakes and looking bad in front of colleagues. They're afraid that they will be blamed for any attempts that are not successful. Bosses who openly castigate employees, or point fingers at those who have taken risks unsuccessfully, create an environment where protecting one's image becomes more important than growing the business. To create and sustain a top-tier organization, you need to ask yourself some questions:

- How do we shift from an environment where people fear risk-taking to one where people embrace it?

- What behaviors and actions support innovative contributions from all?
- How can we coach one another to be comfortable taking risks and experimenting?
- How can we all collaborate to create innovations that expand and grow our brand?
- What do our customers want to see from us?
- How can we constantly reinvent our company?

You can replicate risk-taking throughout your organization, and ensure that it is ongoing, by incorporating generating gene leadership practices to create a culture where people are comfortable with pushing their own envelopes.

Meeting Strategy: Organizational Engagement

Herman Miller has a Monthly Business eXchange (MBX) at all major sites. At the MBX, attended by as many as 400 team leaders, a leader presents a video on a featured topic, such as a tour of the test lab, or a tour of the renovated "Front Door." They may focus on development, reorganization, or whatever is currently going on in the company. They might have a guest speaker. All the videos end with a feature about an employee, for example, a customer rep, scheduler, or someone from the production team. At one meeting, they showed bloopers, which were outtakes from other videos. The feedback from one employee was, "It's great to see management vulnerable like this."

They also do a financial report in the video and then someone from the financial department steps up to add more background to the story. They discuss all the figures and what they need to do in sales and production. And there is always a hot topic—the elephant in the room—which launches the Q & A part of the meeting. The leaders who respond do not give crafted messages; they speak openly and frankly. Then leaders in turn have an MBX with their respective teams. They use the video to bring everyone together.

After the MBX, everyone who attends launches his own MBX for his level, so the information cascades throughout the organization and everyone can be in the know about what is happening. This reduces fear and enables people to sustain the high level of curiosity and wonder that is so characteristic of the culture.

Once a year the company has a corporate-wide employee meeting where the CEO and some of his team visit all major sites within the company, including England, and conduct employee meetings about topics such as product launches, restructuring, and updates about Things that Matter.

The net result of the sizable effort and expense related to these meetings is that every employee feels that he or she matters—and knows how he or she can contribute to the success of the company.

Communication: Scenarios

In the late 70s and 80s, a few companies such as Royal Dutch Shell took a very bold step by pioneering a discipline called "scenario building." Scenario building creates and explores different realities before they occur. The objective is to imagine how the world might unfold in the future.

A scenario example could be what would happen if the company experienced incredible growth in market share, lost market share, or maintained its market share. Executives would then play out the possible repercussions before they occurred so that they would be ready to move swiftly and deftly to be successful—regardless of what actually happened.

The impact on a leader's ability to execute strategy, shift gears, and make critical decisions is dramatic and positive. The gaming process disengages executives from the current playing field, focuses their vision, and presents more possibilities to work with. The path from where they are now, to the future, becomes rich with many alternate routes and bridges to explore.

Scenario building, or scenario planning, is something we can now do on computers. We can create virtual companies, enter data galore, and play out alternative decision-making strategies that enable us to see how different decisions impact other dynamics. Nothing is without connection to something else. At the time Royal Dutch Shell was inventing this discipline, they turned out to be one of the few healthy survivors in a tough marketplace.

At Herman Miller they create different scenarios for a wide variety of audiences, including customer groups who visit the company in search of a partner who can help them create great places to work. The scenarios are intended to help customers—and Herman Miller—imagine and envision what their own world and their own needs will be in the future.

Scenario building revolutionizes how executives plan for the future and adds to their comfort as they approach it. It's a way of working for many forward-thinking companies like Herman Miller.

Individual Development Programs: Creative Futures

"Leadership is temporary and therefore fragile," says Andy Lock, EVP and Chief Administration Officer of Human Resources at Herman Miller. "This is why we focus so much energy on developing our next generation of leaders who can carry our DNA forward." One of their tag lines is, "We help people see their future in a different way." People there own their careers. Herman Miller has an online development plan and individuals choose whether or not they want their leader to have access to it. Any employee can go to the Web site, take an assessment, and discover if she wants to be something other than what she is. Employees might discover they are in the right career and the right place, and would then be more confident in their path. Or they might discover that they could pursue another career and would learn about what they might need to do to enact that change.

Education is one of many career development options. One could apply for a degree in business or another discipline. Herman Miller spends $1 million and more per year on educational assistance. (Company reimbursement for education applies only if the request is related to the business.)

Whether or not the company benefits directly from an individual's career development, employees can build a better future for themselves, whether inside or outside the company.

Innovation Workshops

At Herman Miller, the human resources, information technology, and the real estate departments work together as a team to architect the employee experience. They start with the question, "What should the employee experience be like?" and from there they design environments that open opportunities for high levels of interactivity and conversation. There are "connection zones" where people meet on a casual basis to talk. There are spaces where surprise encounters can take place, where people can ask, "What are you up to?" Instant networks are created and, as a result, a high level of creative energy flows, innovation emerges, new projects are born, and people feel energized by their surroundings.

There is a belief that play or improvisation in the workplace leads to "out of control" outcomes. The assumption is that if we let go of our plan to experiment, we will lose control. We can't predict what will happen. Something could go wrong and we'll get blamed. The fear of making mistakes and getting blamed is so powerful in the human psyche that it produces all sorts of routines and practices that prevent the expression of creativity.

However, what if improvisation brought about more control and greater predictability?

What if it engendered a level of control that was far beyond what was in place before?

Play and improvisation can be staged in controlled environments. It's faulty thinking to believe it's one or the other—control or chaos. One technique that is often used by leaders who play successfully is to initiate improvisation exercises off-site or in safe environments first, and then transfer them to the actual workplace. And remember: the outcomes of experiments need not be implemented. They're just another step in the process. The real hidden value lies in the freedom to test out alternatives—to see more than one pathway and to explore and realize others—and freedom from feared implications.

Improvisation and excitement are a way of interacting that comes from positive intent, exploring the outrageous and impossible, and breaking out of boundaries. Improvisation can show up in the way people test one another in one-on-ones, in how teams "game" together, in how departments restructure, or in how parts of an entire company are taken apart and reassembled. However it is employed, it results in "having fun at work," and outcomes usually exceed expectations.

Sharing Success Stories

When others hear about success related to risk-taking, creativity takes root throughout the entire organization. Herman Miller captures and shares success stories on video and through their intranet. They archive successes and make them available to everyone. Putting the stories into the database inspires others to add theirs.

Your Power Generator

When you think about times in your life that were most joyous for you, you undoubtedly recall memories from your childhood of playing with friends. The interactions were subtle, and impromptu games would regularly take place. There was a dynamic connection that resulted from the excitement that bubbled beneath the surface.

Over time, innocence and wonder get bottled up by doubts and fears. We become more deliberate. We form habits of thought and habits of action that become habits in relationships, both personal and professional. But the child remains within us.

Your new generating gene is the source of power to connect to the other children in your community who are also still there, waiting to play productively with you.

Chapter 7

The *E* Gene: Expressing

"We don't build the future for our children; we build our children for the future."
—*Theodore Roosevelt*

EXPRESSING CULTURES are those where people have a voice, make decisions, push back and challenge authority, and are valued and respected for their contributions. (There is a low level of conflict aversion.) They enable individuals to share their voice without retribution from authority. They can grow their talents, are supported in taking risks, and are energized to take on audacious goals that help the whole enterprise succeed.

The focus of expressing cultures is on developing people and their potential. There is a great sense of shared ownership, accountability, and accomplishment. Expressing cultures encourage and develop the "leadership voice." They are environments where people can challenge each other, can have healthy conflict, and push back. They work to reduce hubris, fear of speaking up, and "telling" behavior. Expressing cultures build "pull energy" by removing artificial restraints that stifle. They give individuals the freedom to use their voices, to join the chorus that heralds progress. This energy extends from the community and envelopes the relationships a company builds with customers, alliance partners, and all others who want to be heard.

Dreyer's and Edy's Grand Ice Cream
An Expressing Success Story: Thank You for Speaking Up!

Few people know what the MOAP is outside of Dreyer's and Edy's Grand Ice Cream—but the 6,500 people inside sure do. The "Mother of All Parties" took place in 1995 to celebrate reaching a fifteen-year company goal—to be the leading premium ice cream company in the United States. At Dreyer's and Edy's, people know about the MOAP and they know what "hoopla" means. They are living in the "Grooves" and love it when CEO Gary Rogers says "You decide."

These terms and concepts, foreign to others, are what shape the culture at Dreyer's. Moreover, it is carried forward from one leadership generation to the next. Their leadership style is "in your face," transparent, and real. There is no tolerance for indirect communication. People say what they mean, and say it to the people who need to hear it. Accountability and ownership are everywhere, and lived by everyone. Conversations may be hard at first, but they're softened by true understanding that results from the pleasurable connections that are made.

Today, Dreyer's and Edy's Grand Ice Cream is a $2 billion company, newly acquired by Nestlé. The culture behind the brand name is as luscious as the ice cream they make, and, as Gary proudly announces, "It's unstoppable. I couldn't stop it if I wanted to." Dreyer's and Edy's Grand Ice Cream is a stellar example of *expressing* because, while they represent all seven genes so well, they are teachers and carriers of the E gene more than any other company in the marketplace. They have ten "Grooves" that make their culture of expression come alive:

1. Management is People
2. Hire Smart
3. Learn Respect for the Individual
4. People Involvement

5. Ownership
6. Hoopla
7. Learn, Learn, Learn
8. Face-to-Face Communication
9. Upside-Down Organization
10. Ready; Fire; Aim

All of the Grooves play a critical role in Dreyer's success, but "hoopla" is the one about rewarding a job well done. Hoopla is all about appreciating and celebrating good effort—especially when someone has taken a bold stand and stretched himself outside of his comfort zone. It is acknowledging others' big, bold, "put your name on the line" achievements. Imagine being asked to come into a boardroom with a dozen senior executives standing up and waiting to tell you what a great job you've done—it's an awe-inspiring experience. Now, imagine that this happens all the time, from a passing comment, to special bonuses, to awards at staff meetings, to formal celebrations. That is what Dreyer's is all about, and it's just one of the many unique "flavors" invented by this truly grand company.

Through the Grooves, employees learn to express their opinions, speak up, and make big decisions and feel ownership for them. Through the Grooves employees learn incredible respect for the value each person brings, and for the importance of individual contributions. Through the Grooves, employees feel they matter and they learn to have confidence in pushing back against authority, and to be on guard whenever these incredible values are violated.

The story of the Grooves began as something concocted by Gary and William F. "Rick" Cronk, old friends who had decided to go into business together. Rick wanted to open a restaurant, but Gary thought that was a lousy idea. "I lost the argument," Gary recalled, "and against my better judgment, we bought a restaurant." After expanding the business, they watched it go south and then shut it down—with no business to replace it. Gary and Rick struggled with little money coming in, and realized they needed to find something else.

Gary was thinking of going back to consulting when he came across an opportunity in late 1976 to buy Dreyer's Grand Ice Cream from a man named Ken Cook. Cook had failed to get a bank loan he needed to expand the business, but Gary was able to get the financing together to buy the company and invited his friend Rick in on the deal. The Dreyer's culture grew under their leadership.

Along with the Dreyer's brand name came the highest commitment to quality that had been instilled by Bill Dreyer, a professor of dairy science who, in partnership with Joe Edy, founded the company in 1928. Dreyer's was one of the few ice cream companies that delivered directly to stores, which meant the quality and flavor selection were better.

Gary remembers that their original goal was to become the most successful ice cream company in the Bay Area, an ambitious goal for a small $6 million company. The two leaders experimented with their products and their employment policies, adding ingredients to the "rich cream" that was already there. They brought out the best in their people and in themselves, and together they reached their goal.

When the company went public in 1981, they raised their sights, aiming "To become the leading premium ice cream company in the West." When they reached that plateau a few years later they were in position to take on Breyers nationally. In fact, Cronk and Rogers declared their new mission: "To become the leading premium ice cream company in the United States."

The MOAP took place when the company achieved that lofty goal. Gary and Rick chartered four jumbo jets that hop-scotched across the United States, picked up thousands of employees, and winged them to Oakland where they were shuttled to the convention center for a huge rally. Gary stood up there and said, "Starting today, our new mission is to become the pre-eminent ice-cream company in the country."

At the party, the theme "I can" emerged and permeated all the activities that had been arranged: I can jump; I can wrestle; I can climb the wall. That is now part and parcel of their expressive culture, a "pillar of thought" for everyone. At the end of the MOAP, Gary got up in front of the 2,500 people and celebrated the success one more time. "It was like a rock concert," he remembers. His hand hurt from shaking hands all night long.

The party lasted for only a few hours, but the memories still live on. Everyone returned home with a shared success memory like no other. Now they know that when they achieve pre-eminent status, they will have raised the "I can" bar to another level. They will then have the GOAP—the Grandmother of All Parties. What will take them there? The "I Can Make a Difference" expressive DNA.

"Even though the restaurant failed, we were still so proud of the things people had done," Gary says. "Our staff was incredibly loyal, and ten of our original Dreyer's hires had been with us at the restaurant company. We were like a family. We were committed to perpetuating that same feeling." It wasn't all smooth sailing. They had lots of meetings about what they wanted. They tried to figure out what makes a great company and got offtrack when they concentrated only on the business side, the procedures, and numbers. They generated an impressive list of eighty-five things that they thought were important. Gary and Rick felt that was too complicated and wanted to simplify things. They found their answer: it came down to people. In 1986 Gary sat down and wrote the Grooves, their philosophy to keep everyone in the company on track together. They believed in hiring smart, whether that was people or ideas. They borrowed good ideas from other places and made no apologies for doing so.

The Dreyer's and Edy's culture is reinforced by underlying practices that allow individuals to lay down some tracks of their own while staying in the Grooves:

Day 1 Attitude: When a new hire walks in for his first day on the job, he wants to have a good experience, to make a contribution. He's probably a little bit anxious and wants to be accepted as an individual. He wants to be who he is, not have to conceal his personality. He's full of energy. Company leaders consider those instincts perfect!

They don't want to drain attributes and aspirations out of a person. They feel their job is not to put ideas in people (except maybe what they don't know about ice cream), but to benefit from ideas they put into the company.

The Power of "You Decide": "This is the most powerful principle I've learned in my whole life," says Gary. "If you have a conversation with someone, with anyone, so that each of you really knows what the other thinks, and at the end you say, 'You decide,' that says, 'I trust you to make the decision.' Think about the mindset of someone hearing those words. What is understood is, 'I better not screw up' and as a result people become responsible for outcomes. When you run a whole company around this practice, it's so empowering. Employees have accountability."

Gary recalls, "One Christmas Eve, I was walking past the reception desk at about three o'clock. Nearly everyone had gone home. The receptionist asked if I thought it was okay for her to forward calls to the answering service and go home, too. That left me with three options: I could have said yes; I could have said no, this is a big company and you need to stay; or I could have said, 'You decide.' I told her, 'You're the expert; you're closer to the action. You decide.' I left, and on Monday morning, my executive assistant told me that the receptionist stayed until 5:30. If I had told her she couldn't leave, she would have stayed while wanting to go. Instead, she stayed with the pride of ownership. Everyone here owns his or her own piece of Dreyer's."

The Joy in Life Comes from the Struggle: Gary continued to reveal his DNA: "We all have goals. I'll play my hardest, and sometimes I'll win and sometimes I'll lose. But I'll get there someday. The joy is in the struggle. We always face tough competitive issues, tough customer issues. Sometimes we get down. But there is joy in the challenges. Just be grateful that the challenges you face are worthy of your talents and experience."

It's Not about Mistakes; It's about Learning and Developing:
"If we're not making mistakes we're not learning. The only way to
develop good judgment is to exercise bad judgment," says Gary. "But
think about what the cost was, what you did and what the lessons
were, so you don't make the same mistake again. We try to distinguish
between decisions and outcomes. You look outside and the weather
is good, so you don't take an umbrella. Then it rains. Good decision,
bad outcome. Regardless of the outcome, you need to find out if a
decision was a good one or not, and why. That's how we learn. We
constantly encourage people to try. We celebrate experimenting, as
long as people learn and better themselves and the company in the
process."

Measuring and Monitoring Evolution: "You can't impose a philosophy on anyone. You have to start small," explains Gary. "You
have to expose people to the philosophy and have them digest it and
embrace it. People here talk about it all the time. Everyone works
on it and we have an anonymous Grooves Survey every year. Questions address areas such as personal job satisfaction, whether a person feels respected, and how a person feels his coworkers are doing.
We have over 6,500 employees. Better than 80 percent of them fill
out the survey. The commitment to this is awesome. Over the entire
company we average a 7.8 score out of a possible 10. Some locations
score above 9. We take our temperature all the time. It's who we are.
The Grooves are the single most important thing we do—without
question. They are the primary reason for our success."

Within the collective, the focus is on the individual. Everyone
brings unique talent and personality to his or her job. Dreyer's and
Edy's doesn't tell people what to do or how to do it. They don't have
job descriptions. Individuals figure it out and are expected to become
experts in their positions while doing their jobs their way. "I'm best
at arranging travel for my boss," or, "I'm the best at oiling a compres-
sor." That's what ownership is to them. That's how people become

invigorated and enthusiastic, and feel privileged to be part of the company. If someone doesn't pull his weight, employees notice it and take action before the manager does. They feel comfortable enough to pull someone aside and talk to that person because they care deeply about a community of shared responsibility. Once a year they have a Hall of Fame induction when they honor twelve front-line employees who represent the "I Can Make a Difference" philosophy. They take a tour, have lunch, tell their stories, and then go to dinner with the Executive Committee. The honorees explain why their peers selected them that year.

At Dreyer's and Edy's, work is an extension of a person's personal life. People are eager to get to work every day at a place where they feel they belong. They are the same people at work as they are at home. "We want you to integrate your life and your job," Gary explains. "We don't expect you to check your personality at the reception desk when you come to work. We want you to be free to be who you are and to take every opportunity to be better."

▷ LEADERSHIP PRINCIPLE
Developing vs. Dictating

Leaders like Rick Cronk and Gary Rogers pay attention to their leadership impact and put incredible energy into bringing out the best in others. They decided together that they wanted to create a workplace where everyone could grow and develop to realize his or her greatest potential. They experimented and played with ideas for creating an open environment where they were not the authorities on everything. They encouraged dialogue and debate, enabling people to find their leadership voice.

What Rick and Gary instinctively knew was that great leaders believe in developing the voice of the next generation of leaders. They nurture the unborn potential in others, through conversation and debate, and by leaving space for others to step up and make decisions. They know that a culture of trust and respect produces unstoppable power for growth. Their leadership DNA enables other expressive leaders to emerge.

I-Centric vs. WE-Centric Leadership

I-centric leaders focus on the success of the past to define their present. Once a pattern has been established, they keep people in compliance with it, rather than questioning or changing it to continuously improve. Their power comes from being the boss and dictating the way. They are believers in the status quo, because it's easier than self-examination and confronting change. The primary downfall is that they get locked into patterns and are not open to shifting perceptions or looking at alternatives when circumstances require that. I-centric leaders allow entropy to affect organizational stability instead of mustering the power of others to control events. In the face of change, they cling to what was. In the face of crisis, they close ranks. In the face of something new, they seek refuge in the old. I-centric leaders just want to be the boss, the authority.

WE-centric leaders believe that the past is a wonderful storehouse of experiences and knowledge—a reference encyclopedia that can be used to manage the present and create a new "volume" for the future. They lead by nurturing growth and development in others, not by demanding strict adherence to set formulas. They establish environments where aspirations can emerge, where colleagues can find their unique voices and express them without fear of repercussion.

WE-centric leaders express themselves by challenging others to express their thoughts and feelings. Together, the extraordinary energy of wonder and excitement is released, resulting in remarkable company-wide achievement. WE-centric leaders understand that to aspire is to breathe, and that expression is sharing air with others. These leaders open the space for individuals to shape the collective reality.

INTENTION ─────────────────── **IMPACT** ─●

Leader Story: Failure to Ask

"I don't tell people what to do; I show them the way."

Eight years ago Meredith had been hired to establish a benefits department in a growing advertising company. The firm was hiring people in the United States and in Europe, and a formal benefits program would attract better people to the company. Meredith had an accounting and actuarial background. She was one of the best in the industry, and when she was hired everyone was pleased she had accepted the offer. Within a few months, she had finished two research projects, sizing up the challenge and designing the foundation for what would become one of the industry's best benefits programs. The company knew it had chosen the right person for the job.

Meredith searched thoroughly for people to join her team, and hired two women whom she felt had the talent and ability to be her partners. One was like her, with strong quantitative skills, while the other had exemplary people skills. They made a dynamic team. As people throughout the company became aware of Meredith's department, tremendous demand arose for the benefits team to deliver programs to thousands of employees spread out across two continents. Over the next year, they had to put compensation and benefits practices in place company-wide. Meredith's team was stretched thin, and so she hired two more people to help them with program implementation and administration. The pressure from outside raised the pressure inside the team. Meredith's high standards were not to be compromised by the increased workload. She was very prescriptive and didn't tolerate mistakes. She was a perfectionist about how all work looked before going out to the other departments. After months of high demands, something changed inside Meredith's team.

The increased visibility of her department and the complexity of managing more people and programs taxed Meredith's leadership skills. She was great with numbers, but supervising a staff to deliver programs distressed her. Being an introvert, she kept everything inside. She was unable to relieve her own stress, let alone the mounting pressure her team felt to meet her demanding timetables.

To complicate matters further, Meredith was elected head of the EBC (Executive Benefits Committee), giving her even more visibility and stature in the company. In this role she was to ensure that all benefits complied with government regulations while conforming to the high standards set by her company. She ran meetings on a regular basis; the executives who attended would sign off on any new programs. Meredith took on the added responsibilities and felt it. Those around her felt it, too.

Not having been trained in leadership skills, the only way that Meredith knew how to get work done, was to either do it herself or tell other people what to do. Meredith pushed her people to produce more to meet expectations. As the workload increased, she increased the pressure. This meant staying late at night and coming in early in the morning. It meant redoing work until it was perfect and it meant putting business targets before feelings and relationships.

Meredith got upset when one of her people had to take off for a long-awaited appointment with an out-of-state medical specialist. This clashed with a new benefits launch. Meredith was relentless about getting the program out and told her direct report she could not go to the doctor. This upset the employee greatly because the appointment was necessary for her health and just about impossible to reschedule in the near future. Meredith relented and let her go, but she reminded her repeatedly upon her return that leaving at such a critical time was unacceptable.

A short time later, the environment became unbearably stressful for everyone. When Meredith's employees tried to push back on her Attila-the-Hun leadership style, she didn't listen or respond to their needs. People whispered behind her back about her insensitivity. It was as though the only thing that mattered was work, and her timetable. A new and exciting department had deteriorated to the point where people dreaded coming to work. There was no comfort there, and no sense of belonging or accomplishment. All signs of fun had disappeared. The impact of task over relationship—dictate over develop—took its toll:

- One person left the department, claiming she didn't see any growth opportunities.
- Another left saying that he could not work in a place where he was constantly criticized.
- Meredith was labeled as someone without feelings.
- Performance remained high but communication remained "behind her back" and turned vicious.
- People stopped respecting Meredith's leadership.
- Meredith withdrew further.

When the first two people resigned they did exit interviews with Human Resources. Each person had reasons to leave the company that were directly related to Meredith's leadership. "This is not the right place for me to grow" and "I can't work with a boss who puts so much pressure on me" were representative comments.

Within the next three months, other direct reports visited with HR to discuss the problems they were experiencing in the benefits department. The result was that Meredith was relieved of her leadership position and put into a strategic consulting role where she could use her strengths of trending, forecasting, and future planning.

Meredith exerted pressure on her team to get the work done without showing any signs of sensitivity to their personal and professional needs. Without realizing it, she had sent mixed messages to her team.

Fear of Speaking Up

Those like Meredith who are asked to lead for the first time are desperate to meet their assigned objectives and often become more of a dictator than a true leader who recruits others to meet goals. Leaders who put a high level of focus on tasks versus relationships create the impression that they have no heart, that it's "my way or the highway." Leaders who, under pressure, fail to listen to feedback give the impression they don't care. Leaders who start out as dictators find it hard to change their style because they usually get quick responses initially from employees when they exert their power, and this responsiveness reinforces their management style—until the consequences become unmanageable.

In Meredith's case, the consequences were that her team individually and collectively developed a fear of authority and of speaking up. When they even hinted that they needed help or questioned her tough directives, she met them with a cold stare that they translated to mean, "How can you disappoint me this way?"

When we fear our authority figures, we develop self-doubt that dredges up "noise in the attic," those childhood experiences when parents and teachers criticized us. We remember feeling diminished and devalued. We all have these memories and they surface anew under poor leadership. The fear deepens as employees:

- Are unable to read the leader's mind
- Become insecure about the leader's influence over their future job security
- Lose confidence in their own abilities
- Lack a mechanism for pushing back on authority
- Endure an ongoing lack of trust
- Withdraw from others, feeling they are the ones who are weak and helpless and wanting to keep that a secret

If people feel weak they will not have the strength to function well. As a leader, you must ensure that fear of speaking up does not infect your workplace and degrade the performance of your work force. Your ability to manage fear of authority and to create a culture of speaking up is integral to your organization's growth and success.

A great leader understands that "positional power" has an incredible impact on others. It can threaten their confidence even before a conversation takes place. Employees "filter" conversations with bosses before they have them because they don't want to appear ignorant or make a mistake. This filtering process usually removes vital information the boss really needs to hear because people are afraid it is going to be too controversial. Filtering removes the very elements needed to make critical decisions.

When you remove the fear of authority, you create energetic workplaces where your people thrive and reach their potential while helping you to reach yours.

FIGURE 7.1

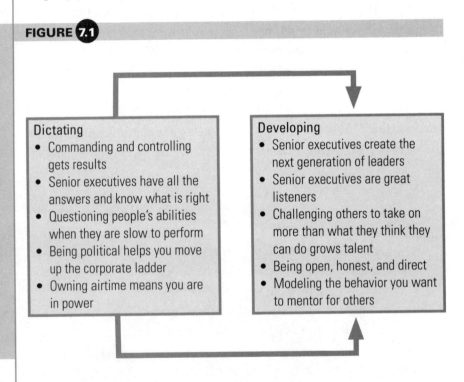

Dictating
- Commanding and controlling gets results
- Senior executives have all the answers and know what is right
- Questioning people's abilities when they are slow to perform
- Being political helps you move up the corporate ladder
- Owning airtime means you are in power

Developing
- Senior executives create the next generation of leaders
- Senior executives are great listeners
- Challenging others to take on more than what they think they can do grows talent
- Being open, honest, and direct
- Modeling the behavior you want to mentor for others

The "Do What I Say" Meta-Message

When leaders say they want to get performance and results, yet fail to solicit staff input about how to deliver that, they send a dictating meta-message. When leaders order others around, they reveal distrust of employee abilities—another meta-message. Once trust is broken, informal conversations—those where learning and sharing happen—stop taking place, and formal conversations—those where you need to get on another's calendar to talk, where learning and self-correction are absent—take over.

When leaders are insensitive to employee feelings and their desires to make original contributions, employees get the message to retreat into protective behavior. They stop taking risks. They lose faith in their leader and stop asking questions to clarify their understanding. When a leader continues to dictate, the meta-message to direct reports is, "You are not smart enough to know how to do this on your own so I'll just tell you."

Meta-messages cause employees to spend time worrying, not performing. These mixed messages create a separation between those who have positional power from individuals who have the collective power to truly advance the organization.

Leader Profile

Let's look at Meredith's profile through a number of lenses:

How she communicates: Meredith is an introvert with incredible strengths in quantitative analysis. She manipulates numbers with extraordinary skill, and is incredibly talented at thinking through a plan and organizing it. Her solid grasp of figures led to a hands-on, command-and-control style that matched her "fill in the Excel spread sheet" approach. To stay on task, she avoids any conflict by dictating so that there will be no push back. She does not accept "no" and she interprets questions as excuses for not doing the work. Because she is so structured and rigid, there is little improvisation, discovery, or learning. She is very smart; when people question her, she quickly communicates her "knowingness" with arrogance. Her positional power, especially when she's frustrated and overwhelmed, easily intimidates people.

How she motivates others: Meredith uses fear to get the performance she wants. She tells people what to do once, and they know she expects them to deliver. She is not available for their needs. Overall, the atmosphere is one of pleasing the boss, not one of learning and discovery. People don't seek rewards from Meredith because they believe they won't measure up to her expectations.

How she listens or doesn't: Meredith focuses on telling to get results. She is a taskmaster, not a relationship master. While she may hear what people say, she is processing their conversation through a filter of judgment. Are they meeting her standards? Are they delivering? Are they listening to her when they don't respond quickly enough?

How she uses or abuses power: Meredith knows she has to deliver results. While tough on the outside, she is fragile inside. She knows she has not been trained to lead and worries that she is not good at it. Her solution is to seek refuge in the power of her position to get things done. The effects on her staff go unnoticed. Inside, she sees herself as lacking power, yet outside she translates that fear into a dictating and task-oriented style. In her mind, it's black or white.

Progressive leaders are effective because they understand that they have one mouth, two eyes, and two ears. They see and hear twice as much as they speak and learn much that can be used to be effective stewards. Their employees are thereby challenged to share what they know, and to learn from others at the same time. Without being told, each individual develops personally and that advances all.

The Negative Ripple Effect

Meredith failed to engage with her employees in taking on the challenges they were facing together. In any environment where priorities expand with the business challenges, there are tradeoffs that need discussion so that everyone is part of the decision-making process. Meredith's staff was not able to tackle the real issues it faced.

Meredith certainly felt resistance to the work, but she ascribed it to talent deficiencies or lack of urgency. Once she came to that conclusion, she could not accurately assess events as they unfolded. All that ever mattered to her was getting the job done. And she would show them all how to do it. She made waves that carried everyone in the same way to the same place. The cascading impact is that people felt:

- Anger from being stifled
- Professionally unfulfilled
- Unhappy because they were not contributing
- Concerned about job security
- Unable to see a way out of their situation
- Aversion to their boss

Junk DNA: Leadership Mythologies

Many of us think that leaders tell people what to do. Especially when projects are just starting out, it's assumed that the leader knows more than everyone else and will make all the decisions. Leaders learn this behavior from their mentors and repeat it with their direct reports. On top of this, we've all been brought up to respect positional power, and have been taught not to challenge authority.

As a result, we have old archetypes of leadership in our minds, causing us to fear speaking up. We can either allow those old visions to continue, or we can consciously challenge them to progress, to improve, and to achieve great heights as Rick Cronk and Gary Rogers did at Dreyer's and Edy's. The dictator defines a leader with an outmoded strain of DNA who believes that:

- Leaders need to tell people what to do or else they won't know what to do.
- What you see is what you get, and when people aren't performing you need to assume it's because they can't or won't.
- Positional authority should automatically confer employee deference.

There are red flags, "mutations" that indicate a leader is expressing old DNA that limits diversity:

- Conversations are usually formal, not informal.
- Clans begin to form for protection from the boss.
- People quickly blame others so they can avoid the bullet.
- There is little mention of controversial topics.
- There is little to no expressed conflict.

To evolve, you need to break the bonds of old DNA and connect to new beliefs. Research shows that extraordinary leaders are not autocratic. They see their role as one of service to the organization and its employees. They feel their job is to grow talent, to ensure that everyone leverages individual strengths, and that there are robust opportunities to learn and grow. They know that when people grow, the business grows. Development-oriented leaders help their organizations discover, experience, and perpetuate.

When Meredith lost staff, her boss decided to move her into a more strategic role so that she could continue to contribute to the organization without having to manage. In addition, coaching was recommended and Meredith received support in redefining how she would work. Having her move out of the department while still working with her previous direct reports was difficult for everyone at first.

In response to this challenge, the company—much to its credit— offered a larger leadership intervention for the whole team to enable Meredith and her two previous direct reports to redefine their roles. The whole team embraced the intervention with incredible commitment and passion. The 360-degree process provided the means to explore its impact, to learn how to adapt, and to see roles in a new light. Within a couple of months, the benefits department was reborn.

Allowing expression by every individual is not without its difficulties, not without bumps in the road. But hearing from everybody ultimately avoids heading down a dead end.

▷ THE LEADERSHIP STEP
Elevate Dialogue

The expressing leader understands that fear of authority reduces or eliminates employee feedback, as well as the leader's own success. To diminish this fear in the workplace, leaders must shift from a dictating style to a developing style, and eliminate the meta-messages related to positional power, as those only serve to create fear in the workplace. People are less fearful and consequently more secure and more productive when leaders are open and transparent in their roles, discussing how decisions are being made and being genuinely interested in questions and debates, even during the toughest of business challenges. Leaders should actively solicit input from everyone so that speaking up and asking difficult questions become a normal way of working. This leads to the healthy conversations that identify real needs and produce real solutions.

How can you build an environment where people feel safe to open up, to push back, to challenge your point of view, and to contribute their all? Instead of allowing meta-messages to silence your staff, set the context for their expression.

The Twenty-First-Century Leader Can *See* the Way to Develop Voices

To keep your organization moving forward, advance all employees. Rather than telling your employees how to do things, remove imposed restraints and let them evolve to reach whatever level their talents permit. Authoritarian behavior smothers conversation that could provide invaluable information as well as productive solutions and strategies. The following three leadership practices keep the lines of communication open at all times.

Share Strengths

"We focus on individual strengths, not weaknesses," says Gary Rogers. "Every 'I' is critical to the team. We all want to make personal contributions; there are things you're good at or I'm good at. We find ways to leverage everyone." Combining individual strengths in their cultural mix is as pivotal to the success of Dreyer's as the individual ingredients in its product mixes.

Practices for yourself:
- Open your mind, not just your door, to others. Be receptive to their unique talents and suggestions.
- Value differences, not conformity.
- Acknowledge people for what they know rather than chasten them for what they don't.
- Admit to not being the expert on everything, and invite others into conversations about how to tackle key challenges

Practices with your staff:
- Challenge individuals to discover and use their strengths.
- Assign projects that stretch employees' current skills.

- Create environments where employees are publicly recognized in front of their peers for extraordinary efforts.
- Ask everyone, "What do you know?"

Establish an Encouraging Environment

At Dreyer's, people become widely recognized for what they do through informal networks. People say, "Get Robin; she's good at that." As a result, informal mentoring takes place. It happens over lunch, in hallways, in carpools. That's where a lot of business gets done. Dreyer's doesn't do as much formal training as some companies. They are, by nature, an environment that encourages self-expression.

Practices for yourself:
- Set a collegial atmosphere.
- Be committed to developing the leadership voice.
- Select employees who are willing to encourage others.
- Teach others through your actions, not by lecturing.

Practices with your staff:
- Be receptive to others who want to learn about your job.
- Ask others to ask others.
- Encourage employees to bring in others on their projects.
- Promote cross-training.
- Ask, "Whom can you help?"

Encourage Talent Development

Talent development at Dreyer's comes from throwing people into the fray to learn as they go. They are given responsibility before they are ready for it. They expect people to step up and leaders to say, "We trust you."

Practices for yourself:
- Trust that people can do more than you might think. Think bigger for them.
- Communicate your desire to help them grow and suggest possibilities that might be of interest to them.
- Be receptive when people want to stretch their skills and try new things.

Practices with your staff:
- Promote leadership development, continuing education, and advanced training in meetings.
- Communicate self-improvement successes that people achieve.
- Ask, "What would you like to do?"

When one person always speaks for all, the message is likely to fall upon deaf ears. When everyone is respected and invited into the mix, the truth will emerge and be heard loud and clear. Leaders who develop the voices of others ensure the steady flow of information and ideas upon which difficult decisions can be based.

FIGURE 7.2

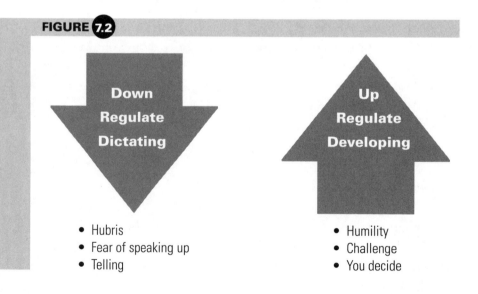

Down
Regulate
Dictating

- Hubris
- Fear of speaking up
- Telling

Up
Regulate
Developing

- Humility
- Challenge
- You decide

Up- and Down-Regulating

We can't and shouldn't take away all positional power from leaders. We also can't and shouldn't lose our respect for it. What we can and should do, however, is express the leadership that removes artificial constraints on invaluable individual contributions, and instills a culture of participation.

Down-Regulate

Sometimes leaders say a lot by saying little. A choir with voices in one octave is not as pleasing to the ear as one where the entire range of notes sings out. To be a skilled conductor within your organization, be sure one voice—including your own—doesn't drown out all others, and tone down those tendencies that cause employees to sing offkey.

Hubris

Pride in one's work and accomplishments is a positive trait; excessive pride, or chest-thumping, raises one person by lowering others. Minimize the risk of unchecked egos silencing the voices that need to be heard by spreading these tenets:

- Having a title doesn't entitle you to bully others.
- People are hired for their talent—appreciate them!
- No one is right all the time, and position or knowledge base does not automatically trump others' ideas.

Fear of speaking up

If one person who wants to speak is stifled, everyone should hear a message loud and clear: silence is an impediment to progress. To prevent a lost voice, leaders must:

- Acknowledge the need for input.
- Eliminate chastisement for questioning.
- Reward people for expressing opinions.

Telling

Dictating to others is analogous to giving them a fish to eat; developing others is analogous to teaching them how to catch fish. You sustain your organization when everyone learns how to sustain himself or herself so:

- Experiment, experiment, experiment! Instead of dictating to others, "tell" yourself to ask a question instead.
- Let others find a way before trying to fill the vacuum.
- Ask others to ask questions.

A bass can be appreciated more when complemented by a soprano. Beautiful compositions result when all voices are heard, balanced by a skilled choirmaster. Modulating discordant behavior within your organization prevents missing and/or sour notes.

Dictating language that is part of the Junk DNA in your culture:

- "Just do as I say."
- "I'll show you how it's done."
- "I don't want to hear it."
- "You can't."

Up-Regulate

Just as there are behaviors that silence voices, there are those that bring them out. You can ensure a full chorus by applying leadership practices that involve everybody.

Humility

Leaders rise in stature as they lower their profiles. Admitting fallibility, uncertainty, or a lack of knowledge from time to time inspires others to pitch in. You can develop others by admitting honestly that:

- To lead is to serve others.
- Clerks, salespeople, and account executives who "touch" customers make the difference.
- No one is irreplaceable.

Challenge others at every opportunity

You will never know how far your organization can go unless you know how strong the people who must carry it are. You demonstrate your own strength when you:

- Give people opportunities to get onto task forces and key projects.
- Expect inspiration from others.
- Say "You decide" and mean it, and be prepared to live with the consequences.

Ask questions constantly

Socrates taught by demonstrating the value of thoughtful queries. Reporters do their jobs by asking six basic questions: Who? What? Where? Why? How? When? Leaders gain useful knowledge with honest probing to:

- Find out what they don't know.
- Draw people out and into the mix.
- Understand what people want to say, rather than jumping in with an opinion.

As your employees are able to express their voices, they will be proud to be a part of a group effort. They will realize that the whole is greater than the sum of its parts. As a result, your organization won't miss a beat.

Language that supports development in your workplace:

- "How do you feel about this?"
- "What should we do here?"
- "Is there something I'm missing?"

Expressing Conversations

The most powerful way to change a culture is to be the change. Just because you have a big title doesn't mean you have to be a big boss. The key is to have an opinion but not be arrogant. The key is to decide not to make every decision. The key is to realize that the people who touch the customer are just as important as you are to the enterprise. Enlightened leaders serve the employees who serve the customer.

The best bosses create environments where others can grow. But don't just give lip service to staff development. When your employees feel genuinely challenged and inspired by you, they grow into their greatness. They are then more able to inspire growth in others. Leaders who mentor and coach create other mentors and coaches. Together, you'll "coach" your company to greatness.

Drawing out the best in others is a trait of real leaders. Your approach and attitude should include the following:

- *There's no such thing as a dumb question:* Silent employees are stagnant employees. Inquiring minds learn and grow. Encourage others to ask questions by saying, "That was a great question. I'm glad you asked it." Then ask someone else what she thinks about it before you respond.
- *Listen actively:* You have two ears and one mouth; hear twice as much as you say. Allow open dialogue and debate to go on

until they reach a natural conclusion. Make it fun to participate. Disagree and referee where appropriate.

- *Share knowledge and learn from others:* Everyone can be an
  expert at something and can be more willing to participate
  with others to share and teach what he or she knows. There
  is nothing more stimulating that getting together highly talented people and giving them room to perform.
- *Challenge others to grow:* Let people know you are not always
  right so that they feel more comfortable speaking up. After
  a healthy discussion, there is nothing more powerful for a
  leader to say than "You decide." It builds judgment, confidence, ownership, and responsibility for the business.

Knockout Genes

Be sensitive to language that silences people. Make a conscious
effort to remove the following from your conversations:

- *Position authority:* "I already know that."
- *Status quo:* "Why would you want to change that; it's not
  broken."
- *Caution:* "I'm your boss; my work is not to be questioned."

Gene Splicing

You'll see dramatic effects on morale and performance when you
replace words that silence with ones that encourage speaking up.
Graft the following into your conversations:

- "Let's talk about your personal development."
- "How can I help you with your career advancement?"
- "What type of leadership training would you like to have?"

Communication can either soothe or it can agitate. Twenty-first-century leaders use words that motivate all to come out for the choir in order to develop their voices.

▷ A CULTURE OF DEVELOPMENT
Expression

"A community is like a ship; everyone ought to be prepared to take the helm."
—*Henrik Ibsen*

Growing and developing the next generation is a part of leadership DNA. Too often, however, we follow old role models and methods and just go along for the ride. Even when we want to change we hesitate because we think we would be giving up power. We revert to telling others what to do. Real leadership power comes from harnessing the energy that everyone is waiting to express.

Lakota Pipe Talking

The Lakota people live with a spiritual and holistic understanding of their connection to everything in the universe. The ceremonial use of the pipe, which serves as a portable altar, is a simple but powerful symbolic ritual. Fundamental to the pipe ceremony is the symbolic pairing of the male (stem) and female (bowl) powers that results in new life and creation.

The pipe is offered to each tribal member in a circle with the stem pointed to one of the four compass directions. The ritual reflects the connection between the natural and supernatural worlds. The rings of smoke and the communal aspect of the ritual represent interaction with all creation. The center is the self, or the individual holding the pipe. Next come the circles of human relationships: family, clan, and nation. Further outward is the sphere of animal relationships, and the last circle contains the most powerful spirits: earth, wind, fire, and water.

To preserve harmony, each pipe smoker speaks, without interruption, what is in his heart. The smoke symbolizes the participant's visible breath and stands for truthful speech, actions, and spirit. As his story unfolds, each talker maintains his balance with the larger community. He signifies the unity between the heavens and the earth, and his connection to all, by inhaling from the pipe or by raising it upward and then touching it to the ground before passing it along.

The pipe and its respective holders are a force to preserve and disseminate the culture. The Lakota value the words of each tribal member. In the pipe-passing ceremony, the person holding the pipe brings his breath into the world and reveals his unique attachment to it. He becomes a new source of wisdom adding his insights to the wisdom of the community and the universe. Each voice is solemnly honored in turn and strengthens the whole.

Replicating Organizational Development

In business, too, the individual is integrally connected to the whole. Leaders must learn to ritually include development of others as part of their agenda, not as an afterthought. At Dreyer's, Grooves-related activities are part of every meeting, every event, and every discussion.

Employees respond to "knowingness" and positional power with fear. When fear sets in, productivity goes away, respect goes away, and sometimes employees go away. When you understand the dimension of dictating, you will begin to see its reflections in how you interact with your peers and staff, from the way you stand to how you speak and respond to crisis.

To perpetuate the growth of both your people and your organization, you need to ask yourself some questions:

- How do I shift from a telling leader to an asking one?
- What behaviors and actions support a mentoring and coaching culture?
- How can I grow talent and the business at the same time?
- How can I make development part of everyone's agenda?

You can replicate development and influence throughout your organization, and ensure that it is ongoing, by incorporating expressive gene leadership practices to create a culture where people reveal and contribute their unique talents.

Meetings: Workouts

Expressing organizations make it easy to speak up, express a point of view, celebrate success, and push back on authority. They "train" their ritual "muscles" to support the open environment they want to have. When someone has done something great, public recognition from a boss can be just as important as a monetary reward. Expressing companies take the time to officially celebrate achievement.

In expressing companies, meetings take place more frequently. They're not just those formally scheduled gatherings; they're every informal get-together taking place in a hallway and across a cubicle or phone line. Everyone is free to flex his or her dialogue muscles to express unique talent and ability. Meetings are expressing "workouts" that are the fabric of the culture.

Communication: Open Dialogue

"Tough" conversations solve tough problems. In expressive cultures, open and frank dialogue is a way of life. Coaching in this skill, from the top of the organization to the bottom, is vital. Honest talk is not mean talk; honest talk reinforces the focus on the group mission. Having tough conversations is integral to an expressive culture. You have to start out by hiring people who can handle that. Then everyone needs to practice it every day. Once a culture evolves with this skill clearly embedded in the way people talk with one another, it becomes "the way we do things around here." Consistency makes all the difference. Giving one another feedback when you are not living at this level of conversation is vital.

Individual Development Plans: Coaching Techniques

Leaders in expressing companies focus on coaching that is designed to develop, not criticize. They encourage people to take more risks, to speak up with the pride of having a voice and the pride of ownership, and to grow individually so that the company grows collectively.

Developmental coaching looks to the future, and conversations reflect that a leader expects others to expect more from themselves. Questions are effectively used to focus on what can be: What do you think we should do? How would you like to help? Where do you see yourself next year? And then the most important development question a leader can ask is: How can I help you?

When you coach developmentally, you become better equipped to take on larger challenges because your talent pool is larger.

Raise Questions for which There Are No Pat Answers

One of the most important elements of an expressing culture is that leaders are comfortable living inside of questions. They actually train each other to down-regulate telling and up-regulate asking. Leaders monitor each other's behavior of asking over telling.

In most companies, declarative statements outweigh the questions by a large margin—85 percent to 15 percent is not unusual.

Expressing cultures raise the bar dramatically on questions, and they are better-crafted questions that get people to think about issues, to challenge each other's thinking, and to actively own a piece of the discussion and a portion of the solution. People become comfortable with challenging authority as a way of life.

Your Expressive Voice

You can replicate development and growth throughout your organization, and ensure that it is ongoing, by incorporating new leadership DNA practices to create a culture where every individual makes a genuine contribution to the whole.

When people sing a cappella, each voice holds its own within the chorus. Each voice has a perfectly suited range, and each person needs to hear the other voices in order to perform well. When people join the chorus, they must fit in with the other talent. If one person drowns out the others, or isn't heard, the composition suffers.

A leader who uses the expressive leadership gene is the maestro who conducts a symphony that is music to everyone's ears.

Chapter 8

The *S* Gene: Spirit of Reinvention

"We must always change, renew, rejuvenate ourselves; otherwise we harden."
—*Johann Wolfgang von Goethe*

SPIRIT EXISTS WHEN people feel connected to each other and to a higher purpose. Cultures with spirit are those where people rise above the territoriality and pushback of everyday life. There is continuous value creation and ongoing transformation. People communicate about what they want the desired outcome to be. In companies and organizations with spirit, people work together seamlessly toward a higher purpose. They are energized to take on audacious goals that help the whole enterprise succeed. Why? Because the organization is imbued with a spirit of reinvention. Thus, a shared future takes precedence over dogma and compliance with long-established norms. This commitment to reinvention drives the organization forward. This energy extends from the culture or organization, and emboldens the relationships with customers, alliance partners, and others who interact with the organization.

IBM
A Spirit Success Story: Creating Our Winning Team!

One hundred years ago, Thomas Watson founded IBM on three basic beliefs: respect for the individual, the best customer service, and the pursuit of excellence. When Sam Palmisano took over as CEO in 2002, he revisited those beliefs, and while they were still steeped in IBM history and legacy, they needed to be reinvented for the company to survive the historic shifts and contractions in the IT industry. In 2003, Sam implemented an astounding process called a ValuesJam.

Imagine what it would take to engage 350,000 people in a conversation for twenty-four hours, then try to visualize it going on for seventy-two hours. Many of us would think it impossible that a conversation with this many people could even take place. Yet it did, indeed, happen, and more than once—each time making it clearer what the pivotal issues were for growth. IBM, in its desire to sustain its core DNA, and continue its transformation, morphed into a whole new company.

Imagine a company as large as IBM becoming incredibly agile and sensitive to customers' changing needs—in fact, to the changing needs of the entire industry. Imagine that an organization this big can become incredibly responsive and efficient, contrary to what one would expect based on size alone. With its DNA so bound to the customer from its very beginning, IBM took on one of its largest transformations ever, yet did so while preserving what makes it IBM.

During a seventy-two-hour Values Jam, 350,000 IBMers could visit the company's internal Web site to offer comments about their relationship with the company and one another. Sam learned that the old values had taken on a dull shine, reflective of the autocratic culture that IBM had become in the early 1980s. Respect for the individual had taken on a meaning of entitlement, pursuit of excellence had become arrogance, and IBM had stopped listening to its customers. The Values Jam wasn't to debate Thomas' basic beliefs, but rather to discover what IBMers valued about the company and their relationships with other employees and clients. It was a true experiment in creating a companywide conversation where the voices of all employees were heard. Everyone had access to the site, and everyone could see the comments pouring in: millions of words, expressing the sentiments of tens of thousands of employees.

As with any experiment, the outcome would be unknown until it was over. Early in the Values Jam some comments from employees were brutal: "The only value in IBM today is the stock price"; "We talk a lot about trust and taking risks, but we have endless audits, mistakes are punished, and managers' decisions are constantly questioned." Twenty-four hours into the experiment, some senior executives wanted to pull the plug. Once the early venting subsided, and people felt self-expressed, the mood shifted as did the comments. They became constructive, and it was clearer what employees were trying to articulate. They wanted values that better reflected the present culture.

IBM had experienced the worst downturn in its history during the 1990s. Former CEO Louis Gerstner then capably repositioned the company from mainframe production to one that delivered integrated hardware, networking, and software solutions. Sam wanted to re-energize the company that had withstood major blows to its bottom line, and, in his mind, there was no better way to do that than to involve the whole organization in defining what the company would stand for, and what deeply mattered to everyone.

The million words of text that poured in from employees were analyzed by executives and the project team until new themes emerged. Then Sam shaped them into a version that more aptly represented the current IBM. Some might say the words are not much different, but if you ask an IBMer, he or she will say they are miles apart. Launched in 2004, these values give new life and breadth to the IBM heritage and culture:

- Dedication to every client's success
- Innovation that matters . . . for our company and the world
- Trust and personal responsibility in all our relationships

Sam knew that value statements can be nothing more than window dressing, and so he chartered a new project to determine what gaps existed between the new values and the existing practices.

In October of 2004, a second jam—called the "World Jam"—took place to identify gaps. This seventy-two-hour event (followed by an archive site) was intended to change the culture of IBM by providing a platform where employees could talk with and help each other.

Value Jam and World Jam revolutionized IBM's culture. In the old IBM, hubris abounded and the company believed that it owned the world. Prior successes bred a myopia that turned into blindness, ensuring that IBM missed seeing the emergence of competitors and new market shifts that threatened its very existence. IBM had to let go of 400,000 employees, and for a company that pledged employment for life, this was devastating to its heritage, values, and overall morale. Sam believed that the old values—IBM's DNA—were still meaningful, but needed to be transformed. Adaptability and flexibility came to the fore, challenging IBM's former structure.

Tara Sexton, VP of Communications, Integrated Supply Chain (ISC), highlighted the key impact the jams had on the culture: "The process got buy-in. It wasn't a mandate. People personally stood up and committed; it was living our values." Fostering this kind of culture was the only way IBM would be able to deliver on its strategy called "on demand," which would require a more open and collaborative environment where teams of people could come together as needed for clients.

In the former IBM, employees were hard-wired to their brand, isolated in their own subculture. As a result of the jamming sessions, and a new vision that Sam had for the company, IBM today is hard-wired to the customer. IBM's new culture is exhibited in its new supply chain organization.

In 2002, IBM established the integrated supply chain (ISC), consisting of 19,000 employees from across the company. "Our goal was an on-demand supply chain," says Bob Moffat, senior VP, Integrated Supply Chain, "so our business could respond quickly, flexibly, and at much lower cost to whatever the world throws at it."

The trigger event for the ISC was really the state of the industry. For the first time, the IT industry was contracting. There are two ways to respond to this kind of environment: hunker down and wait for growth to return, or do dramatic things to change the way you operate your business.

"One of the ways we were going to change the way we operate," describes Tara, "was to view and run the supply chain differently. We were going to integrate it on a global scale and use it as a competitive advantage, and not view it as just a cost of doing business."

At the launch of the ISC, Bob explained that the strategy was not fully formed, and that it would develop as the ISC team interacted within the company—a revolutionary shift for a company that had always been top-down hierarchical.

"This journey," he says, "will be guided by a strategy that is dynamic and anticipatory. We will respond rapidly to real changes as they occur, and seize opportunities as they arise. The strategy we create to execute our supply chain will be large enough, broad enough, and yet generic enough that they can respond to change and inspire it as well."

"One of the biggest challenges," says Tara, "was to evolve the culture from command-and-control to one that was more inclusive and collaborative. Some of the senior leadership weren't sure they could make the leap. They were used to telling people what to do, because at the end of the quarter when you need to get boxes out the door, you don't need people at every level thinking differently. Leaders understood what they needed to do vertically, but not across the company. Overcoming such cultural challenges kept the project on track."

While senior leadership may talk the talk, unless they walk the walk, it disenfranchises the employee population. They begin to see this as just a vision shared and driven by a few who are espousing the new principles but managing in the old way. "We tracked this disparity," explains Tara. "And we worked on narrowing the gap. Our leaders had to believe the vision, not just talk about it. We learned we couldn't force-fit old management styles into a new 'script.' If we did, the employees would not get onboard."

Pulse Surveys are taken regularly to identify how people feel about the organization's progress. When new needs are identified, teams are put together to work on them. Employees discuss what to do about gaps. Larger groups meet, and then break up into smaller ones. They synthesize ideas and vote on solutions. Identifying and closing gaps is the way IBM regularly runs its business.

Being able to "loosen control without losing control" expressed the real issue: it was a challenge for the leadership team to let go of the reins a bit, step back, set the direction, and let people fail. They did this through "leading by example"—and this was the same challenge for everyone on the leadership team.

Tara expressed the key behind the transformation's success: "The goal was to let people see this as something really different, not just a change to their reporting structure. What emerged was something beyond the elimination of redundancies. It was a spirit of reinvention that marked the IBM culture with its new DNA."

That new and stronger DNA is driven by communication, engagement, and employee commitment. It is reversing the effect of years of command-and-control and is enabling the work force to be integrally linked to each other and the customer.

Both Sam and Bob are very passionate about leadership. They talk about it all the time. Bob ends every employee communication with what has become his tag line: "Leadership makes a difference."

At IBM today, with a new culture of interconnection, every employee can be a leader who makes a difference.

▷ LEADERSHIP PRINCIPLE
Compliance vs. Commitment

Leaders like Sam Palmisano and Bob Moffat put incredible energy into creating leadership spirit. The Integrated Spply Chain initiative provided an opportunity for IBM employees to drive the business forward. By creating an ISC, the company works as an organism, where all parts are interconnected and more responsive to the customer. The ISC not only saved money for IBM, but, more importantly, rallied employees to a larger purpose. Instead of blind compliance to a rigid structure, there is a sense of shared ownership of innovative approaches. The jams swept everyone at IBM into the fervor of being heard, of having a direct impact on the company brand and its future direction. Leaders who engender such spirit think WE not I.

I-Centric vs. WE-Centric Leadership

I-centric leaders believe that to change organizations you must demand that people buy into a new way of working. Such leaders do not tolerate resistance, and rather than being a source of inspiration, these individuals use force, power, and a heavy hand to get results. I-centric leaders use senior management to create the values, vision, mission, and purpose of the company, and expect everyone else to fall in line. They fail to engage employees when their companies need to be reinvented in response to changing times.

WE-centric leaders understand that organizational change starts with a personal decision to change. Change cannot be mandated. Compliance does not inspire passion and spirit. Engaging with others in ongoing dialogue and celebrating success creates a powerful, energetic environment where everyone is synchronized around a vision and purpose. It can be "we together" by providing clarity of direction, by inspiring people to find a place of value and importance and a way to contribute to the larger process. WE-centric leaders are releasers of energy and set a tone for greatness that transforms people and transforms a business. WE-centric leaders think WE all the time and create organizational spaces where individuals and teams are part of something big, purposeful, meaningful, and wonderful.

Abstracted from "Leading When Business is Good" *Harvard Business Review*, December 2004.

INTENTION ———————————— **IMPACT** ————•

Leader Story: Failure to Focus on Purpose

"I don't want control; I just want results."

Jack spent his entire career in a growing technology company. He was tall and had a commanding presence. In a roomful of people, his charm was felt and people would often gravitate toward him. It was not uncommon for him to be the center of attention, and he enjoyed the spotlight. Early on, Jack was tagged as a high performer, and thus his name was always put into the mix when larger opportunities arose. Jack started out as a sales manager in the northeast region, but was quickly promoted to national accounts, supervising a staff of 250 people. He was a natural leader, and as a result sales trended upward every quarter. Management was pleased.

Jack was asked to become the worldwide head of sales, and in his new responsibility he had quadrupled the number of people on his staff. At first, he saw this as a wonderful next step in his career. Then, as he traveled and saw what it really took to sustain sales, he unearthed issues in the company that shook his confidence both in himself and in the company's future. He did not know how to transfer his personal charm and success to so many others, and so he resorted to commanding it.

Jack was a perfectionist and if he saw people straying too far from what he thought the strategy should be, he became more overbearing in his style. He was showing up for meetings and driving the agendas to "make sure everyone got the plan." People started to notice that he was not listening to their issues.

As time passed, employees who had been successful sales managers in their own right, faltered in reaching their numbers. It was not clear if it was the increased competition in the marketplace or something else. Jack turned up the heat, expecting they would make up the shortfall. The environment became more stressful for everyone. Jack's pressure on his team caused them to feel that he:

- Valued numbers over people
- Micromanaged
- Ignored interdependence and shared goals
- Lacked clear communication about direction
- Caused the steady down-trending of sales

Jack's internal anxiety about meeting the numbers translated into him being heavy-handed within the organization. He became distanced from the team he needed to inspire. He focused more on his team's failure to deliver than on their strategies for how to deliver. He wanted them to sustain their prior record of success, yet he wanted them to do it his way. Without realizing it, Jack had sent mixed messages to his people.

Fear of Sustaining Success

Leaders like Jack exist in all organizations. They are hired for their competencies, their skills, and their ability to get the job done. Yet when the promotions come, there is often increased "performance anxiety" about getting results. Some leaders talk about the "impostor" syndrome: feeling that they are not capable of handling increased responsibility, and fearing that their shortcomings will be exposed. These leaders want to be seen as the winners they have always been. At the intersection of these internal and external pressures, a leader can become excessively controlling, which dampens morale.

Jack did not share his worries with his peers, boss, or staff. He resorted to pressure to achieve results. The distance between Jack and his employees widened as their relationship dynamics took a turn for the worse. Employees were:

- Unable to gain access to Jack's strategies for improving the business
- Directionless and felt out of the loop

- Unsure of their own abilities
- Passing the pressure on to customers

When you understand how to shift the emphasis from compliance to commitment, you create energetic workplaces where employees thrive and are more able to reach their potential while helping you sustain your own record of success.

FIGURE 8.1

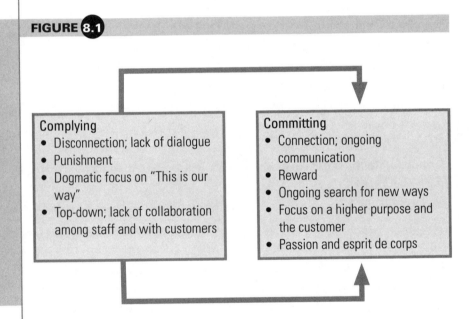

Complying	Committing
• Disconnection; lack of dialogue	• Connection; ongoing communication
• Punishment	• Reward
• Dogmatic focus on "This is our way"	• Ongoing search for new ways
• Top-down; lack of collaboration among staff and with customers	• Focus on a higher purpose and the customer
	• Passion and esprit de corps

The "Bottom-Line" Meta-Message

When leaders say they want bottom-line results, and yet fail to engage employees in developing the strategy, they send a meta-message. When they punish failed initiatives, they cut off future attempts at innovation—another meta-message. When leaders demand that others "do what I say" they send a clear message: "Don't bother wasting time and passion on what you think is important."

Mixed signals that tell people to take responsibility but put the leash on them at the same time break trust. Once trust is broken, the divide between management and employees widens, vital communication is reduced or disappears, and employee spirit is broken. These meta-messages cause employees to doubt both themselves and their leadership. They spend time worrying about what to believe in, how to direct their work, and what will be rewarded. Mixed messages separate organizations from the employee drive that can truly advance the business.

Leader Profile

Let's look at Jack's profile through a number of lenses:

How he communicates: Jack is assertive and an extrovert. He has a dominant personality and likes to indoctrinate others in his ways. He talks down to others and expects them to deliver the results that he prescribes.

How he motivates others: Jack uses fear of negative consequences to get the performance he wants. He tells people that if they don't deliver they are out. He has been known to fire people publicly, making them a symbol of what not to do. People don't see Jack as supportive or empathetic. They assume he won't be there to provide advice.

How he listens or doesn't: Jack has one thing in mind: making the numbers and getting results. He doesn't want to hear any "no's" or "can'ts" and thus he is impatient when people are having difficulty. People believe he won't tolerate feedback.

How he uses or abuses power: Jack is a driver, and when people question his authority he gets more demanding. He is a "do, don't think" leader who expresses his positional power to gain compliance. He does not like informal conversation even when it's to clarify goals and strategies. He feels too much discussion distracts people from the maximum effort that is required of them.

Leaders who demand blind fealty do not see the dead end that awaits—for themselves, for employees, or for the organization. Forced deference enforces detachment. It relieves those who must take personal responsibility for their actions, and severs a personal connection to the outcomes that result from their efforts. Ennui sets in, and a general malaise spreads among individuals, which erodes the collective zeal.

The Negative Ripple Effect

Jack failed to engage with his employees in brainstorming about the strategies, challenges, and the larger purpose for the organization. As a result, he fostered silo mentality and caused others to feel they needed to protect their own self-interest. People were under the gun to produce results, and it caused them to compete with each other. To them, *team* was an empty word.

Jack was an I-centric leader who created waves that battered everyone. The cascading impact was that people felt:

- Territorial
- Competitive with others on the team
- Fearful of failure, blame, and public humiliation
- Deferential to Jack
- Uninspired

Junk DNA: Leadership Mythologies

Some leaders believe that their job is to demand conformance with established organizational practices and procedures. There is associated language that such executives adopt, such as "get them on the bus" or "get everyone onboard." The larger concept is alignment with the one common set of beliefs about where the company is going and how it will get there.

On the surface, these beliefs have merit. An organization is like an orchestra that is playing one song with a chorus of singers sharing the same songbook. But a satisfying composition is much more than a string of notes that is played with technical perfection. The key is for leaders to move up from practices and procedures to interpretation and passion. By inspiring others about the larger purpose of the organization, leaders "pull" instead of "push" them to support business goals.

Employees love to be motivated to higher goals and to feel they are contributing to something bigger than they could do alone. Employees do not feel inspired and committed by force, domination, or pressure of compliance.

Compliant leadership is an outmoded strain of DNA that reinforces old beliefs that:

- Leaders need to control what others do or else they will do the wrong things.
- Strategy gets created at the top and implemented at the bottom.
- You get "buy-in" by demanding it.

There are red flags, "mutations" that indicate a leader is expressing old DNA that limits spirit:

- Conversations between management and employees are formal and minimal.
- Clans form to try to figure out the organizational direction.
- People do only what they are asked to do.
- There is little to no sense of ownership and accountability.
- There is little passion or enthusiasm.

To evolve, you need to break the bonds of old beliefs and connect to new ones. Research shows that extraordinary leaders are not compliance-driven; they instead focus on creating commitment to a higher purpose. They see their role as one of inspiring others to see the goal and work together to figure out the strategies for getting there. They are determined to be inclusive, to create a true sense of community, and to set the context for organization-wide engagement.

▷ THE LEADERSHIP STEP
Get into the Spirit

The spirit leader understands that change is challenging and shakes the core of a culture. They also understand that what people need at a time of major change is to feel interconnected. When people are striving for a goal together they feel supported in the face of change.

At IBM, Bob Moffat stepped up into his new leadership role and learned how to create a context for spirit to emerge. His communication was inspiring and motivating. The focus on creating an environment that could lift up others to achieve the goal was instrumental to the success of this initiative. And he created a process where strategy could be owned by the organization rather than only by the leadership team. Bob brings spirit into his communication—and others feel it: "Our new ISC leadership model is all about trust, respect, and relationships. It's about creating an environment that enables people to work together to maximize their collective strengths. The purpose—as it's always been—is not just to inform, but to inspire. Inspire new ideas . . . renew the enthusiasm . . . and build stronger connections between the leaders and the entire organization."

How can you build an environment where people feel engaged in the strategy and linked to the higher purpose of your brand? How can you help employees see the journey as ongoing, and transformation as something that everyone needs to own?

The Twenty-First-Century Leader Can *See* the Way to Commitment

To build a passionate environment where everyone attaches himself or herself to outcomes, replace a demanding posture with one that solicits participation. While compliance engenders fear and resentment, commitment results in a climate of reinvention that perpetuates growth. The following three leadership practices infuse esprit de corps everywhere.

Share Passion with Everyone

During the ISC effort, Bob spent 80 percent of his time visiting ISC sites for all-hands meetings. He instituted these to ensure that everyone involved in the initiative would be in the conversation and could share in the passion and excitement of the ongoing progress.

Practices for yourself:
- Keep your mind on the larger goals.
- Frame challenges as opportunities.
- Keep your ear to the ground for issues and concerns that need to be addressed.
- After reaching milestones—even minor ones—share the results so everyone can get excited together.

Practices with your staff:
- Ensure employees interact more freely and frequently.
- Share excitement at the beginning of every meeting.
- Create environments where employees can see themselves as active participants, able to shape their reality by creating their future, rather than just reacting to the present.
- Reward employees publicly; people need to know what "good" looks like so it can be replicated.

Establish Success Communication

During the ISC project, leaders communicated regularly to employees to update them on the progress. The communication was inspiring and gave a picture of the successes and what else they needed to focus on to move forward. They also encouraged employees to share success stories with one another.

Practices for yourself:
- Make communication a priority.
- Create space in agendas for storytelling.
- Ask employees to draw out the success principles and lessons from shared stories.
- Be a champion of your employees' success.

Practices with your staff:
- Find people who are good at communication and enlist them in the process of crafting success stories.
- At meetings, ask people to share their success stories with others.
- Recognize employees for their stories—each story contains wisdom and lessons learned that others can learn from.
- Promote cross-divisional best-practice sharing.

Encourage Employee and Management Dialogue

The IBM ISC project has mechanisms for employees to post questions through the Web site. They also run manager roundtables at each location and accessibility is encouraged at all levels.

Practices for yourself:
- Communicate your desire to be available and accessible.

- Trust your people to come up with ideas and strategies that you have not yet thought of.
- Be receptive when employees want to talk to you.

Practices with your staff:
- Schedule regular meetings to ensure understanding of the strategy.
- Don't use e-mail for important conversations—use teleconferences instead.
- Ask, "What needs clarification?"

Employees, like soldiers, will march in lockstep if commanded to do so. And they will work (fight) when they have to. But they will succeed phenomenally (conquer decisively) when they want to help their colleagues (protect their buddies) and see the larger picture (believe in a righteous cause). The best leaders—wherever they do battle—are those who enlist everyone in the fight.

FIGURE 8.2

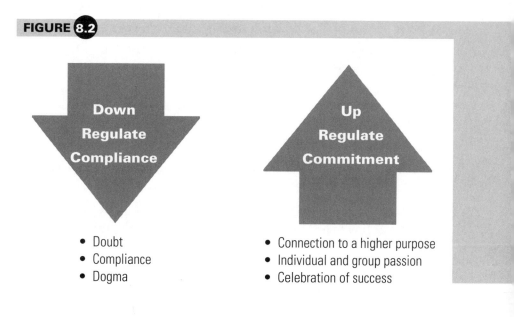

- Doubt
- Compliance
- Dogma

- Connection to a higher purpose
- Individual and group passion
- Celebration of success

Up- and Down-Regulating

WE leadership DNA is expressed by removing doubt, improving clarity of purpose and methods, and engaging managers and employees. It inspires a willingness to adapt when the need arises, and it fosters excitement about overcoming challenges.

Down-Regulate

It is the leader's responsibility to rally the troops—not by superficial cheerleading displays, but by exposing the enemy within.

Doubt

Uncertainty is a part of business. But an unknown future should not be cause for employees to lose faith during the struggle or despair. Morale is bolstered when you:

- Give employees updates so they can see forward movement.
- Remove cynicism by providing fair assessments of what is working and what is not.
- Challenge others publicly to remove the gap between what is said and what is done.

Compliance

Forced agreement is seductive because it supposedly achieves concerted effort. But the effect is cosmetic; beneath the surface, employees seethe with resentment that eventually leads to resistance and jeopardizes real progress. Ensure an attachment to the mission by:

- Creating an environment where people can question the rules
- Eliminating rules that create inefficiencies and get in the way of the larger mission
- Valuing and rewarding innovation and creativity

Dogma

While it is beneficial and perhaps appropriate for some practices to be written in stone, most employees benefit from re-evaluation, reassessment, and revision. You can reap the benefits that change brings by:

- Creating company-wide conversations so that employees and management can talk about how to create desired changes
- Enabling employees to push back and speak up without being chastised
- Empowering employees to identify what the culture should be and the things that have to change to support it

Development, progress, and growth are challenging enough to achieve when everyone is onboard. However, they are nearly impossible to accomplish if you have defectors within the ranks, so be on guard for those things that may cause a breach in your lines.

Compliance language that is part of the Junk DNA in your culture:

- "We're spending too much time talking about this."
- "You are making this too complicated."
- "Just keep your nose to the grindstone."
- "The strategy is not up for discussion."

Up-Regulate

History has demonstrated, and studies have proven, that people will extend themselves beyond what was thought possible for the good of others whom they care about or for a cause in which they believe. You can inspire commitment by embracing the following practices.

Connecting everyone to a higher purpose

Sometimes the obvious becomes obscured in the heat of battle. Ensure that everyone keeps the big picture in mind by:

- Reminding everyone that the whole is greater than the sum of its parts
- Emphasizing group goals that foster teamwork
- Focusing employees on the importance of serving customers

Stoking individual and group passion

Encouraging each person is infectious and builds collective spirit. Instill passion across the board by:

- Rewarding individual initiative publicly to spread excitement
- Framing goals as team challenges to bind people together
- Relating effort to the big picture so that no one feels isolated or insignificant

Regular celebration of success stories

Major achievements are the result of a progression of much smaller ones. Rather than waiting for significant milestones to be reached before celebrating, acknowledge the stops along the way that made the trip a success by:

- Awarding individuals who take on a challenge, set their own course for success, and take a risk, even if they don't achieve the intended target
- Giving out nonmonetary awards such as plaques, desk items, or Web site postings when someone does something special
- Planning official time-outs at meetings to verbally recognize outstanding achievement

As you embody spirit you will see it spread among employees who get caught up in the fervor—not the temporary kind as seen at a sporting event, but the kind that builds a "can do" attitude that moves mountains. As a result, your organization becomes one that thrives even in the most difficult times.

Language that supports commitment in your workplace:

- "We've got to keep the drumbeat going!"
- "We are blazing a path through uncharted territory."
- "I'm honored to make this journey with you. I'm humbled by your accomplishments."

Committed Conversations

Reinvention is an ongoing process that requires an incredible amount of ongoing communication. The importance of communication can't be overemphasized. When communication takes place it needs to be navigational, to give people a sense of clarity about where you've been and where you are going. It needs to include what is working and what needs to change. And it needs to be motivational.

The most powerful way to change a culture is to be the change. The best leaders create environments where the direction is clear and progress is apparent. People become motivated and enthusiastic when they are part of ongoing communication where issues are identified early, and where they are part of creating strategies for addressing them. People feel committed when they can measure success, where they are able to see accomplishments and celebrate milestones together. Employees lose commitment when they can't see the connection between what they are doing and where the organization is going.

Knockout Genes

Be sensitive to language that creates compliance without commitment. Remove the following from your conversations:

- "Do as I say, not as I do."
- "The only thing that counts is the bottom line."
- "This is not about relationships; it's about getting results."

Gene Splicing

When you are aware of the impact that your words have on others, you'll see dramatic effects on morale, motivation, and performance when you replace words that demand compliance with ones that encourage commitment. Graft the following into your conversations:

- "Our story is about the power of inspiration and innovation."
- "Our success is directly related to people thinking and behaving differently."
- "We're all in this together."

Language is powerful, but on its own it is insufficient to overcome challenges or accomplish great things. E-mails, newsletters, speeches, voice mail, and direct orders will not result in coordinated efforts on a consistent basis unless the communication relates tangibly to common desires and beliefs. Twenty-first-century leaders use words that articulate a cause to which everyone can be dedicated.

▷ A CULTURE OF COMMITMENT
Spirit of Reinvention

"Never tell people how to do things. Tell them what to do and they will surprise you with their ingenuity."
—George S. Patton

Instilling purpose and passion is part of leadership DNA. Too often, however, we get caught up in short-term goals and dampen the spirit that is necessary to achieve greatness. When we feel connected to a larger purpose, we act as a community and we naturally want to see everyone succeed. Real leadership harnesses group dynamics to achieve long-term objectives.

Native American wisdom says that we are all connected and that we have the privilege and responsibility of being the custodians for Mother Earth. Native Americans believe that the earth is truly our mother and that we have to be conscientious in all that we do. This foundation is based on a personal connection between an individual and the Creator Spirit. This spirit resides in plants, animals, earth, water, fire, and air.

To live in harmony and balance with life, we must ask ourselves some challenging questions and draw on sacred principles. Anthropologist Angeles Arrien calls these principles the Four-Fold Way:

1. *Show up and choose to be present—* the way of the warrior.
2. *Pay attention to what your heart tells you—* the way of the healer.
3. *Tell the truth without blame or judgment—* the way of the visionary.
4. *Be open to outcome, not attached to it—* the way of the teacher.

Instead of complaining about the state of the world, we are inspired to join together in sacred ceremony and envision a new and better one. We can always reinvent ourselves, our community, and our businesses as long as we have a strong connection to our spirit.

Spiritual Journey: A Hopi Elder Speaks

"You have been telling the people that this is the Eleventh Hour, now you must go back and tell the people that this is the Hour. And there are things to be considered. . . .

Where are you living?

What are you doing?

What are your relationships?

Are you in right relation?
Where is your water?
Know your garden.
It is time to speak your Truth.
Create your community.
Be good to each other.
And do not look outside yourself for the leader."

Then he clasped his hands together, smiled, and said, "This could be a good time! There is a river flowing now very fast. It is so great and swift that there are those who will be afraid. They will try to hold on to the shore. They will feel they are being torn apart and will suffer greatly.

"Know the river has its destination. The elders say we must let go of the shore, push off into the middle of the river, keep our eyes open, and our heads above the water.

"And I say, see who is in there with you and celebrate. At this time in history, we are to take nothing personally. Least of all, ourselves. For the moment that we do, our spiritual growth and journey comes to a halt.

"The time of the lone wolf is over. Gather yourselves!

"Banish the word struggle from your attitude and your vocabulary. All that we do now must be done in a sacred manner and in celebration.

"We are the ones we've been waiting for."

—*Oraibi, Arizona*

Replicating Reinvention

As an executive and organizational coach, I meet, talk with, and sometimes coach C-level executives who are in the process of creating dramatic changes in their businesses. The transformations are dramatic: shifting from a domestic to a global company; from a product-centric to a customer-centric company; and from a supply to a demand company. These are major changes and require total engagement of everyone in the organization, with each other and with the customers, to achieve success.

The common challenge expressed by these leaders is how to "turn the ship": how to implement the new strategy and engage everyone when change calls for a new direction.

Replicating reinvention is about creating the networks and the forums for the organization to drive the process of transformation. At IBM, the ISC is an investment in a multiyear process of employee engagement. The success of the ISC business is in direct relation to the organization's ability to drive the change process through their 19,000 employees.

As you think about the spirit of reinvention in your business, you need to ask yourself some questions:

- How do I shift from a compliant leader to a commitment leader?
- What behaviors and actions support full engagement in the culture?
- How can I put into place the right architecture for ongoing communication with employees?
- How can I make reinvention everyone's agenda?

You can replicate the passion of commitment throughout your organization, and ensure that it is ongoing, by incorporating spirit gene leadership practices to ensure employees are engaged and inspired as well as informed.

Meeting Strategy: Creating a Common Language and Shared View of Reality

Every Wednesday morning, the ISC holds an operating team meeting to get a pulse on how things are going. It had ten to twelve representatives from across the company, and at those meetings, people talk about day-to-day activities. They talk about root causes of problems, and identify and fix bottlenecks. They establish end-to-end visibility, which they call "looking left to right."

Prior to the integration of IBM's supply chain, each function (manufacturing, procurement, and logistics) had its own language that the other functions didn't understand. To improve functional communication, people were challenged to stop talking in their functional language and start talking in a common language that all employees and departments could understand.

Language is how we create a shared experience. As a transformational leader, create a shared language that envelopes your change process. Create new language and new definitions with your employees so that all are part of the experience of change. Talk about what you are doing with others. Stories shape people's perception of reality, so be sensitive to how you shape perception. If your stories are about how you collectively took on challenges with vigor, commitment, and success, people will feel forward movement. Make your stories true and compelling to engage and motivate.

Communication: Up, Down, and Sideways

Taking the organizational pulse during a major transformation is vital to its success. By implementing surveys a leader will know what's working and what's not, can readjust the direction, and provide needed support. Every other month, the ISC team uses a "Global Pulse Survey" to measure the mood of employees against some key indexes.

Through this intense communication process, the leaders can see where the breakdowns are and understand how they can address them swiftly. When the ISC launched its strategy, Bob Moffat sent a message to all employees: "Our ability to execute comes down to two very fundamental things: how well you understand the various aspects of the plan, and how quickly you make a meaningful connection between your jobs and the strategic direction of ISC. Translating the strategy into action is the key to our continued success." Ongoing communication is vital, and so they use more than the traditional means to stay connected.

"The challenge was to inform, align, and empower 19,000 people in fifty-six countries, and do it all in a remarkably short period of time," Bob explains. "Under these circumstances, our traditional methods of communication—a Webcast, an all-hands meeting, a deck of slides—would not cut it." Their approach involved enlisting a team of managers and equipping them to communicate to their peers around the world through a series of workshops. These help managers have better conversations with employees at all levels. "It defied our sensibilities, yet it was not only doable, it's what created the shared conversation that was necessary for the success of the enterprise. When employees and management are in the same conversation, they become one brand thinking with one brain," says Bob.

Another aspect of their nontraditional communications process is a series of ongoing conversations, each building off of the previous ones—another chapter in the larger story. This creates involvement and curiosity, and motivates people to move from the large picture to specific issues. They evaluate interim results of the projects and then move forward to the next conversation. This brings everyone across the globe together in the reinvention process, adding a huge dimension to IBM's new DNA.

Shared Metrics for Success

Creating a strong commitment to the ISC is not a short-term campaign. It is a long-term process to connect everyone permanently to the whole. ISC published a community framework white paper to give insight to employees and others about what they were trying to do. The goal was to promote a culture that values and supports innovation, collaboration, and inclusiveness.

At the beginning of every year, employees at all levels are asked to identify the key objectives they would commit to that would move the business forward. Laying out a map during a multiyear journey gave employees a sense of what each was accomplishing during each phase. Everything couldn't be done in one year, so a journey map helped employees see that the path to success was ongoing and that each set of milestones enabled the next to emerge. Three years after forming the organization, IBM ISC continues to realize the fruits of its labor.

Foster Reinvention

Reinvention is a multifaceted long-term effort to build an ongoing sense of community. Once you feel you are close to the end, the process of reinvention begins again. Reinvention:

- Entails a variety of intentional efforts to organize and strengthen social connections among employees
- Builds common values that promote collective goals and creates new structures and relationships for executing strategy
- Does not replace tactical operational objectives, but complements them
- Engages everyone, but relies on select groups, for example, up-line managers and employees at an early stage in their career
- Uses a disciplined, systematic approach with a strong management and governance model

Organizational Engagement in Creating the Brand

The ISC was a systematic approach for engaging employees in creating the brand. In this light, executives needed to:

- **Define and articulate the purpose:** What does it mean to be a part of a larger community? How does this satisfy the organizational objectives and individuals' goals?
- **Gain commitment:** Start with the leadership team. Begin the conversation about the need to create a community and its relevancy to overall objectives.
- **Take stock:** Use data and input on all major initiatives to frame current and desired states and establish priorities.
- **Facilitate understanding:** Articulate and promote a positive community model among employees and managers; come to a common understanding of what the organization will evolve to.
- **Engage:** Involve critical constituents early on in the discussion.
- **Sustain:** Leaders play an important role in sustaining community structures and processes. Develop a managing system to ensure you stay on track toward stated objectives.

Sometimes we can get caught up in doing business—the *content* of our work—and lose sight of the *context* in which it takes place, of the importance of building and nurturing relationships on a broad basis so that both business and relationships are self-perpetuating. People fight for causes they believe in and for people they care about. Valuing and maintaining connections to others should be on every leader's daily to-do list so that spirit is preserved company-wide.

Template for "Living the Brand"

The ISC has strengthened the IBM culture. By rewiring how communication, engagement, learning, and doing business take place, a new template for "living the brand" emerged. A brand is much more than a company's products and services. It's the way employees and management work together with the customer to realize a greater value that benefits all. Each company has its unique DNA and when all are engaged together in sustaining and building the DNA, it becomes strong and transferable from generation to generation.

The key points are:

- Employees will be involved with managers in the creation of the environment.
- Alignment with the myriad initiatives under the framework takes place and sets the stage for the critical focus areas moving forward.
- The transformation uses a disciplined, systematic approach with a strong management and governance model.

Raising Your Spirit

Spirit is the vital principle of conscious life, animating the body and mediating between the body and soul. Spirit is the invisible dimension that inspires people and moves them to action. Spirit represents courage, integrity, vigor, and firmness of intent.

Spirit instills a vigorous sense of membership in a group. It connects to language in that it is the general meaning or intent of a statement, as opposed to its literal meaning. Spirit relates to nurturing in that it is the act of encouragement, and of compassion in that it recognizes feelings or moods. Spirit is the power that connects human beings to themselves and to others, and activates profound changes in the world.

In the Navajo culture, the spirit line is a thread that is woven into all blankets. It may look like it's a mistake because one thread seems to come out of the design and ends as a separate thread in the fringe. This is intentional; it symbolizes the spirit being released from the design on the blanket. It means that in life, while we make our designs and live life within a pattern that we create together, we still need to leave a thread—spirit—that enables survival to the next generation.

A leader who creates environments where people feel connected to a higher purpose uses the spirit leadership gene to enable everyone to rise up together to achieve audacious business goals.

Chapter 9

Replicating and Evolving Your New DNA

"We don't accomplish anything in this world alone . . . and whatever happens is the result of the whole tapestry of one's life and all the weavings of individual threads from one to another that creates something."
—*Sandra Day O'Connor*

PERHAPS YOU'VE HEARD the story about the leader who, when faced with a crisis of momentous proportion, went alone to a mountain retreat to meditate and seek inspiration. He sweated over which option he would choose that would determine the future of his group: continue to battle the forces that threatened its survival, likely at great cost, or cut losses and move on in search of a new way. After tortured contemplation, this great leader decided to accept a new approach, and that changed everything about his culture and ensured its long-term survival.

Could this be about a CEO at a *Fortune* 100 company, or about a valiant entrepreneur at a high-tech start-up? It could be, but it isn't. It's the story of Moses.

As I mentioned in the introduction, and affirmed in each of the seven leadership gene chapters, the wisdom of the ages is available—and eminently useful—to all of us now. But it doesn't take divine intervention to lead boldly and effectively in the face of challenge. What it takes is an awareness that to master change you must first change yourself. And that requires a willingness to learn and the courage to apply the lessons learned.

Why do some companies thrive in both bull and bear markets, while others seem to be constantly beset by organizational and financial setbacks? It has to do with the way leadership DNA is expressed. The remarkable success of Starbucks, which went from less than 100 locations to over 8,000 in fifteen years, is not just because of a great product and a good business plan. It's because they see every employee as a partner who delivers an "experience" to millions of customers, one at a time.

Companies like Starbucks and the others profiled in this book have leaders who consistently express the WE half of each of the seven leadership genes to positively impact their leadership teams and employees. They understand that success, despite capital and technology, comes down to how people work together to creatively shape the future. They know that what they say and do shapes their environments, and that environments are their brands. They know that the "I" alone is not what leadership is about; it's the "I inside the WE" that needs to come alive.

Evolution and growth take place in healthy cultures that handle conflict and change effectively. This is done best when the thinking and the energy that solutions require come from the collective whole instead of from one person or from a small group. I-centric leaders dictate and imitate, and their organizations are stagnant when confronted by change. WE-centric leaders integrate, differentiate, and innovate, and their organizations capitalize on change and constantly move forward. In healthy organizations the "I" can differentiate its uniqueness inside of the "WE"–one of the most powerful concepts of this book.

The DNA of Leadership shows you how to bond with others inside and outside of your organization so that the "I's" transform into a healthy WE. Each DNA gene chapter examines leadership from the words (micro) to the behaviors and practices (macro) that combine to create a growth environment. Compelling use of your leadership genes reshapes your organization from a territorial one to a community that gels with a shared view—not because of forced compliance, but because of a genuine commitment to common and far-reaching goals.

Forward-thinking leaders are not limited by narrow thinking. They challenge old ways and upset the status quo if it stands in the way of progress. Most of all, they are driven by an overriding purpose: to release the unbounded potential of WE.

You are the leader of your future. As your coach, my desire is to help you scale your own mountain where you find the wisdom and inspiration for setting new courses, as change always dictates. The following exercises will get you in shape for the climb.

From Desiring to Doing: Your DNA Exercises

We evolve our DNA in the context of others—in a community. In the gene chapters, we saw how leadership can be practiced to nurture an environment for healthy growth. The exercises that follow will help you leverage the strengths and best aspects of your DNA. They are specific to each leadership gene, and will result in the emergence of a cultural aspect that help your organization continuously evolve.

TABLE 9.1 DNA Exercises

Leadership Gene	Cultural Aspect	Exercise(s)
Community	Inclusion	Open Space Technology
Humanizing	Appreciation	Self-Disclosure; Examining Judgments; Moving from Blame to Honoring; Yes and. . . .
Aspiration	Striving	Appreciative Inquiry Dreaming
Navigating	Learning	Celebrating the Different; Benchmarking with a Difference; Best-Practices Sharing
Generating	Innovation	Brain Walking
Expressing	Initiative	Workout; An Issue of Success; Learner as Teacher; Unpacking the Suitcase of Strong Emotion
Spirit	Reinvention	Weekly Synchronization Meetings; Evolutionary Mapping

COMMUNITY

Leadership Step: Co-Creation | Culture: Inclusion

The C leadership gene exercise creates a collective culture of open communication where everyone feels involved in strategy, engaged in the business, and accountable for results.

Open Space Technology

"Holding space" is the establishment of a safe container (a block of time and a location) and inviting a team, a division, or the whole company to come together to talk about what they care about most. It allows conversation to take place. It is a time where you withhold judgment and actively listen and reflect on what you hear from others.

An amazing process to hold space is called Open Space Technology (OST) developed by Harrison Owen. OST is an emergent process for conducting a meeting that enables groups of people to deal with issues constructively and speedily. (For more on OST, see Owen's book, *Open Space Technology: A User's Guide* [Berrett-Koehler, 1997].) OST creates the space for a group to discuss what they really care about. If you are to co-create, you need to invite others to share their voice about issues or projects they are willing to take responsibility for. In Open Space meetings, participants create and manage their own meeting agenda of parallel working sessions around a central theme of strategic importance.

OST is based on four principles and one law.

The Four Principles of Open Space
1. Whoever attends are the right people.
2. Whatever happens is the only thing that should happen.
3. Whenever it starts is the right time.
4. When it's over, it's over.

The Law of Two Feet: if you find yourself in a situation where you are neither learning nor contributing, use your two feet. In other words, take yourself to a session where you can make a contribution or have an interest in participating.

Holding an Open Space Meeting

Identify a theme or issue of strategic importance. The event runs on two fundamentals: passion and responsibility. Those who come will have issues about which they are passionate. They will also be required to be responsible when they raise that issue. You should invite participants representing all stakeholders.

The meeting begins as a circle with a facilitator in the middle. The facilitator invites participants to identify some issue for which they feel a great deal of passion and for which they are willing to take responsibility. They are invited to stand up, state their name and the issue, write their name and issue on a sheet of paper, and put it up on the designated wall space. Once the issues are identified, the issue presenter has the responsibility to select the location and time of the meeting and to ensure that the meeting is documented as per the facilitator's directions.

People join those discussions that they are most drawn to. If they at any point are dissatisfied with the discussion or direction a particular meeting is going, they are invited to use the Law of Two Feet.

By the end of the gathering, the following will have occurred:

1. Every issue of concern to anybody will have been raised, provided they took responsibility for doing that.
2. All issues will have received full discussion, to the extent desired.
3. A full report of issues and discussions will be in the hands of all participants.
4. Priorities will be set and action plans will be made.

Using Open Space Technology activates the C gene for a culture of inclusion.

HUMANIZING

Leadership Step: Embrace Your Humanity | Culture: Appreciation

The H leadership gene exercises create an atmosphere that values uniqueness and diversity, and respects the talents of each individual.

Self-disclosure

When was the last time you admitted that you didn't have the answer? The next time someone comes in with a question that you do not have the answer for, reply with, "I don't know," and let there be silence. Try to do this as often as you are comfortable with and see what happens. By admitting to subordinates that you don't know, you are demonstrating that you are human just like them. This breaks down barriers and builds stronger relationships. It also gives subordinates the space to be creative and innovative in solving problems.

Each time you try saying I don't know, watch and follow-up with what happens.

Examining Judgments or Checking Assumptions, Interpretations, and Perceptions

Think about someone or a group that you work with that you may be having some difficulties with right now. How would you describe them and the situation in a single sentence?

What if all adjectives and adverbs or modifiers were taken away from our communications? For example:

Sentence #1:
The big red boat pulled up to the creaky, old dock.

Sentence #2:
The boat pulled up to the dock.

Now go back and remove all the adjectives/adverbs/modifiers from your first sentence. Rewrite the situation without interpretation, just writing the observable facts:

_____

_____

Look at what you wrote about the situation without interpretation. If five other people had witnessed the same situation, would their statements read like yours?

Moving from Blame to Honoring

People get upset, hurt, or angry when they feel they didn't get something they deserved. They can then slip into I-centric behavior. Follow these steps to cultivate a more empathetic posture that takes into account others' feelings:

Step #1: Identify frustrations
Identify a person with whom you are having difficulty on your team:

_____

_____

Determine what you want to happen in this relationship:

_____

_____

_____

What things would change in your team if this relationship were working perfectly?

_____

Step #2: Let go and embrace

What beliefs about yourself or that person do you need to let go of that are getting in your way of creating what you want?

_____

_____

What feelings about yourself or that person do you need to let go of that are getting in your way of creating what you want?

_____

_____

What behaviors that you turn to when you are with that person do you need to let go of that are getting in your way of creating what you want?

_____

_____

_____

What patterns of speaking and communicating do you need to let go of that are getting in your way of creating what you want?

_____

_____

Make a commitment to yourself to let go of those things that are working against you and to live fully in the new space you are embracing.

Step #3: Coach yourself

Give yourself permission to be your own coach, or to find someone to coach you when you are having trouble and reverting to your old behaviors and beliefs. When you find yourself backsliding, have the following conversation with yourself:

"I have been doing a great job of creating a new future. I am proud of myself for putting effort into these things":

_____

_____

"I am making great progress and will change the following things":

_____

_____

"In the future, I will do _____ instead of _____."
Then picture yourself doing the things you plan to do.

Celebrate Your Success

It is not so much the behavior of another person but what our expectations and needs are that cause frustration and blame. Using the Examining Our Judgments exercise, you can identify where those expectations began. If you can get in touch with what those expectations and needs were, you are moving away from blame. Once you understand your own needs and expectations, you create a space and openness to begin thinking in terms of the other person's expectations and needs and are more likely to have a conversation that moves toward resolution rather than separation.

Yes and . . .

In the field of improv, one of the first exercises/games one learns is "Yes and . . ." The idea is that any comment offered should be perceived as a gift, and then you add your own information. Rather than negating the offered comment, you accept the gift and build upon it with, "Yes and . . ."

Go back and look at some of your personal e-mails or memos. Scan them for use of the words *but* and *however*. Now look at those memos/e-mails and see if you could rewrite the sentence replacing the *but* or *however* with an *and*. How might the whole impact of that memo shift if you were to do that? How has the message changed? How much more likely is it that your message will be heard?

In a conversation, when you reply to someone by beginning your sentence with "But," you are negating what was just said. The other person probably stopped listening to what you were saying as soon as she heard "but" and is probably thinking about how she will defend what she just said. If you are giving a compliment followed by a "but," the listener will be focusing on the sentence following the "but" and will forget the compliment. Communication has stopped.

When we use *and*, we are taking what was said before and building upon it. So we are honoring what comes before. Watch your use of the words *but* and *however*. Listen for the replies and observe the nonverbal behavior of the people you are talking to. Listen for how often *but* or *however* are used by others and how it impacts the communication between the parties involved. Watch for your own reactions to the use of these words in memos and e-mails from others.

ASPIRING

Leadership Step: Dare to Dream | Culture: High-Performance

The A leadership gene exercise marshals the wonder of shared imagination and possibilities.

Appreciative Inquiry Dreaming

Appreciative Inquiry is a philosophical mindset and process of looking at what's right and what works well in your organization. Initially created by David L. Cooperrider, professor at Case Western Reserve in Ohio, it delves into stories of "when we have been at our best." It looks for and explores internal best practices, root causes of success, strengths, achievements, strategic opportunities, assets, tacit wisdom, core competencies, vital traditions, and visions of possibility. (For a more in-depth discussion of this process, see *Appreciative Inquiry Handbook* [Lakeshore Communications, 2003] by David L. Cooperrider, Diana L. Whitney, and Jacqueline M. Stavros.)

The process follows four phases:

1. *Discovery:* exploring what gives life to the organization and identifying the positive core
2. *Dream:* images and visions of the future, what we aspire to become
3. *Design:* what can make the aspirations possible
4. *Destiny:* the actions to achieve those aspirations

The next time you and your team are facing a particular challenge, have a conversation about whether you are focusing on the outcome/objective/results or on the problem. As a group, discuss answers to the following questions and build on answers as you proceed:

1. What is our intention or desired state?
2. What is working well and where?
3. What strengths do we have?
4. What possibilities exist that we have not thought about yet?
5. What do we as a team want to make happen?
6. As a team, how can we make it happen?

The appreciative inquiry process should culminate in a specific plan of action. What single small change could you make right now that would have a significant impact? What bolder change might you want to consider?

NAVIGATING

Leadership Step: Never Operate in a Vacuum | Culture: Learning

Celebrating the Different

Throughout any organization there are pockets of individual or group excellence that we can identify if we just open our eyes and look for them. In a May 2000 article in the *Harvard Business Review*, Jerry Sternin and Robert Choo described this phenomenon as "Positive Deviancy." It represents a framework for thinking about individual and organizational change and the issue of how to adopt new behaviors. (The part of this concept related to change was further developed in a May 2005 *Harvard Business Review* article by Sternin, Choo, and Richard T. Pascale titled, "Your Company's Secret Change Agents.") The idea is to seek out pockets of excellence or effectiveness within your organization and invite those pockets to share what makes them excellent and/or effective. Look for positive examples of people doing things outside of the norm—the positive deviants. Look for those who are creating successes despite organizational, resource, or other limitations. Think of it as celebrating the different. Seek it out on a regular basis and find new and interesting ways of sharing these differences with the rest of the company.

Benchmarking with a Difference

There are a number of traditional benchmarking approaches that are used: internal business units, competitive performance/process, industry performance/process, or performance/process from outside your industry.

Conduct this exercise to stimulate innovation and creativity by nontraditional benchmarking: think about the critical elements—practices, processes, and human aspects—that go into superior performance on a project. Pose the question to your team, "What would make this effort excellent?" Let the conversation go on for a while, and then ask, "What can we take from this discussion that is applicable for the task at hand?"

GENERATING

Leadership Step: Risk-Taking | Culture: Innovation

The G leadership gene exercise nurtures innovation and "next generation" thinking that leads to inspired breakthroughs.

Brain Walking

Brain Walking is an exciting technique designed to help coworkers generate "big ideas"/eureka! insights by stimulating connections between seemingly unrelated or random thoughts, facts, insights, intuitions, and/or idea fragments.

You might think of Brain Walking as a kind of interactive suggestion box because of its ability to elicit ideas in a nonthreatening and nonjudgmental way, and because it encourages dynamic and ongoing idea building from a wide variety of employees. Brain Walking:

- Improves the ability of a person, department, or organization to collaborate on generating breakthrough ideas
- Leverages/exploits the inherent ability of the human brain to make connections and recognize patterns
- Captures some of the energy, excitement, and "concept-productivity" that comes from group ideation

The technique entails having coworkers scribble/record ideas against a specific topic/creative challenge on flip charts during a meeting:

Step #1:   Place a group of flip charts in the room.

Step #2:   Decide on a topic/creative challenge for which you want new ideas, and write a short description of it in the center of the flip chart. Example: "How do we cut costs in this department by 15 percent?" or "How do we differentiate ourselves competitively?"

Step #3:   "Seed" the flip chart if you have a few initial ideas by putting down a few facts, idea fragments, or areas for research around the topic/creative challenge.

Step #4: Engage the group by asking them to walk to each flip chart and, using sticky notes, add their ideas, cautions, and valuable suggestions.

Step #5: Try to supercharge the group by asking additional questions so that they can add something to the flip chart if they get "dry"—every idea is important no matter how seemingly insignificant or trivial.

Step #6: Continue a few rounds until you feel the group has exhausted its thinking output. You may add teaser questions such as: Consider the "worst idea" or the "most expensive/least expensive" way to approach this challenge. Encourage your coworkers to add some more ideas.

Step #7: At the end of the allotted time and after the input rounds, divide up the group so that each flip chart has people sorting through the input to come up with the "story" or the "statement of value" or the "rationale" for that challenge.

Step #8: Groups summarize the ideas on the flip chart and present to the larger group. If the group feels the challenge is too big or not of value, eliminate that challenge and move on to the next.

Step #9: Select the creative challenges to work on.

Brain Walking is an extension of brainstorming that places more structure on random, unconnected ideas. It is a method that develops concepts and connects inspirations to each other until something tangible results, or identifies avenues that are unlikely to lead anywhere worthwhile. The mechanism of group evaluation quickly results in proposed courses of action.

EXPRESSING

Leadership Step: Elevate Influence | Culture: Development

The E leadership gene exercises encourage others to speak up, take risks, develop themselves to develop the organization—to lead in their own way.

Workout

The WE workout process is an approach to intensive team problem solving. After a problem is defined, a manager charges the group to solve it and exits. The group spends two or three days brainstorming and developing solutions/recommendations to the problem with the guidance of skilled outside facilitators. Then, in a town hall meeting, recommendations are presented to the manager who decides yes, no, or that he or she needs further information on each recommendation.

As a WE-centric leader, allowing your team to develop recommendations without your influence sends a powerful message of trust and confidence in its abilities. It also enables the development of solutions that comes from a diversity of expertise and shared learning. As a result, these teams are supporting both their own personal growth, as well as the organization's.

An Issue of Success

Whenever someone comes to you with a problem, you might have several recommendations based on your experience. As a way for your team members to express themselves, you can tap into the best of their prior experiences about a particular issue or challenge.

Whenever your team is facing a particular issue or challenge, invite each member of your team to share how he or she overcame it or a similar one. As stories are shared, the group dynamic is strengthened and new ideas are generated.

Learner as Teacher

One of the best ways to learn is by having to teach someone else. Here are two ways to apply this approach:

Method #1: *The importance of my division*
To help other divisions better understand the internal workings of the organization, on a monthly basis during a one-hour meeting, have an individual or team by functional or divisional area provide a lesson on that area's responsibilities or processes and how they fit in with other areas:

1. What are its critical success factors?
2. Who are its internal and/or external customers?
3. What are its core processes and where does it experience bottlenecks?
4. What are its key deliverables for the year?
5. What aspirations do they have?

By creating the space for diverse areas to share their role within the organization, everyone gains greater understanding of the whole organization. The preparation for the presentations allows these areas to review what they do, and in the process, find ways to improve methods. And, finally, in explaining what they do within the company, it gives them a chance to have a voice in front of the rest of the organization.

Method #2: Professors of the new

Once a month have a team research and present/teach about any of the following:

- A hot new topic
- An innovative company within your industry
- An innovative company outside your industry to bring fresh insights and ideas to the company
- The core ideas of new bestsellers, and where they see evidence of the positive practices of what's discussed in the book throughout the company
- An outside hobby and what skills, tools, and resources are required for it, and how that relates to company processes

The presenting team carries the title "Professors of the New," with the idea that whatever will be presented will help stimulate new thoughts. There is no right or wrong thinking; it becomes a dialogue about ideas. It is a fun way to spur creativity within the organization, and people consider it an honor to be Professors of the New.

Unpacking the Suitcase of Strong Emotions

This exercise comes from the work of Dr. Marshall Rosenberg, the author of *Nonviolent Communication* (PuddleDancer Press, 1999). Emotions in the workplace can get in the way of allowing individuals or groups to move forward. Recognizing and naming those emotions for ourselves or helping others to do so can pave a much more positive path to productivity.

When a negative emotion is stimulated, take a moment to identify what you are feeling and what need is not being fulfilled. Keep repeating to yourself, "I am feeling _____ because I needed _____." For example: "I feel angry and frustrated because I needed cooperation and effectiveness."

Once it has been clearly identified, you can "unpack it" from the suitcase you carry around with you. You will actually sense a release of tension in your body when you discard the counterproductive emotion.

You can help a team member through the unpacking process as well. Marshall calls it empathic guessing. When someone is in the throws of a negative emotion, you can assist by guessing (in the form of a question, not a statement—remember, it is the other person's emotion and need), for example, "Are you angry because you really needed to deliver your project on time?" The other person will guide you: "Yes, that's it," or, "No, it's more about XYZ." And then you can guess again. This process can be very helpful to diffuse intense situations and to bring people and groups back to equilibrium.

SPIRIT

Leadership Step: Inspiration | Culture: Commitment

The S leadership gene exercises create a sense of ongoing accomplishment, celebration, and evolution so that everyone is excited about pulling together toward the future.

Weekly Synchronization Meetings

An effective means to develop a coordinated team where all contributions are valued is a weekly staff meeting, usually lasting no longer than an hour. Executives share all necessary information from the home office or from those above their level, quickly review status on projects due from the strategic plan, celebrate (acknowledge) team and individual accomplishments, and then turn it over to the rest of the staff. Going around the room, each staff member has the opportunity to quickly share information about her respective projects, identify deliverables for the week, make requests for support, and/or discuss what she will need from others. If there is little change from the previous week, the staff member can pass. In the space of one hour the whole team knows all it needs for the week, and the team has been fully synchronized.

Evolutionary Mapping

To identify strengths as well as weaknesses and potential roadblocks, create a visual map of where you have been, where you are now, and where you are going. Hang a ten- to twenty-foot-long sheet of butcher paper on a meeting-room wall. Select a significant time frame going back at least ten years and forward at least five years, and write the years across the top of the paper. Draw a horizontal line across the center of the paper, and write the numbers 1 to 10 vertically up the left edge, as follows:

FIGURE 9.1

	1990	1995	2000	2005	2010
High					
10					
9					
8					
7					
6					
5					
4					
3					
2					
1					
Low					

Past

Have individuals create their own personal version on a sheet of paper. This will be strictly for their eyes only. Have them look into their own personal history within the organization or in their previous position and ask them to map their own "personal" high points and low points on the map. Then, using a different color of writing implement (to the degree they were part of the organization during the various time frames), have them then write in, from their perspectives, what they feel were the "organizational" high points and low points both for their area of responsibility and for the company/organization as a whole.

After people have had the time to get their ideas down, invite individuals to share just the event and not the rating of high or low points. Then discuss the event as a group. Place it on the Evolutionary Map at the appropriate date aligned with the high or low rating based on the overall group's general consensus. (Be careful here to just discuss the event in terms of a high or low point. Do not let it descend into a "who's to blame" exercise. The important area to focus on is how the team/organization was able to move forward.)

For any events that fell below a five on the chart, discuss as a group how the organization was able to move beyond that event to a new high point later on the map. For the high points, discuss what made them happen. What were the contributing factors? What role did they personally play? How did they contribute to that high point? Does this high point coincide with their personal high points? How so?

Present

Discuss what projects are currently ongoing, what events are taking place both inside and outside the organization from all stakeholder perspectives. (Alternative approaches to do this is a SWOT analysis where you identify Strengths, Weaknesses, Opportunities, and Threats, or a SOAR analysis where you specify Strengths, Opportunities, Aspirations, and Results.) Have a dialogue about what everyone sees as working very well, things that are working moderately well, and things they believe could be improved. After discussion, post the project/event on the map at the appropriate rating point. There will be a growing awareness of where and how resources—personnel, financial, and technological—are being used. A dialogue about "Are we investing in the right things at the right time, given the events that are occurring both within and outside the organization?" will continue throughout the discussion about the future.

Future

The dialogue moves to where you are going in the future. Draw out what has already been identified as organizational goals and objectives. Using sticky notes, have the team members brainstorm critical issues facing the team. When they are ready, have them place their critical issues on the chart with 10 being the highest priority and 1 being the lowest priority. Have a dialogue about each and move them to the appropriate level as the group's consensus-building evolves.

At each step of the conversation, new insights emerge that will move things up or down the scale. On a regular basis, be sure to go around the group ensuring that each person has an opportunity to speak and share insights.

Through the dialogue, you have in effect mapped out your team or organizational DNA as well as created a common frame of reference for everyone involved as to where you have been, where you are, and where you are going.

A Culture of Replication and Evolution

Cultures continually evolve and express "how we do things here." They result from leadership DNA, with a leader's focus on defining and exemplifying practices and behaviors. Leaders who realize that cultures evolve understand the underlying elegance of evolution, as does Lindsay Farrell, CEO of Open Door, a nonprofit health care organization in Ossining, New York.

Open Door was started by a group of community volunteers to provide medical services to a community where people were unable to afford it. The health center provided a safe place where minorities could get more than medical care. It offered life skills that provided grounding and enabled people to sustain healthy lives.

Lindsay joined Open Door twenty years ago, starting there as a volunteer driver. Today, there are four centers and she is helping the organization perpetuate its culture that nourishes both staff and patients. "To affix the culture," she believes, "we need to constantly work with our patients and on ourselves."

Lindsay remembers how the organization had become too employee-centric in the late 1990s. She and her staff realized that they needed to open their approach to create an external focus as well as an internal focus: "It was a challenge to shift more toward meeting our patients' needs, but the shift took hold and we work every day to sustain this orientation. It requires an ongoing re-evaluation about how we are doing, and the willingness to communicate and make changes to the way we work."

On April 2, 2005, Open Door launched a Journey Meeting where management representatives from across the organization came together to look back at what the past year had brought, and to look forward to affirm the vision for the next year. In this dynamic session, the leaders celebrated their evolution and worked to define new challenges to take on at all levels to sustain the momentum for future success. In this session, a feeling of "one brain, one brand" emerged. There was a commitment to work together across the organization. Conversations became transparent, issues were put on the table in a no-blame environment, and there was a shared view of how everyone needed to work together for mutual growth.

They created a number of large journey maps that painted pictures of the environment that Open Door had created and wanted to sustain. Everyone could see the big picture graphically; the maps synchronized the organization and provided a guide for their culture to move forward.

While each best-in-breed company we visited in each chapter has its own unique DNA, they all have some things in common. They honor and value relationships, knowing that business growth can only come from people working well together and valuing each other's contributions. Leaders in those companies recognize that they set the tone and guide others through their actions. Healthy, open, honest conversations are the bedrock of good relationships, which are the foundation for the evolution of a culture.

Those leaders devote significant attention to communication. It is more frequent and more intensely focused on narrowing the gap between what is desired and what is taking place. In their organizations, they down-regulate fear of speaking up and up-regulate support for articulating a view of organizational challenges that enables each person to participate in creating the future and achieving the desired goals. Blame is transformed into accountability and coaching so people can get feedback on their efforts to grow. The view looks forward, toward creating the future, not backward toward punishing unmet expectations.

Best-in-breed leaders spend more time on creating a psychologically safe environment for experimentation, for risk-taking. They appreciate that growth cannot be imposed—it comes from within. Implementing best practices that come from in-house sources is essential for collective development. Organizations that "discover" what they are and what they value, and that celebrate their identity reaffirm their cultures and their brands and self-generate a spirit of renewal.

In the early 1980s, benchmarking was a new trend for the industry and for me. It inspired my company's name: Benchmark Communications, Inc. At the time, I believed that studying the best companies would provide a blueprint for duplicating their organizational success at other companies where I consulted. I thought by studying world-class companies, we could all learn how to become great.

I discovered, however, that benchmarking was not the all-purpose answer for helping companies succeed in the face of new challenges. I learned that it offered something from the outside as a wake-up call to catalyze an organization, to trigger and inspire new ways of doing business, not a step-by-step formula. Every company was unique and had to graft lessons onto their own cultures for them to be useful. Too often, as a result of benchmarking a team would surface great ideas and turn them into a report that ended up in a file. Or, when trying to implement the benchmarking discoveries, a team faced roadblock after roadblock because people who were not involved in the process didn't buy into it. People inherently resist change, especially when it is presented as "you change this because someone else is doing it better than you are."

The essence of what I learned changed the way I work with clients and propelled me into the work I embarked upon. *The DNA of Leadership* was born.

The lessons we learn from others—the substance of this book—are, indeed, important. But it's what's inside of leaders and their organizations that make or break survival and growth. Looking outside creates the initial impetus to change, but the real benefit comes when we look inside. Mining our own resources is more valuable in the long term.

I have learned that benchmarking as a "change management technology" yields greater benefits when companies focus their efforts on internal benchmarking activities before or during external benchmarking. Rather than getting bogged down in arguments about the rightness of a point of view, they synthesize multiple points of view. They don't assume there is one magic solution or approach that someone else has; they are open to outside knowledge, but know that enlightenment resides within.

With the hindsight of years of client work, I realized something we may have known but forgotten. Human beings have an extraordinary capacity for wisdom and brilliance that we must tap into. It all comes down to the importance of leadership DNA. When leaders create a container for the discovery of their own and others' unique talent and abilities, and when they implement communication and learning practices in their companies, an incredible thing happens: organizations dramatically and successfully transform themselves into WE-centric cultures.

Too often, organizations and people inside organizations become stale; they take on the resignation of the environment they are in, and become themselves psychologically toxic. Baggage from the past lingers around in the present, keeping us trapped in patterns that limit rather than enhance our ability to be as successful as we can be now and into the future.

The purpose of this book is to revitalize your thinking, to give you visionary ways of getting unstuck, and to position yourself to make magnificent changes in your life that you never thought possible. Whether you are starting a business, working in an organization, changing jobs or the way you build your teams and your organization, you will find extraordinary value from applying the lessons of this book.

The DNA of Leadership is an operating manual for leaders who want to learn how to challenge themselves and take responsibility for playing an important role in transforming a workplace from an I-centric into a WE-centric environment. It delivers the message for how you can successfully handle change: The source for innovation, solutions, and growth is within *you* . . . and the people you work with every day.

Index